MW01267729

COLLECTED WORKS OF
MARTIN LUTHER

CONTENTS

MARTIN LUTHER'S LARGE CATECHISM

CONCERNING CHRISTIAN LIBERTY

THE SMALCALD ARTICLES.

MARTIN LUTHER'S 95 THESES

MARTIN LUTHER'S LARGE CATECHISM

Translated by F. Bente and W. H. T. Dau

PREFACE

A Christian, Profitable, and Necessary Preface and Faithful, Earnest Exhortation of Dr. Martin Luther to All Christians, but Especially to All Pastors and Preachers, that They Should Daily Exercise Themselves in the Catechism, which is a Short Summary and Epitome of the Entire Holy Scriptures, and that they May Always Teach the Same.

We have no slight reasons for treating the Catechism so constantly [in Sermons] and for both desiring and beseeching others to teach it, since we see to our sorrow that many pastors and preachers are very negligent in this, and slight both their office and this teaching; some from great and high art [giving their mind, as they imagine, to much higher matters], but others from sheer laziness and care for their paunches, assuming no other relation to this business than if they were pastors and preachers for their bellies' sake, and had nothing to do but to [spend and] consume their emoluments as long as they live, as they have been accustomed to do under the Papacy.

And although they have now everything that they are to preach and teach placed before them so abundantly, clearly, and easily, in so many [excellent and] helpful books, and the true Sermones per se loquentes, Dormi secure, Paratos et Thesauros, as they were called in former times; yet they are not so godly and honest as to buy these books, or even when they have them, to look at them or read them. Alas! they are altogether shameful gluttons and servants of their own bellies who ought to be more properly swineherds and dog-tenders than care-takers of souls and pastors.

And now that they are delivered from the unprofitable and burdensome babbling of the Seven Canonical Hours, oh, that, instead thereof, they would only, morning, noon, and evening, read a page or two in the Catechism, the Prayer-book, the New Testament, or elsewhere in the Bible, and pray the Lord's Prayer for themselves and their parishioners, so that they might render, in return, honor and thanks to the Gospel, by which they have been delivered from burdens and troubles so manifold, and might feel a little shame because like pigs and dogs they retain no more of the Gospel than such a lazy, pernicious, shameful, carnal liberty! For, alas! as it is, the common people regard the Gospel altogether too lightly, and we accomplish nothing extraordinary even though we use all diligence. What, then, will be achieved if we shall be negligent and lazy as we were under the Papacy?

To this there is added the shameful vice and secret infection of security and satiety, that is, that many regard the Catechism as a poor, mean teaching, which they can read through at one time, and then immediately know it, throw the book into a corner, and be ashamed, as it were, to read in it again.

Yea, even among the nobility there may be found some louts and scrimps, who declare that there is no longer any need either of pastors or preachers; that we have everything in books, and every one can easily learn it by himself; and so they are content to let the parishes decay and become desolate, and pastors and preachers to suffer distress and hunger a plenty, just as it becomes crazy Germans to do. For we Germans have such disgraceful people, and must endure them.

But for myself I say this: I am also a doctor and preacher, yea, as learned and experienced as all those may be who have such presumption and security; yet I do as a child who is being taught the Catechism, and every morning, and whenever I have time, I read and say, word for word, the Ten Commandments, the Creed, the Lord's Prayer, the Psalms, etc. And I must still read and study daily, and yet I cannot master it as I wish, but must remain a child and pupil of the Catechism, and am glad so to remain. And yet these delicate, fastidious fellows would with one reading promptly be doctors above all doctors, know everything and be in need of nothing. Well, this, too, is indeed a sure sign that they despise both their office and the souls of the people, yea, even God and His Word. They do not have to fall, they are already fallen all too horribly, they would need to become children, and begin to learn their alphabet, which they imagine that they have long since outgrown.

Therefore I beg such lazy paunches or presumptuous saints to be persuaded and believe for God's sake that they are verily, verily! not so learned or such great doctors as they imagine; and never to presume that they have finished learning this [the parts of the Catechism], or know it well enough in all points, even though they think that they know it ever so well. For though they should know and understand it perfectly (which, however, is impossible in this life), yet there are manifold benefits and fruits still to be obtained, if it be daily read and practiced in thought and speech; namely, that the Holy Ghost is present in such reading and repetition and meditation, and bestows ever new and more light and devoutness, so that it is daily relished and appreciated better, as Christ promises, Matt. 18, 20: Where two or three are gathered together in My name, there am I in the midst of them.

Besides, it is an exceedingly effectual help against the devil, the world, and the flesh and all evil thoughts to be occupied with the Word of God, and to speak of it, and meditate upon it, so that the First Psalm declares those blessed who meditate upon the law of God day and night. Undoubtedly, you will not start a stronger incense or other fumigation against the devil than by being engaged upon God's commandments and words, and speaking, singing, or thinking of them. For this is indeed the true holy water and holy sign from which he flees, and by which he may be driven away.

Now, for this reason alone you ought gladly to read, speak, think and treat of these things if you had no other profit and fruit from them than that by doing so you can drive away the devil and evil thoughts. For he cannot hear or endure God's Word; and God's Word is not like some other silly prattle, as that about Dietrich of Berne, etc., but as St. Paul says, Rom. 1, 16, the power of God. Yea, indeed, the power of God which gives the devil burning pain, and strengthens, comforts, and helps us beyond measure.

And what need is there of many words ? If I were to recount all the profit and fruit which God's Word produces, whence would I get enough paper and time? The devil is called the master of a thousand arts. But what shall we call God's Word, which drives away and brings to naught this master of a thousand arts with all his arts and power? It must indeed be the master of more than a hundred thousand arts. And shall we frivolously despise such power, profit, strength, and fruit—we, especially, who claim to be pastors and preachers? If so, we should not only have nothing given us to eat, but be driven out, being baited with dogs, and pelted with dung, because we not only need all this every day as we need our daily bread but must also daily use it against the daily and unabated attacks and lurking of the devil, the master of a thousand arts.

And if this were not sufficient to admonish us to read the Catechism daily, yet we should feel sufficiently constrained by the command of God alone, who solemnly enjoins in Deut. 6, 6 ff. that we should always meditate upon His precepts, sitting, walking, standing, Lying down, and rising, and have them before our eyes and in our hands as a constant mark and sign. Doubtless He did not so solemnly require and enjoin this without a purpose; but because He knows our danger and need, as well as the constant and furious assaults and temptations of devils, He wishes to warn, equip, and preserve us against them, as with a good armor against their fiery darts and with good medicine against their evil infection and suggestion.

Oh, what mad, senseless fools are we that, while we must ever live and dwell among such mighty enemies as the devils are, we nevertheless despise our weapons and defense, and are too lazy to look at or think of them! And what else are such supercilious, presumptuous saints, who are unwilling to read and study the Catechism daily, doing than esteeming themselves much more learned than God Himself with all His saints, angels [patriarchs], prophets, apostles, and all Christians For inasmuch as God Himself is not ashamed to teach these things daily, as knowing nothing better to teach, and always keeps teaching the same thing, and does not take up anything new or different, and all the saints know nothing better or different to learn, and cannot finish learning this, are we not the finest of all fellows to imagine, if we have once read or heard it, that we know it all, and have no further need to read and learn, but can finish learning in one hour what God Himself cannot finish teaching, although He is engaged in teaching it from the beginning to the end of the world, and all prophets, together with all saints, have been occupied with learning it and have ever remained pupils, and must continue to be such ?

For it needs must be that whoever knows the Ten Commandments perfectly must know all the Scriptures, so that, in all affairs and cases, he can advise, help, comfort, judge, and decide both spiritual and temporal matters and is qualified to sit in judgment upon all doctrines, estates, spirits, laws, and whatever else is in the world. And what, indeed, is the entire Psalter but thoughts and exercises upon the First Commandment? Now I know of a truth that such lazy paunches and presumptuous spirits do not understand a single psalm, much less the entire Holy Scriptures; and yet they pretend to know and despise the Catechism, which is a compend and brief summary of all the Holy Scriptures.

Therefore I again implore all Christians, especially pastors and preachers, not to be doctors too soon, and imagine that they know everything (for imagination and cloth unshrunk [and false weights] fall far short of the measure), but that they daily exercise themselves well in these studies and constantly treat them; moreover, that they guard with all care and diligence against the poisonous infection of such security and vain imagination, but steadily keep on reading, teaching, learning, pondering, and meditating, and do not cease until they have made a test and are sure that they have taught the devil to death and have become more learned than God Himself and all His saints.

If they manifest such diligence, then I will promise them, and they shall also perceive, what fruit they will obtain, and what excellent men God will make of them, so that in due time they themselves will acknowledge that the longer and the more they study the Catechism, the less they know of it, and the more they find yet to learn; and then only, as hungry and thirsty ones, will they truly relish that which now they cannot endure because of great abundance and satiety. To this end may God grant His grace! Amen.

SHORT PREFACE OF
DR. MARTIN LUTHER.

This sermon is designed and undertaken that it might be an instruction for children and the simple-minded. Hence of old it was called in Greek catechism, i.e., instruction for children, what every Christian must needs know, so that he who does not know this could not be numbered with the Christians nor be admitted to any Sacrament, just as a mechanic who does not understand the rules and customs of his trade is expelled and considered incapable. Therefore we must have the young learn the parts which belong to the Catechism or instruction for children well and fluently and diligently exercise themselves in them and keep them occupied with them.

Therefore it is the duty of every father of a family to question and examine his children and servants at least once a week and to ascertain what they know of it, or are learning and, if they do not know it, to keep them faithfully at it. For I well remember the time, indeed, even now it is a daily occurrence that one finds rude, old persons who knew nothing and still know nothing of these things, and who, nevertheless, go to Baptism and the Lord's Supper, and use everything belonging to Christians, notwithstanding that those who come to the Lord's Supper ought to know more and have a fuller understanding of all Christian doctrine than children and new scholars. However, for the common people we are satisfied with the three parts, which have remained in Christendom from of old, though little of it has been taught and treated correctly until both young and old who are called and wish to be Christians, are well trained in them and familiar with them. These are the following:

First.

THE TEN COMMANDMENTS OF GOD.

1. Thou shalt have no other gods before Me.
2. Thou shalt not take the name of the Lord, thy God, in vain [for the Lord will not hold him guiltless that taketh His name in vain].
3. Thou shalt sanctify the holy-day. [Remember the Sabbath-day to keep it holy.]
4. Thou shalt honor thy father and mother [that thou mayest live long upon the earth].
5. Thou shalt not kill.
6. Thou shalt not commit adultery.
7. Thou shalt not steal.
8. Thou shalt not bear false witness against thy neighbor.
9. Thou shalt not covet thy neighbor's house.
10. Thou shalt not covet thy neighbor's wife, nor his man-servant, nor his maidservant, nor his cattle [ox, nor his ass], nor anything that is his.

Secondly.

THE CHIEF ARTICLES OF OUR FAITH.

1. I believe in God the Father Almighty, Maker of heaven and earth.
2. And in Jesus Christ, His only Son, our Lord; who was conceived by the Holy Ghost, born of the Virgin Mary; suffered under Pontius Pilate, was crucified, dead and buried; He descended into hell; the third day He rose again from the dead; He ascended into heaven, and sitteth on the right hand of God the Father Almighty; from thence He shall come to judge the quick and the dead.

3. I believe in the Holy Ghost, the holy Christian Church, the communion of saints, the forgiveness of sins, the resurrection of the body, and the life everlasting. Amen.

Thirdly.

THE PRAYER, OR "OUR FATHER," WHICH CHRIST TAUGHT

Our Father who art in heaven.
  1. Hallowed be Thy name.
  2. Thy kingdom come.
  3. Thy will be done on earth as it is in heaven.
  4. Give us this day our daily bread.
  5. And forgive us our trespasses as we forgive those who trespass against us.
  6. And lead us not into temptation.
  7. But deliver us from evil. [For Thine is the kingdom and the power and the glory, forever and ever.] Amen.

These are the most necessary parts which one should first learn to repeat word for word and which our children should be accustomed to recite daily when they arise in the morning when they sit down to their meals, and when they retire at night; and until they repeat them, they should be given neither food nor drink. Likewise every head of a household is obliged to do the same with respect to his domestics, ma-servants and maid-servants and not to keep them in his house if they do not know these things and are unwilling to learn them. For a person who is so rude and unruly as to be unwilling to learn these things is not to be tolerated, for in these three parts everything that we have in the Scriptures is comprehended in short, pain, and simple terms. For the holy Fathers or apostles (whoever they were) have thus embraced in a summary the doctrine, life, wisdom, and art of Christians, of which they speak and treat, and with which they are occupied. Now, when these three arts are apprehended, it behooves a person also to know what to say concerning our Sacraments, which Christ Himself instituted, Baptism and the holy body and blood of Christ, namely, the text which Matthew [28, 19 ff.] and Mark [16, 15 f.] record at the close of their Gospels when Christ said farewell to His disciples and sent them forth.

OF BAPTISM.

Go ye and teach all nations, baptizing them in the name of the Father, and of the Son, and of the Holy Ghost. He that believeth and is baptized shall be saved; but he that believeth not shall be damned. So much is sufficient for a simple person to know from the Scriptures concerning Baptism. In like manner, also, concerning the other Sacrament in short, simple words, namely the text of St. Paul [1 Cor. 11, 23 f.].

OF THE SACRAMENT

Our Lord Jesus Christ, the same night in which He was betrayed, took bread; and when He had given thanks, He brake it, and gave it to His disciples and said, Take, eat; this is My body, which is given for you: this do in remembrance of Me.

After the same manner also He took the cup, when He had supped, gave thanks, and gave it to them, saying, Drink ye all of it; this cup is the new testament in My blood, which is shed for you for the remission of sins: this do ye, as oft as ye drink it, in remembrance of Me.

Thus, ye would have, in all, five parts of the entire Christian doctrine which should be constantly treated and required [of children] and heard recited word for word. For you must not rely upon it that the young people will learn and retain these things from the sermon alone. When these parts have been well learned, you may, as a supplement and to fortify them. lay before them also some psalms or hymns, which have been composed on these parts, and thus lead the young into the Scriptures, and make daily progress therein.

However, it is not enough for them to comprehend and recite these parts according to the words only, but the young people should also be made to attend the preaching, especially during the time which is devoted to the Catechism, that they may hear it explained and may learn to understand what every part contains, so as to be able to recite it as they have heard it, and, when asked, may give a correct answer, so that the preaching may not be without profit and fruit. For the reason why we exercise such diligence in preaching the Catechism so often is that it may be inculcated on our youth, not in a high and subtle manner, but briefly and with the greatest simplicity, so as to enter the mind readily and be fixed in the memory. Therefore we shall now take up the above mentioned articles one by one and in the plainest manner possible say about them as much as is necessary.

PART FIRST.
THE TEN COMMANDMENTS.

THE FIRST COMMANDMENT.

Thou shalt have no other gods before Me.

That is: Thou shalt have [and worship] Me alone as thy God. What is the force of this, and how is it to be understood? What does it mean to have a god? or, what is God? Answer: A god means that from which we are to expect all good and to which we are to take refuge in all distress, so that to have a God is nothing else than to trust and believe Him from the [whole] heart; as I have often said that the confidence and faith of the heart alone make both God and an idol. If your faith and trust be right, then is your god also true; and, on the other hand, if your trust be false and wrong, then you have not the true God; for these two belong together faith and God. That now, I say, upon which you set your heart and put your trust is properly your god.

Therefore it is the intent of this commandment to require true faith and trust of the heart which settles upon the only true God and clings to Him alone. That is as much as to say: "See to it that you let Me alone be your God, and never seek another," i.e.: Whatever you lack of good things, expect it of Me, and look to Me for it, and whenever you suffer misfortune and distress, creep and cling to Me. I, yes, I, will give you enough and help you out of every need; only let not your heart cleave to or rest in any other.

This I must unfold somewhat more plainly, that it may be understood and perceived by ordinary examples of the contrary. Many a one thinks that he has God and everything in abundance when he has money and possessions; he trusts in them and boasts of them with such firmness and assurance as to care for no one. Lo, such a man also has a god, Mammon by name, i.e., money and possessions, on which he sets all his heart, and which is also the most common idol on earth. He who has money and possessions feels secure, and is joyful and undismayed as though he were sitting in the midst of Paradise. On the other hand, he who has none doubts and is despondent, as though he knew of no God. For very few are to be found who are of good cheer, and who neither mourn nor complain if they have not Mammon. This [care and desire for money] sticks and clings to our nature, even to the grave.

So, too, whoever trusts and boasts that he possesses great skill, prudence, power, favor friendship, and honor has also a god, but not this true and only God. This appears again when you notice how presumptuous, secure, and proud people are because of such possessions, and how despondent when they no longer exist or are withdrawn. Therefore I repeat that the chief explanation of this point is that to have a god is to have something in which the heart entirely trusts.

Besides, consider what in our blindness, we have hitherto been practicing and doing under the Papacy. If any one had toothache, he fasted and honored St. Apollonia [lacerated his flesh by voluntary fasting to the honor of St. Apollonia]; if he was afraid of fire, he chose St. Lawrence as his helper in need; if he dreaded pestilence, he made a vow to St. Sebastian or Rochio, and a countless number of such abominations, where every one selected his own saint, worshiped him, and called for help to him in distress. Here belong those also, as, e.g., sorcerers and magicians, whose idolatry is most gross, and who make a covenant with the devil, in order that he may give them plenty of money or help them in love-affairs, preserve their cattle, restore to them lost possessions, etc. For all these place their heart and trust elsewhere than in the true God, look for nothing good to Him nor seek it from Him.

Thus you can easily understand what and how much this commandment requires, namely, that man's entire heart and all his confidence be placed in

God alone, and in no one else. For to have God, you can easily perceive, is not to lay hold of Him with our hands or to put Him in a bag [as money], or to lock Him in a chest [as silver vessels]. But to apprehend Him means when the heart lays hold of Him and clings to Him. But to cling to Him with the heart is nothing else than to trust in Him entirely. For this reason He wishes to turn us away from everything else that exists outside of Him, and to draw us to Himself, namely, because He is the only eternal good. As though He would say: Whatever you have heretofore sought of the saints, or for whatever [things] you have trusted in Mammon or anything else, expect it all of Me, and regard Me as the one who will help you and pour out upon you richly all good things.

Lo, here you have the meaning of the true honor and worship of God, which pleases God, and which He commands under penalty of eternal wrath, namely, that the heart know no other comfort or confidence than in Him, and do not suffer itself to be torn from Him, but, for Him, risk and disregard everything upon earth. On the other hand, you can easily see and judge how the world practices only false worship and idolatry. For no people has ever been so reprobate as not to institute and observe some divine worship; every one has set up as his special god whatever he looked to for blessings, help, and comfort.

Thus, for example, the heathen who put their trust in power and dominion elevated Jupiter as the supreme god; the others, who were bent upon riches, happiness, or pleasure, and a life of ease, Hercules, Mercury, Venus or others; women with child, Diana or Lucina, and so on; thus every one made that his god to which his heart was inclined, so that even in the mind of the heathen to have a god means to trust and believe. But their error is this that their trust is false and wrong for it is not placed in the only God, besides whom there is truly no God in heaven or upon earth. Therefore the heathen really make their self-invented notions and dreams of God an idol, and put their trust in that which is altogether nothing. Thus it is with all idolatry; for it consists not merely in erecting an image and worshiping it, but rather in the heart, which stands gaping at something else, and seeks help and consolation from creatures saints, or devils, and neither cares for God, nor looks to Him for so much good as to believe that He is willing to help, neither believes that whatever good it experiences comes from God.

Besides, there is also a false worship and extreme idolatry, which we have hitherto practiced, and is still prevalent in the world, upon which also all ecclesiastical orders are founded, and which concerns the conscience alone that seeks in its own works help, consolation, and salvation, presumes to wrest heaven from God, and reckons how many bequests it has made, how often it has fasted, celebrated Mass, etc. Upon such things it depends, and of them boasts, as though unwilling to receive anything from God as a gift, but desires itself to earn or merit it superabundantly, just as though He must serve us and were our debtor, and we His liege lords. What is this but reducing God to an idol, yea, [a fig image or] an apple-god, and elevating and regarding ourselves as God ? But this is slightly too subtle, and is not for young pupils.

But let this be said to the simple, that they may well note and remember the meaning of this commandment, namely, that we are to trust in God alone, and look to Him and expect from Him naught but good, as from one who gives us body, life, food, drink, nourishment, health, protection, peace, and all necessaries of both temporal and eternal things. He also preserves us from misfortune, and if any evil befall us, delivers and rescues us, so that it is God alone (as has been sufficiently said) from whom we receive all good, and by whom we are delivered from all evil. Hence also, I think, we Germans from ancient times call God (more elegantly and appropriately than any other language) by that name from the word good as being an eternal fountain which gushes forth abundantly nothing but what is good, and from which flows forth all that is and is called good.

For even though otherwise we experience much good from men, still whatever we receive by His command or arrangement is all received from God. For our parents, and all rulers, and every one besides with respect to his neighbor, have received from God the command that they should do us all manner of good, so that we receive these blessings not from them, but, through them, from God. For creatures are only the hands, channels, and means whereby God gives all things, as He gives to the mother breasts and milk to offer to her child, and corn and all manner of produce from the earth for nourishment, none of which blessings could be produced by any creature of itself.

Therefore no man should presume to take or give anything except as God has commanded, in order that it may be acknowledged as God's gift, and thanks may be rendered Him for it, as this commandment requires. On this account also these means of receiving good gifts through creatures are not to be rejected, neither should we in presumption seek other ways and means than God has commanded. For that would not be receiving from God, hut seeking of ourselves.

Let every one, then, see to it that he esteem this commandment great and high above all things, and do not regard it as a joke. Ask and examine your heart diligently, and you will find whether it cleaves to God alone or not. If you have a heart that can expect of Him nothing but what is good, especially in want and distress, and that, moreover renounces and forsakes everything that is not God, then you have the only true God. If on the contrary, it cleaves to anything else, of which it expects more good and help than of God, and does not take refuge in Him, but in adversity flees from Him, then you have an idol, another god.

In order that it may be seen that God will not have this commandment thrown to the winds, but will most strictly enforce it, He has attached to it first a terrible threat, and then a beautiful, comforting promise which is also to be urged and impressed upon young people, that they may take it to heart and retain it:

[Exposition of the Appendix to the First Commandment.]

For I am the Lord, thy God, strong and jealous, visiting the iniquity of the fathers upon the children unto the third and fourth generation of them that hate Me; and showing mercy unto thousands of them that love Me and keep My commandments.

Although these words relate to all the commandments (as we shall hereafter learn), yet they are joined to this chief commandment because it is of first importance that men have a right head; for where the head is right, the whole life must be right, and vice versa. Learn, therefore, from these words how angry God is with those who trust in anything but Him, and again, how good and gracious He is to those who trust and believe in Him alone with the whole heart; so that His anger does not cease until the fourth generation, while, on the other hand, His blessing and goodness extend to many thousands lest you live in such security and commit yourself to chance, as men of brutal heart, who think that it makes no great difference [how they live]. He is a God who will not leave it unavenged if men turn from Him, and will not cease to be angry until the fourth generation, even until they are utterly exterminated. Therefore He is to be feared, and not to be desisted.

He has also demonstrated this in all history, as the Scriptures abundantly show and daily experience still teaches. For from the beginning He has utterly extirpated all idolatry, and, on account of it, both heathen and Jews; even as at the present day He overthrows all false worship, so that all who remain therein must finally perish. Therefore, although proud, powerful, and rich worldlings [Sardanapaluses and Phalarides, who surpass even the Persians in wealth] are now to be found, who boast defiantly of their Mammon, with utter disregard whether God is angry at or smiles on them, and dare to withstand His wrath, yet they shall not succeed, but before they are aware, they shall be wrecked, with all in which they trusted; as all others have perished who have thought themselves more secure or powerful. And just because of such hardened heads who imagine because God connives and allows them to rest in security, that He either is entirely ignorant or cares nothing about such matters, He must deal a smashing blow and punish them, so that He cannot forget it unto children's children; so that every one may take note and see that this

30

is no joke to Him. For they are those whom He means when He says: Who hate Me, i.e., those who persist in their defiance and pride; whatever is preached or said to them, they will not listen; when they are reproved, in order that they may learn to know themselves and amend before the punishment begins, they become mad and foolish so as to fairly merit wrath, as now we see daily in bishops and princes.

But terrible as are these threatenings, so much the more powerful is the consolation in the promise, that those who cling to God alone should be sure that He will show them mercy that is, show them pure goodness and blessing not only for themselves, but also to their children and children's children, even to the thousandth generation and beyond that. This ought certainly to move and impel us to risk our hearts in all confidence with God, if we wish all temporal and eternal good, since the Supreme Majesty makes such sublime offers and presents such cordial inducements and such rich promises.

Therefore let everyone seriously take this to heart, lest it be regarded as though a man had spoken it. For to you it is a question either of eternal blessing, happiness, and salvation, or of eternal wrath, misery, and woe. What more would you have or desire than that He so kindly promises to be yours with every blessing, and to protect and help you in all need?

But, alas! here is the failure, that the world believes nothing of this, nor regards it as God's Word, because it sees that those who trust in God and not in Mammon suffer care and want, and the devil opposes and resists them, that they have neither money, favor, nor honor, and, besides, can scarcely support life; while, on the other hand, those who serve Mammon have power, favor, honor, possessions, and every comfort in the eyes of the world. For this reason, these words must be grasped as being directed against such appearances; and we must consider that they do not lie or deceive, but must come true.

Reflect for yourself or make inquiry and tell me: Those who have employed all their care and diligence to accumulate great possessions and wealth, what have they finally attained? You will find that they have wasted their toil and labor, or even though they have amassed great treasures, they have been dispersed and scattered, so that the themselves have never found happiness in their wealth, and afterwards never reached the third generation. Instances of this you will find a plenty in all histories, also in the memory of aged and experienced people. Only observe and ponder them.

Saul was a great king, chosen of God and a godly man; but when he was established on his throne, and let his heart decline from God, and put his trust in his crown and power, he had to perish with all that he had, so that none even of his children remained. David, on the other hand, was a poor, despised man, hunted down and chased, so that he nowhere felt secure of his life; yet he had to remain in spite of Saul, and become king. For these words had to abide and come true, since God cannot lie or deceive. Only let not the devil and the world deceive you with their show, which indeed remains for a time, but finally is nothing.

Let us, then, learn well the First Commandment, that we may see how God will tolerate no presumption nor any trust in any other object, and how He requires nothing higher of us than confidence from the heart for everything good, so that we may proceed right and straightforward and use all the blessings which God gives no farther than as a shoemaker uses his needle, awl, and thread for work, and then lays them aside, or as a traveler uses an inn, and food, and his bed only for temporal necessity, each one in his station, according to God's order, and without allowing any of these things to be our food or idol. Let this suffice with respect to the First Commandment, which we have had to explain at length, since it is of chief importance, because, as before said, where the heart is rightly disposed toward God and this commandment is observed, all the others follow.

THE SECOND COMMANDMENT.

Thou shalt not take the name of the Lord, thy God, in vain.

As the First Commandment has instructed the heart and taught [the basis of] faith, so this commandment leads us forth and directs the mouth and tongue to God. For the first objects that spring from the heart and manifest themselves are words. Now, as I have taught above how to answer the question, what it is to have a god, so you must learn to comprehend simply the meaning of this and all the commandments, and to apply it to yourself. If, then, it be asked: How do you understand the Second Commandment, or what is meant by taking in vain, or misusing God's name? answer briefly thus: It is misusing God's name when we call upon the Lord God no matter in what way, for purposes of falsehood or wrong of any kind. Therefore this commandment enjoins this much, that God's name must not be appealed to falsely, or taken upon the lips while the heart knows well enough, or should know, differently; as among those who take oaths in court, where one side lies against the other. For God's name cannot be misused worse than for the support of falsehood and deceit. Let4this remain the exact German and simplest meaning of this commandment.

From this every one can readily infer when and in how many ways God's name is misused, although it is impossible to enumerate all its misuses. Yet, to tell it in a few words, all misuse of the divine name occurs, first, in worldly business and in matters which concern money, possessions, honor, whether it be publicly in court, in the market, or wherever else men make false oaths in God's name, or pledge their souls in any matter. And this is especially prevalent in marriage affairs where two go and secretly betroth themselves to one another, and afterward abjure [their plighted troth].

But. the greatest abuse occurs in spiritual matters, which pertain to the conscience, when false preachers rise up and offer their Lying vanities as God's Word. Behold, all this is decking one's self out with God's name, or making a pretty show, or claiming to be right, whether it occur in gross, worldly business or in sublime, subtle matters of faith and doctrine. And among liars belong also blasphemers, not alone the very gross, well known to every one, who disgrace God's name without fear (these are not for us, but for the hangman to discipline); but also those who publicly traduce the truth and God's Word and consign it to the devil. Of this there is no need now to speak further.

Here, then, let us learn and take to heart the great importance of this commandment, that with all diligence we may guard against and dread every misuse of the holy name, as the greatest sin that can be outwardly committed. For to lie and deceive is in itself a great sin, but is greatly aggravated when we attempt to justify it, and seek to confirm it by invoking the name of God and using it as a cloak for shame, so that from a single lie a double lie, nay, manifold lies, result.

For this reason, too, God has added a solemn threat to this commandment, to wit: For the Lord will not hold him guiltless that taketh His name in van. That is: It shall not be condoned to any one nor pass unpunished. For as little as He will leave it unavenged if any one turn his heart from Him, as little will He suffer His name to be employed for dressing up a lie. Now alas! it is a common calamity in all the word that there are as few who are not using the name of God for purposes of Lying and all wickedness as there are those who with their heart trust alone in God. For by nature we all have within us this beautiful virtue, to wit, that whoever has committed a wrong would like to cover up and adorn his disgrace, so that no one may see it or know it; and no one is so bold as to boast to all the world of the wickedness he has perpetrated, all wish to act by stealth and without any one being aware of what thy do. Then, if any one be arraigned, the name of God is dragged into the affair and must make the villainy look like godliness, and the shame like honor. This is the common course of the world, which, like a great deluge, has flooded all lands. Hence we have also as our reward what we seek and deserve: pestilences wars, famines, conflagrations, floods, wayward wives, children, servants, and all sorts of defilement. Whence else should so much misery come? It is still a great mercy that the earth bears and supports us.

Therefore, above all things, our young people should have this commandment earnestly enforced upon them, and they should be trained to hold this and the First Commandment in high regard; and whenever they transgress, we must at once be after them with the rod and hold the commandment before them, and constantly inculcate it, so as to bring them up not only with punishment, but also in the reverence and fear of God.

Thus you now understand what. it is to take God's name in vain, that is (to recapitulate briefly), either simply for purposes of falsehood, and to allege God's name for something that is not so, or to curse, swear, conjure, and, in short, to practice whatever wickedness one may. Besides this you must also know how to use the name [of God] aright. For when saying: Thou shalt not take the name of the Lord thy God, in vain, He gives us to understand at the same time that it is to be used properly. For it has been revealed and given to us for the very purpose that it may be of constant use and profit. Hence it is a natural inference, since using the holy name for falsehood or wickedness is here forbidden, that we are, on the other hand, commanded to employ it for truth and for all good, as when one swears truly where there is need and it is demanded. So also when there is right teaching, and when the name is invoked in trouble or praised and thanked in prosperity etc.; all of which is comprehended summarily and commanded in the passage Ps. 50, 15: Call upon Me in the days of trouble; I will deliver thee, and thou shalt glorify Me. For all this is bringing 't into the service of truth, and using it in a blessed way, and thus His name is hallowed, as we pray in the Lord's Prayer.

Thus you have the sum of the entire commandment explained. And with this understanding the question with which many teachers have troubled themselves has been easily solved, to wit, why swearing is prohibited in the Gospel, and yet Christ, St. Paul, and other saints often swore. The explanation is briefly this: We are not to swear in support of evil, that is, of falsehood, and where there is no need or use; but for the support of good and the advantage of our neighbor we should swear. For it is a truly good work, by which God is praised, truth and right are established, falsehood is refuted, peace is made among men, obedience is rendered, and quarrels are settled. For in this way God Himself interposes and separates between right and wrong, good and evil. If one part swears falsely, he has his sentence that he shall not escape punishment, ad though it be deferred a long time, he shall not succeed; that all that he may gain thereby will slip out of his hands, and he will never enjoy it; as I have seen in the case of many who perjured themselves in their marriage-vows, that they have never had a happy hour or a healthful day, and thus perished miserably in body, soul, and possessions.

Therefore I advise and exhort as before that by means of warning and threatening, restraint and punishment, the children be trained betimes to shun falsehood, and especially to avoid the use of God's name in its support. For where they are allowed to do as they please, no good will result, as is even now evident that the world is worse than it has ever been and that there is no government, no obedience, no fidelity, no faith, but only daring, unbridled men, whom no teaching or reproof helps; all of which is God's wrath and punishment for such wanton contempt of this commandment.

On the other hand, they should be constantly urged and incited to honor God's name, and to have it always upon their lips in everything that may happen to them or come to their notice: For that is the true honor of His Name, to look to it and implore it for all consolation, so that (as we have heard above) first the heart by faith gives God the honor due Him, and afterwards the lips by confession.

This is also a blessed and useful habit and very effectual against the devil, who is ever about us, and lies in wait to bring us into sin and shame, calamity and trouble, but who is very loath to hear God's name, and cannot remain long where it is uttered and called upon from the heart. And, indeed, many a terrible and shocking calamity would befall us if, by our calling upon His name, God did not preserve us. I have myself tried it, and learned by experience that often sudden great calamity was immediately averted and removed during such invocation. To vex the devil, I say, we should always have this holy name in our mouth, so that he may not be able to injure us as he wishes.

For this end it is also of service that we form the habit of daily commending ourselves to God, with soul and body, wife, children, servants, and all that we have, against every need that may occur; whence also the blessing and thanksgiving at meals, and other prayers, morning and evening, have originated and remain in use. Likewise the practices of children to cross themselves when anything monstrous or terrible is seen or heard, and to exclaim: "Lord God, protect us!" "Help, dear Lord Jesus!" etc. Thus, too, if any one meets with unexpected good fortune, however trivial, that he say: "God be praised and thanked; this God has bestowed on me!" etc., as formerly the children were accustomed to fast and pray to St. Nicholas and other saints. This would be more pleasing and acceptable to God than all monasticism and Carthusian sanctity.

Behold, thus we might train our youth in a childlike way and playfully in the fear and honor of God, so that the First and Second Commandments might be well observed and in constant practice. Then some good might take root, spring up and bear fruit, and men grow up whom an entire land might relish and enjoy. Moreover, this would be the true way to bring Up children well as long as they can become trained with kindness and delight. For what must be enforced with rods and blows only will not develop into a good breed and at best they will remain godly under such treatment no longer than while the rod is upon their back.

But this [manner of training] so spreads its roots in the heart that they fear God more than rods and clubs. This I say with such simplicity for the sake of the young, that it may penetrate their minds. For since we are preaching to children, we must also prattle with them. Thus we have prevented the abuse and have taught the right use of the divine name, which should consist not only in words, but also in practices and life, so that we may know that God is well pleased with this and will as richly reward it as He will terribly punish the abuse.

THE THIRD COMMANDMENT.

Thou shalt sanctify the holy day.
[Remember the Sabbath day to keep it holy.]

The word holy day (Feiertag) is rendered from the Hebrew word Sabbath which properly signifies to rest, that is, to abstain from labor. Hence we are accustomed to say, Feierbend machen [that is, to cease working], or heiligen Abend geben [sanctify the Sabbath]. Now, in the Old Testament, God separated the seventh day, and appointed it for rest, and commanded that it should be regarded as holy above all others. As regards this external observance, this commandment was given to the Jews alone, that they should abstain from toilsome work, and rest, so that both man and beast might recuperate, and not be weakened by unremitting labor. Although they afterwards restricted this too closely, and grossly abused it, so that they traduced and could not endure in Christ those works which they themselves were accustomed to do on that day, as we read in the Gospel just as though the commandment were fulfilled by doing no external [manual] work whatever, which, however, was not the meaning, but, as we shall hear, that they sanctify the holy day or day of rest.

This commandment, therefore, according to its gross sense, does not concern us Christians; for it is altogether an external matter, like other ordinances of the Old Testament, which were attached to particular customs, persons, times, and places, and now have been made free through Christ. But to grasp a Christian meaning for the simple as to what God

39

requires in this commandment, note that we keep holy days not for the sake of intelligent and learned Christians (for they have no need of it [holy days]), but first of all for bodily causes and necessities, which nature teaches and requires; for the common people, man-servants and maid-servants, who have been attending to their work and trade the whole week, that for a day they may retire in order to rest and be refreshed.

Secondly, and most especially, that on such day of rest (since we can get no other opportunity) freedom and time be taken to attend divine service, so that we come together to hear and treat of God's and then to praise God, to sing and pray.

However, this, I say, is not so restricted to any time, as with the Jews, that it must be just on this or that day; for in itself no one day is better than another; but this should indeed be done daily; however, since the masses cannot give such attendance, there must be at least one day in the week set apart. But since from of old Sunday [the Lord's Day] has been appointed for this purpose, we also should continue the same, in order that everything be done in harmonious order, and no one create disorder by unnecessary innovation.

Therefore this is the simple meaning of the commandment: since holidays are observed anyhow, such observance should be devoted to hearing God's Word, so that the special function of this day should be the ministry of the Word for the young and the mass of poor people, yet that the resting be not so strictly interpreted as to forbid any other incidental work that cannot be avoided.

Accordingly, when asked, What is meant by the commandment: Thou shalt sanctify the holy day? answer: To sanctify the holy day is the same as to keep it holy. But what is meant by keeping it holy? Nothing else than to be occupied in holy words, works, and life. For the day needs no sanctification for itself; for in itself it has been created holy [from the beginning of the creation it was sanctified by its Creator]. But God desires it to be holy to you. Therefore it becomes holy or unholy on your account, according as you are occupied on the same with things that are holy or unholy.

How, then, does such sanctification take place? Not in this manner, that [with folded hands] we sit behind the stove and do no rough [external] work, or deck ourselves with a wreath and put on our best clothes, but (as has been said) that we occupy ourselves with God's Word, and exercise ourselves therein.

And, indeed, we Christians ought always to keep such a holy day, and be occupied with nothing but holy things, i.e., daily be engaged upon God's Word, and carry it in our hearts and upon our lips. But (as has been said) since we do not at all times have leisure, we must devote several hours a week for the sake of the young, or at least a day for the sake of the entire multitude, to being concerned about this alone, and especially urge the Ten Commandments, the Creed, and the Lord's Prayer, and thus direct our whole life and being according to God's Word. At whatever time, then, this is being observed and practiced, there a true holy day is being kept; otherwise it shall not be called a Christians' holy day. For, indeed, non-Christians can also cease from work and be idle, just as the entire swarm of our ecclesiastics, who stand daily in the churches, singing, and ringing bells but keeping no holy day holy, because they neither preach nor practices God's Word, but teach and live contrary to it.

For the Word of God is the sanctuary above all sanctuaries, yea, the only one which we Christians know and have. For though we had the bones of all the saints or all holy and consecrated garments upon a heap, still that would help us nothing; for all that is a dead thing which can sanctify nobody. But God's Word is the treasure which sanctifies everything, and by which even all the saints themselves were sanctified. At whatever hour then, God's Word is taught, preached, heard, read or meditated upon, there the person, day, and work are sanctified thereby, not because of the external work, but because of the Word which makes saints of us all. Therefore I constantly say that all our life and work must be ordered according to God's Word, if it is to be God-pleasing or holy. Where this is done, this commandment is in force and being fulfilled.

On the contrary, any observance or work that is practiced without God's Word is unholy before God, no matter how brilliantly it may shine! even though it be covered with relics, such as the fictitious spiritual orders which know nothing of God's Word and seek holiness in their own works. Note, therefore, that the force and power of this commandment lies not in the resting but in the sanctifying so that to this day belongs a special holy exercise. For other works and occupations are not properly called holy exercises, unless the man himself be first holy. But here a work is to be done by which man is himself made holy, which is done (as we have heard) alone through God's Word. For this, then, fixed places, times, persons, and the entire external order of worship have been created and appointed, so that it may be publicly in operation.

Since, therefore, so much depends upon God's Word that without it no holy day can be sanctified, we must know that God insists upon a strict observance of this commandment, and will punish all who despise His Word and are not willing to hear and learn it, especially at the time appointed for the purpose.

Therefore not only those sin against this commandment who grossly misuse and desecrate the holy day, as those who on account of their greed or frivolity neglect to hear God's Word or lie in taverns and are dead drunk like swine; but also that other crowd, who listen to God's Word as to any other trifle, and only from custom come to preaching, and go away again, and at the end of the year know as little of it as at the beginning. For hitherto the opinion prevailed that you had properly hallowed Sunday when you had heard a mass or the Gospel read; but no one cared for God's Word, as also no one taught it. Now, while we have God's Word we nevertheless do not correct the abuse; we suffer ourselves to be preached to and admonished, but we listen without seriousness and care.

Know, therefore, that you must be concerned not only about hearing, but also about learning and retaining it in memory, and do not think that it is optional with you or of no great importance, but that it is God's commandment, who will require of you how you have heard, learned, and honored His Word.

Likewise those fastidious spirits are to be reproved who, when they have heard a sermon or two, find it tedious and dull, thinking that they know all that well enough, and need no more instruction. For just that is the sin which has been hitherto reckoned among mortal sins, and is called *achedia*, i.e., torpor or satiety, a malignant, dangerous plague with which the devil bewitches and deceives the hearts of many, that he may surprise us and secretly withdraw God's Word from us.

For let me tell you this, even though you know it perfectly and be already master in all things, still you are daily in the dominion of the devil, who ceases neither day nor night to steal unawares upon you, to kindle in your heart unbelief and wicked thoughts against the foregoing and all the commandments. Therefore you must always have God's Word in your heart, upon your lips, and in your ears. But where the heart is idle, and the Word does not sound, he breaks in and has done the damage before we are aware. On the other hand, such is the efficacy of the Word, whenever it is seriously contemplated heard, and used, that it is bound never to be without fruit, but always awakens new understanding, pleasure, and devoutness, and produces a pure heart and pure thoughts. For these words are not inoperative or dead, but creative, living words. And even though no other interest or necessity impel us, yet this ought to urge every one thereunto, because thereby the devil is put to flight and driven away, and, besides, this commandment is fulfilled, and [this exercise in the Word] is more pleasing to God than any work of hypocrisy, however brilliant.

THE FOURTH COMMANDMENT.

Thou shalt honor thy father and thy mother.

Thus far we have learned the first three commandments, which relate to God. First that with our whole heart we trust in Him, and fear and love Him throughout all our life. Secondly, that we do not misuse His holy name in the support of falsehood or any bad work, but employ it to the praise of God and the profit and salvation of our neighbor and ourselves. Thirdly, that on holidays and when at rest we diligently treat and urge God's Word, so that all our actions and our entire life be ordered according to it. Now follow the other seven, which relate to our neighbor among which the first and greatest is:

To this estate of fatherhood and motherhood God has given the special distinction above all estates that are beneath it that He not simply commands us to love our parents, but to honor them. For with respect to brothers, sisters, and our neighbors in general He commands nothing higher than that we love them, so that He separates and distinguishes father and mother above all other persons upon earth, and places them at His side. For it is a far higher thing to honor than to love one, inasmuch as it comprehends not only love, but also modesty, humility, and deference as to a majesty there hidden, and requires not only that they be addressed kindly and with reverence, but, most of all that both in heart and with the body we so act as to show that we esteem them very highly, and that, next to God, we regard them as the very highest. For one whom we are to honor from the heart we must truly regard as high and great.

We must, therefore impress it upon the young that they should regard their parents as in God's stead, and remember that however lowly, poor, frail, and queer they may be, nevertheless they are father and mother given them by God. They are not to be deprived of their honor because of their conduct or their failings. Therefore we are not to regard their persons, how they may be, but the will of God who has thus created and ordained. In other respects we are, indeed, all alike in the eyes of God; but among us there must necessarily be such inequality and ordered difference, and therefore God commands it to be observed, that you obey me as your father, and that I have the supremacy.

Learn, therefore, first, what is the honor towards parents required by this commandment to wit, that they be held in distinction and esteem above all things, as the most precious treasure on earth. Furthermore, that also in our words we observe modesty toward them, do not accost them roughly, haughtily, and defiantly, but yield to them and be silent even though they go too far. Thirdly, that we show them such honor also by works, that is, with our body and possessions, that we serve them, help them, and provide for them when they are old, sick, infirm, or poor, and all that not only gladly, but with humility and reverence, as doing it before God. For he who knows how to regard them in his heart will not allow them to suffer want or hunger, but will place them above him and at his side, and will share with them whatever he has and possesses.

Secondly, notice how great, good, and holy a work is here assigned children, which is alas! utterly neglected and disregarded, and no one perceives that God has commanded it or that it is a holy, divine Word and doctrine. For if it had been regarded as such, every one could have inferred that they must be holy men who live according to these words. Thus there would have been no need of inventing monasticism nor spiritual orders, but every child would have abided by this commandment, and could have directed his conscience to God and said: "If I am to do good and holy works, I know of none better than to render all honor and obedience to my parents, because God has Himself commanded it. For what God commands must be much and far nobler than everything that we may devise ourselves, and since there is no higher or better teacher to be found than God, there can be no better doctrine, indeed, than He gives forth. Now, He teaches fully what we should do if we wish to perform truly good works, and by commanding them, He shows that they please Him. If, then, it is God who commands this, and who knows not how to appoint anything better, I will never improve upon it."

Behold, in this manner we would have had a godly child properly taught, reared in true blessedness, and kept at home in obedience to his parents and in their service, so that men should have had blessing and joy from the spectacle. However, God's commandment was not permitted to be thus [with such care and diligence] commended, but had to be neglected and trampled under foot, so that a child could not lay it to heart, and meanwhile gaped [like a panting wolf] at the devices which we set up, without once [consulting or] giving reverence to God.

Let us, therefore, learn at last, for God's sake, that, placing all other things out of sight, our youths look first to this commandment, if they wish to serve God with truly good works, that they do what is pleasing to their fathers and mothers, or to those to whom they may be subject in their stead. For every child that knows and does this has, in the first place, this great consolation in his heart that he can joyfully say and boast (in spite of and against all who are occupied with works of their own choice): "Behold, this work is well pleasing to my God in heaven that I know for certain." Let them all come together with their many great, distressing, and difficult works and make their boast, we will see whether they can show one that is greater and nobler than obedience to father and mother, to whom God has appointed and commanded obedience next to His own majesty; so that if God's Word and will are in force and being accomplished nothing shall be esteemed higher than the will and word of parents; yet so that it, too, is subordinated to obedience toward God and is not opposed to the preceding commandments.

Therefore you should be heartily glad and thank God that He has chosen you and made you worthy to do a work so precious and pleasing to Him. Only see that, although it be regarded as the most humble and despised you esteem it great and precious, not on account of our worthiness, but because it is comprehended in, and controlled by, the jewel and sanctuary, namely, the Word and commandment of God. Oh, what a high price would all; Carthusians, monks, and nuns pay, if in all their religious doings they could bring into God's presence a single work done by virtue of His commandment, and be able before His face to say with joyful heart: "Now I know that this work is well pleasing to Thee." Where will these poor wretched persons hide when in the sight of God and all the world they shall blush with shame before a young child who has lived according to this commandment, and shall have to confess that with their whole life they are not worthy to give it a drink of water? And it serves them right for their devilish perversion in treading God's commandment under foot that they must vainly torment themselves with works of their own device, and, in addition, have scorn and loss for their reward.

Should not the heart, then, leap and melt for joy when going to work and doing what is commanded, saying: Lo, this is better than all holiness of the Carthusians, even though they kill themselves fasting and praying upon their knees without ceasing? For here you have a sure text and a divine testimony that He has enjoined this, but concerning the other He did not command a word. But this is the plight and miserable blindness of the world that no one believes these things; to such an extent the devil has deceived us with false holiness and the glamour of our own works.

Therefore I would be very glad (I say it again) if men would open their eyes and ears and take this to heart, lest some time we may again be led astray from the pure Word of God to the lying vanities of the devil. Then, too, all would be well; for parents would have more joy, love, friendship, and concord in their houses; thus the children could captivate their parents' hearts. On the other hand, when they are obstinate, and will not do what they ought until a rod is laid upon their back, they anger both God and their parents, whereby they deprive themselves of this treasure and joy of conscience and lay up for themselves only misfortune. Therefore, as every one complains, the course of the world now is such that both young and old are altogether dissolute and beyond control, have no reverence nor sense of honor, do nothing except as they are driven to it by blows, and perpetrate what wrong and detraction they can behind each other's back; therefore God also punishes them, that they sink into all kinds of filth and misery. As a rule, the parents, too, are themselves stupid and ignorant; one fool trains [teaches] another, and as they have lived, so live their children after them.

This, now, I say should be the first and most important consideration to urge us to the observance of this commandment; on which account, even if we had no father and mother we ought to wish that God would set up wood and stone before Us, whom we might call father and mother. How much more, since He has given us living parents, should we rejoice to show them honor and obedience, because we know it is so highly pleasing to the Divine Majesty and to all angels, and vexes all devils, and is, besides, the highest work which we can do, after the sublime divine worship comprehended in the previous commandments, so that giving of alms and every other good work toward our neighbor are not equal to this. For God has assigned this estate the highest place, yea, has set it up in His own stead, upon earth. This will and pleasure of God ought to be a sufficient reason and incentive to us to do what we can with good will and pleasure.

Besides this, it is our duty before the world to be grateful for benefits and every good which we have of our parents. But here again the devil rules in the world, so that the children forget their parents, as we all forget God, and no one considers how God nourishes, protects, and defends us, and bestows so much good on body and soul; especially when an evil hour comes we are angry and grumble with impatience and all the good which we have received throughout our life is wiped out [from our memory]. Just so we do also with our parents, and there is no child that understands and considers this [what the parents have endured while nourishing and fostering him], except the Holy Ghost grant him this grace.

God knows very well this perverseness of the world; therefore He admonishes and urges by commandments that every one consider what his parents have done for him and he will find that he has from them body and life, moreover, that he has been fed and reared when otherwise he would have perished a hundred times in his own filth. Therefore it is a true and good saying of old and wise men: Deo, parentibus et magistris non potest satis gratiae rependi, that is, To God, to parents, and to teachers we can never render sufficient gratitude and compensation. He that regards and considers this will indeed without compulsion do all honor to his parents, and bear them up on his hands as those through whom God has done him all good.

Over and above all this, another great reason that should incite us the more [to obedience to this commandment] is that God attaches to this commandment a temporal promise and says: That thou mayest live long upon the land which the Lord, thy God, giveth thee.

Here you can see yourself how much God is in earnest in respect to this commandment, inasmuch as He not only declares that it is well pleasing to Him, and that He has joy and delight therein; but also that it shall be for our prosperity and promote our highest good; so that we may have a pleasant and agreeable life, furnished with every good thing. Therefore also St. Paul greatly emphasizes the same and rejoices in it when he says, Eph. 6, 2. 3: This is the first commandment with promise: That it may be well with thee, and thou mayest live long on the earth. For although the rest also have their promises contained in them, yet in none is it so plainly and explicitly stated.

Here, then, you have the fruit and the reward, that whoever observes this commandment shall have happy days, fortune, and prosperity; and on the other hand, the punishment, that whoever is disobedient shall the sooner perish, and never enjoy life. For to have long life in the sense of the Scriptures is not only to become old, but to have everything which belongs to long life, such as health, wife, and children, livelihood, peace, good government, etc., without which this life can neither be enjoyed in cheerfulness nor long endure. If, therefore, you will not obey father and mother and submit to their discipline, then obey the hangman; if you will not obey him, then submit to the skeleton-man, i.e., death [death the all-subduer, the teacher of wicked children]. For on this God insists peremptorily: Either if you obey Him rendering love and service, He will reward you abundantly with all good, or if you offend Him, He will send upon you both death and the hangman.

Whence come so many knaves that must daily be hanged, beheaded, broken upon the wheel, but from disobedience [to parents], because they will not submit to discipline in kindness, so that, by the punishment of God, they bring it about that we behold their misfortune and grief? For it seldom happens that such perverse people die a natural or timely death.

But the godly and obedient have this blessing, that they live long in pleasant quietness and see their children's children (as said above) to the third and fourth generation. Thus experience also teaches, that where there are honorable, old families who fare well and have many children, they owe their origin to the fact, to be sure, that some of them were brought up well and were regardful of their parents. On the other hand, it is written of the wicked, Ps. 109,13: Let his posterity be cut off; and in the generation following let their name be blotted out. Therefore heed well how great a thing in God's sight obedience is since He so highly esteems it, is so highly pleased with it, and rewards it so richly, and besides enforces punishment so rigorously on those who act contrariwise.

All this I say that it may be well impressed upon the young. For no one believes how necessary this commandment is, although it has not been esteemed and taught hitherto under the papacy. These are simple and easy words, and everybody thinks he knew them a fore; therefore men pass them lightly by, are gaping after other matters, and do not see and believe that God is so greatly offended if they be disregarded, nor that one does a work so well pleasing and precious if he follows them.

In this commandment belongs a further statement regarding all kinds of obedience to persons in authority who have to command and to govern. For all authority flows and is propagated from the authority of parents. For where a father is unable alone to educate his [rebellious and irritable] child, he employs a schoolmaster to instruct him; if he be too weak, he enlists the aid of his friends and neighbors; if he departs this life, he delegates and confers his authority and government upon others who are appointed for the purpose. Likewise, he must have domestics, man-servants and maid-servants, under himself for the management of the household, so that all whom we call masters are in the place of parents and must derive their power and authority to govern from them. Hence also they are all called fathers in the Scriptures, as those who in their government perform the functions of a father, and should have a paternal heart toward their subordinates. As also from antiquity the Romans and other nations called the masters and mistresses of the household patres- et matresfamiliae that is, housefathers and housemothers. So also they called their national rulers and overlords patres patriae, that is fathers of the entire country, for a great shame to us who would be Christians that we do not likewise call them so, or, at least do not esteem and honor them as such.

Now, what a child owes to father and mother, the same owe all who are embraced in the household. Therefore man-servants and maid-servants should be careful not only to be obedient to their masters and mistresses but also to honor them as their own fathers and mothers, and to do everything which they know is expected of them, not from compulsion and with reluctance, but with pleasure and joy for the cause just mentioned, namely that it is God's command and is pleasing to Him above all other works. Therefore they ought rather to pay wages in addition and be glad that they may obtain masters and mistresses to have such joyful consciences and to know how they may do truly golden works;

51

a matter which has hitherto been neglected and despised, when, instead, everybody ran in the devil's name, into convents or to pilgrimages and indulgences, with loss [of time and money] and with an evil conscience.

If this truth, then, could be impressed upon the poor people, a servant-girl would leap and praise and thank God; and with her tidy work for which she receives support and wages she would acquire such a treasure as all that are esteemed the greatest saints have not obtained. Is it not an excellent boast to know and say that, if you perform your daily domestic task, this is better than all the sanctity and ascetic life of monks? And you have the promise, in addition, that you shall prosper in all good and fare well. How can you lead a more blessed or holier life as far as your works are concerned? For in the sight of God faith is what really renders a person holy, and alone serves Him, but the works are for the service of man. There you have everything good, protection and defense in the Lord, a joyful conscience and a gracious God besides, who will reward you a hundredfold, so that you are even a nobleman if you be only pious and obedient. But if not, you have, in the first place, nothing but the wrath and displeasure of God, no peace of heart, and afterwards all manner of plagues and misfortunes.

Whoever will not be influenced by this and inclined to godliness we hand over to the hangman and to the skeleton-man. Therefore let every one who allows himself to be advised remember that God is not making sport, and know that it is God who speaks with you and demands obedience. If you obey Him, you are His dear child; but if you despise to do it, then take shame, misery, and grief for your reward.

The same also is to be said of obedience to civil government, which (as we have said) is all embraced in the estate of fatherhood and extends farthest of all relations. For here the father is not one of a single family, but of as many people as he has tenants, citizens, or subjects. For through them, as through our parents, God gives to us food, house and home, protection and security. Therefore since they bear such name and title with all honor as their highest dignity, it is our duty to honor them and to esteem them great as the dearest treasure and the most precious jewel upon earth.

He, now, who is obedient here, is willing and ready to serve, and cheerfully does all that pertains to honor, knows that he is pleasing God and that he will receive joy and happiness for his reward. If he will not do it in love, but despises and resists [authority] or rebels, let him also know, on the other hand, that he shall have no favor nor blessing, and where he thinks to gain a florin thereby, he will elsewhere lose ten times as much, or become a victim to the hangman, perish by war, pestilence, and famine, or experience no good in his children, and be obliged to suffer injury, injustice, and violence at the hands of his servants, neighbors, or strangers and tyrants; so that what we seek and deserve is paid back and comes home to us.

If we would ever suffer ourselves to be persuaded that such works are pleasing to God and have so rich a reward, we would be established in altogether abundant possessions and have what our heart desires. But because the word and command of God are so lightly esteemed, as though some babbler had spoken it, let us see whether you are the man to oppose Him. How difficult, do you think, it will be for Him to recompense you! Therefore you would certainly live much better with the divine favor, peace, and happiness than with His displeasure and misfortune. Why, think you, is the world now so full of unfaithfulness, disgrace, calamity, and murder, but because every one desires to be his own master and free from the emperor, to care nothing for any one, and do what pleases him? Therefore God punishes one knave by another, so that, when you defraud and despise your master, another comes and deals in like manner with you, yea, in your household you must suffer ten times more from wife, children, or servants.

Indeed, we feel our misfortune, we murmur and complain of unfaithfulness, violence, and injustice, but will not see that we ourselves are knaves who have fully deserved this punishment, and yet are not thereby reformed. We will have no favor and happiness, therefore it is but fair that we have nothing but misfortune without mercy. There must still be somewhere upon earth some godly people because God continues to grant us so much good! On our own account we should not have a farthing in the house nor a straw in the field. All this I have been obliged to urge with so many words, in hope that some one may take it to heart, that we may be relieved of the blindness and misery in which we are steeped so deeply, and may truly understand the Word and will of God, and earnestly accept it. For thence we would learn how we could have joy, happiness, and salvation enough, both temporal and eternal.

Thus we have two kinds of fathers presented in this commandment, fathers in blood and fathers in office, or those to whom belongs the care of the family, and those to whom belongs the care of the country. Besides these there are yet spiritual fathers; not like those in the Papacy, who have indeed had themselves called thus, but have performed no function of the paternal office. For those only are called spiritual fathers who govern and guide us by the Word of God; as St. Paul boasts his fatherhood 1 Cor. 4, 15, where he says: In Christ Jesus I hove begotten you through the Gospel. Now, since they are fathers they are entitled to their honor, even above all others. But here it is bestowed least; for the way which the world knows for honoring them is to drive them out of the country and to grudge them a piece of bread and, in short, they must be (as says St. Paul 1 Cor. 4, 13) as the filth of the world and everybody's refuse and footrag.

Yet there is need that this also be urged upon the populace, that those who would be Christians are under obligation in the sight of God to esteem them worthy of double honor who minister to their souls, that they deal well with them and provide for them. For that, God is willing to add to you sufficient blessing and will not let you come to want. But in this matter every one refuses and resists, and all are afraid that they will perish from bodily want, and cannot now support one respectable preacher, where formerly they filled ten fat paunches. In this we also deserve that God deprive us of His Word and blessing, and again allow preachers of lies to arise to lead us to the devil, and, in addition, to drain our sweat and blood.

But those who keep in sight God's will and commandment have the promise that everything which they bestow upon temporal and spiritual fathers, and whatever they do to honor them, shall be richly recompensed to them, so that they shall have, not bread, clothing, and money for a year or two, but long life, support, and peace, and shall be eternally rich and blessed. Therefore only do what is your duty, and let God take care how He is to support you and provide for you sufficiently. Since He has promised it, and has never yet lied, He will not be found lying to you.

This ought indeed to encourage us, and give us hearts that would melt in pleasure and love toward those to whom we owe honor, so that we would raise our hands and joyfully thank God who has given us such promises, for which we ought to run to the ends of the world [to the remotest parts of India]. For although the whole world should combine, it could not add an hour to our life or give us a single grain from the earth. But God wishes to give you all exceeding abundantly according to your heart's desire. He who despises and casts this to the winds is not worthy ever to hear a word of God. This has now been stated more than enough for all who belong under this commandment.

In addition, it would be well to preach to the parents also, and such as bear their office, as to how they should deport themselves toward those who are committed to them for their government. For although this is not expressed in the Ten Commandments, it is nevertheless abundantly enjoined in many places in the Scriptures. And God desires to have it embraced in this commandment when He speaks of father and mother. For He does not wish to have in this office and government knaves and tyrants; nor does He assign to them this honor, that is, power and authority to govern, that they should have themselves worshiped; but they should consider that they are under obligations of obedience to God; and that, first of all, they should earnestly and faithfully discharge their office, not only to support and provide for the bodily necessities of their children, servants, subjects, etc., but, most of all, to train them to the honor and praise of God. Therefore do not think that this is left to your pleasure and arbitrary will, but that it is a strict command and injunction of God, to whom also you must give account for it.

But here again the sad plight arises that no one perceives or heeds this, and all live on as though God gave us children for our pleasure or amusement, and servants that we should employ them like a cow or ass, only for work, or as though we were only to gratify our wantonness with our subjects, ignoring them, as though it were no concern of ours what they learn or how they live; and no one is willing to see that this is the command of the Supreme Majesty, who will most strictly call us to account and punish us for it; nor that there is so great need to be so seriously concerned about the young. For if we wish to have excellent and apt persons both for civil and ecclesiastical government we must spare no diligence, time, or cost in teaching and educating our children, that they may serve God and the world, and we must not think only how we may amass money and possessions for them. For God can indeed without us support and make them rich, as He daily does. But for this purpose He has given us children, and issued this command that we should train and govern them according to His will, else He would have no need of father and mother. Let every one know therefore, that it is his duty, on peril of losing the divine favor, to bring up his children above all things in the fear and knowledge of God, and if they are talented, have them learn and study something, that they may be employed for whatever need there is [to have them instructed and trained in a liberal education, that men may be able to have their aid in government and in whatever is necessary].

If that were done, God would also richly bless us and give us grace to train men by whom land and people might be improved and likewise well educated citizens, chaste and domestic wives, who afterwards would rear godly children and servants. Here consider now what deadly injury you are doing if you be negligent and fail on your part to bring up your child to usefulness and piety, and how you bring upon yourself all sin and wrath, thus earning hell by your own children, even though you be otherwise pious and holy. And because this is disregarded, God so fearfully punishes the world that there is no discipline, government, or peace, of which we all complain, but do not see that it is our fault; for as we train them, we have spoiled and disobedient children and subjects. Let this be sufficient exhortation; for to draw this out at length belongs to another time.

THE FIFTH COMMANDMENT.

Thou shalt not kill.

We have now completed both the spiritual and the temporal government, that is, the divine and the paternal authority and obedience. But here now we go forth from our house among our neighbors to learn how we should live with one another, every one himself toward his neighbor. Therefore God and government are not included in this commandment nor is the power to kill, which they have taken away. For God has delegated His authority to punish evil-doers to the government instead of parents, who aforetime (as we read in Moses) were required to bring their own children to judgment and sentence them to death. Therefore, what is here forbidden is forbidden to the individual in his relation to any one else, and not to the government.

Now this commandment is easy enough and has been often treated, because we hear it annually in the Gospel of St. Matthew, 5, 21 ff., where Christ Himself explains and sums it up, namely, that we must not kill neither with hand, heart, mouth, signs, gestures, help, nor counsel. Therefore it is here forbidden to every one to be angry, except those (as we said) who are in the place of God, that is, parents and the government. For it is proper for God and for every one who is in a divine estate to be angry, to reprove and punish, namely, on account of those very persons who transgress this and the other commandments.

But the cause and need of this commandment is that God well knows that the world is evil, and that this life has much unhappiness; therefore

58

He has placed this and the other commandments between the good and the evil. Now, as there are many assaults upon all commandments, so it happens also in this commandment that we must live among many people who do us harm, so that we have cause to be hostile to them.

As when your neighbor sees that you have a better house and home [a larger family and more fertile fields], greater possessions and fortune from God than he, he is sulky, envies you, and speaks no good of you.

Thus by the devil's incitement you will get many enemies who cannot bear to see you have any good, either bodily or spiritual. When we see such people, our hearts, in turn, would rage and bleed and take vengeance. Then there arise cursing and blows, from which follow finally misery and murder. Here, now, God like a kind father steps in ahead of Us, interposes and wishes to have the quarrel settled, that no misfortune come of it, nor one destroy another. And briefly He would hereby protect, set free, and keep in peace every one against the crime and violence of every one else; and would have this commandment placed as a wall, fortress, and refuge about our neighbor, that we do him no hurt nor harm in his body.

Thus this commandment aims at this, that no one offend his neighbor on account of any evil deed, even though he have fully deserved it. For where murder is forbidden, all cause also is forbidden whence murder may originate. For many a one, although he does not kill, yet curses and utters a wish, which would stop a person from running far if it were to strike him in the neck [makes imprecations, which if fulfilled with respect to any one, he would not live long]. Now since this inheres in every one by nature and it is a common practice that no one is willing to suffer at the hands of another, God wishes to remove the root and source by which the heart is embittered against our neighbor, and to accustom us ever to keep in view this commandment, always to contemplate ourselves in it as in a mirror, to regard the will of God, and with hearty confidence and invocation of His name to commit to Him the wrong which we suffer. Thus we shall suffer our enemies to rage and be angry, doing what they can, and we learn to calm our wrath, and to have a patient, gentle heart, especially toward those who give us cause to be angry, that is, our enemies.

Therefore the entire sum of what it means not to kill is to be impressed most explicitly upon the simple-minded. In the first place that we harm no one, first, with our hand or by deed. Then, that we do not employ our tongue to instigate or counsel thereto. Further, that we neither use nor assent to any kind of means or methods whereby any one may be injured. And finally, that the heart be not ill disposed toward any one, nor from anger and hatred wish him ill, so that body and soul may be innocent in regard to every one, but especially those who wish you evil or inflict such upon you. For to do evil to one who wishes and does you good is not human, but diabolical.

Secondly, under this commandment not only he is guilty who does evil to his neighbor, but he also who can do him good, prevent, resist evil, defend and save him, so that no bodily harm or hurt happen to him and yet does not do it. If, therefore, you send away one that is naked when you could clothe him, you have caused him to freeze to death; you see one suffer hunger and do not give him food, you have caused him to starve. So also, if you see any one innocently sentenced to death or in like distress, and do not save him, although you know ways and means to do so, you have killed him. And it will not avail you to make the pretext that you did not afford any help, counsel, or aid thereto for you have withheld your love from him and deprived him of the benefit whereby his life would have been saved.

Therefore God also rightly calls all those murderers who do not afford counsel and help in distress and danger of body and life, and will pass a most terrible sentence upon them in the last day, as Christ Himself has announced when He shall say, Matt.25, 42f.: I was an hungered, and ye gave Me no meat; I was thirsty, and ye gave Me no drink; I was a stranger, and ye took Me not in; naked, and ye clothed Me not; sick and in prison and ye visited Me not. That is: You would have suffered Me and Mine to die of hunger thirst, and cold, would have suffered the wild beasts to tear us to pieces, or left us to rot in prison or perish in distress. What else is that but to reproach them as murderers and bloodhounds? For although you have not actually done all this, you have nevertheless, so far as you were concerned, suffered him to pine and perish in misfortune.

It is just as if I saw some one navigating and laboring in deep water [and struggling against adverse winds] or one fallen into fire, and could extend to him the hand to pull him out and save him, and yet refused to do it. What else would I appear, even in the eyes of the world, than as a murderer and a criminal?

Therefore it is God's ultimate purpose that we suffer harm to befall no man, but show him all good and love; and, as we have said it is specially directed toward those who are our enemies. For to do good to our friends is but an ordinary heathen virtue as Christ says Matt. 5, 46.

Here we have again the Word of God whereby He would encourage and urge us to true noble and sublime works, as gentleness patience, and, in short, love and kindness to our enemies, and would ever remind us to reflect upon the First Commandment, that He is our God, that is, that He will help, assist, and protect us, in order that He may thus quench the desire of revenge in us.

This we ought to practice and inculcate and we would have our hands full doing good works. But this would not be preaching for monks; it would greatly detract from the religious estate, and infringe upon the sanctity of Carthusians, and would even be regarded as forbidding good works and clearing the convents. For in this wise the ordinary state of Christians would be considered just as worthy, and even worthier, and everybody would see how they mock and delude the world with a false, hypocritical show of holiness, because they have given this and other commandments to the winds, and have esteemed them unnecessary, as though they were not commandments but mere counsels, and have at the same time shamelessly proclaimed and boasted their hypocritical estate and works as the most perfect life, in order that they might lead a pleasant, easy life, without the cross and without patience, for which reason, too, they have resorted to the cloisters, so that they might not be obliged to suffer any wrong from any one or to do him any good. But know now that these are the true, holy, and godly works, in which, with all the angels He rejoices, in comparison with which all human holiness is but stench and filth, and besides, deserves nothing but wrath and damnation.

THE SIXTH COMMANDMENT.

Thou shalt not commit adultery.

These commandments now [that follow] are easily understood from [the explanation of] the preceding; for they are all to the effect that we [be careful to] avoid doing any kind of injury to our neighbor. But they are arranged in fine [elegant] order. In the first place, they treat of his own person. Then they proceed to the person nearest him, or the closest possession next after his body namely, his wife, who is one flesh and blood with him, so that we cannot inflict a higher injury upon him in any good that is his. Therefore it is explicitly forbidden here to bring any disgrace upon him in respect to his wife. And it really aims at adultery, because among the Jews it was ordained and commanded that every one must be married. Therefore also the young were early provided for [married], so that the virgin state was held in small esteem, neither were public prostitution and lewdness tolerated (as now). Therefore adultery was the most common form of unchastity among them.

But because among us there is such a shameful mess and the very dregs of all vice and lewdness, this commandment is directed also against all manner of unchastity, whatever it may be called; and not only is the external act forbidden, but also every kind of cause, incitement, and means, so that the heart, the lips, and the whole body may be chaste and afford no opportunity, help, or persuasion to unchastity. And not only this, but that we also make resistance, afford protection and rescue wherever there is danger and need; and again, that we give help and counsel, so as to maintain our neighbor's honor. For whenever you omit this when you could make resistance, or connive at it as if it did not concern you, you are as truly guilty as the one perpetrating the deed. Thus, to state it in the briefest manner, there is required this much, that every one both live chastely himself and help his neighbor do the same, so that God by this commandment wishes to hedge round about and protect [as with a rampart] every spouse that no one trespass against them.

But since this commandment is aimed directly at the state of matrimony and gives occasion to speak of the same, you must well understand and mark, first, how gloriously God honors and extols this estate, inasmuch as by His commandment He both sanctions and guards it. He has sanctioned it above in the Fourth Commandment: Honor thy father and thy mother; but here He has (as we said) hedged it about and protected it. Therefore He also wishes us to honor it, and to maintain and conduct it as a divine and blessed estate; because, in the first place, He has instituted it before all others, and therefore created man and woman separately (as is evident), not for lewdness, but that they should [legitimately] live together, be fruitful, beget children, and nourish and train them to the honor of God.

Therefore God has also most richly blessed this estate above all others, and, in addition, has bestowed on it and wrapped up in it everything in the world, to the end that this estate might be well and richly provided for. Married life is therefore no jest or presumption; but it is an excellent thing and a matter of divine seriousness. For it is of the highest importance to Him that persons be raised who may serve the world and promote the knowledge of God, godly living, and all virtues, to fight against wickedness and the devil.

Therefore I have always taught that this estate should not be despised nor held in disrepute, as is done by the blind world and our false ecclesiastics, but that it be regarded according to God's Word, by which it is adorned and sanctified, so that it is not only placed on an equality with other estates, but that it precedes and surpasses them all, whether they be that of emperor, princes, bishops, or whoever they please. For both ecclesiastical and civil estates must humble themselves and all be found in this estate as we shall hear. Therefore it is not a peculiar estate, but the most common and noblest estate, which pervades all Christendom, yea which extends through all the world.

In the second place, you must know also that it is not only an honorable, but also a necessary state, and it is solemnly commanded by God that, in general, in all conditions, men and women, who were created for it, shall be found in this estate; yet with some exceptions (although few) whom God has especially excepted, so that they are not fit for the married estate, or whom He has released by a high, supernatural gift that they can maintain chastity without this estate. For where nature has its course, as it is implanted by God, it is not possible to remain chaste without marriage. For flesh and blood remain flesh and blood, and the natural inclination and excitement have their course without let or hindrance, as everybody sees and feels. In order, therefore, that it may be the more easy in some degree to avoid unchastity, God has commanded the estate of matrimony, that every one may have his proper portion and be satisfied therewith; although God's grace besides is required in order that the heart also may be pure.

From this you see how this popish rabble, priests, monks, and nuns, resist God's order and commandment, inasmuch as they despise and forbid matrimony, and presume and vow to maintain perpetual chastity, and, besides, deceive the simple-minded with lying words and appearances [impostures]. For no one has so little love and inclination to chastity as just those who because of great sanctity avoid marriage, and either indulge in open and shameless prostitution, or secretly do even worse, so that one dare not speak of it, as has, alas! been learned too fully. And, in short, even though they abstain from the act, their hearts are so full of unchaste thoughts and evil lusts that there is a continual burning and secret suffering, which can be avoided in the married life. Therefore all vows of chastity out of the married state are condemned by this commandment, and free permission is granted, yea, even the command is given, to all poor ensnared consciences which have been deceived by their monastic vows to abandon the unchaste state and enter the married life, considering that even if the monastic life were godly, it would nevertheless not be in their power to maintain chastity, and if they remain in it, they must only sin more and more against this commandment.

Now, I speak of this in order that the young may be so guided that they conceive a liking for the married estate, and know that it is a blessed estate and pleasing to God. For in this way we might in the course of time bring it about that married life be restored to honor, and that there might be less of the filthy, dissolute, disorderly doings which now run riot the world over in open prostitution and other shameful vices arising from disregard of married life. Therefore it is the duty of parents and the government to see to it that our youth be brought up to discipline and respectability, and when they have come to years of maturity, to provide for them [to have them married] in the fear of God and honorably; He would not fail to add His blessing and grace, so that men would have joy and happiness from the same.

Let me now say in conclusion that this commandment demands not only that every one live chastely in thought, word, and deed in his condition, that is, especially in the estate of matrimony, but also that every one love and esteem the spouse given him by God. For where conjugal chastity is to be maintained, man and wife must by all means live together in love and harmony, that one may cherish the other from the heart and with entire fidelity. For that is one of the principal points which enkindle love and desire of chastity, so that, where this is found, chastity will follow as a matter of course without any command. Therefore also St. Paul so diligently exhorts husband and wife to love and honor one another. Here you have again a precious, yea, many and great good works, of which you can joyfully boast, against all ecclesiastical estates, chosen without God's Word and commandment.

THE SEVENTH COMMANDMENT.

Thou shalt not steal.

After your person and spouse temporal property comes next. That also God wishes to have protected, and He has commanded that no one shall subtract from, or curtail, his neighbor's possessions. For to steal is nothing else than to get possession of another's property wrongfully, which briefly comprehends all kinds of advantage in all sorts of trade to the disadvantage of our neighbor. Now, this is indeed quite a wide-spread and common vice, but so little regarded and observed that it exceeds all measure, so that if all who are thieves, and yet do not wish to be called such, were to be hanged on gallows the world would soon be devastated and there would be a lack both of executioners and gallows. For, as we have just said, to steal is to signify not only to empty our neighbor's coffer and pockets, but to be grasping in the market, in all stores, booths, wine-and beer-cellars, workshops, and, in short, wherever there is trading or taking and giving of money for merchandise or labor.

As, for instance, to explain this somewhat grossly for the common people, that it may be seen how godly we are: When a manservant or maid-servant does not serve faithfully in the house, and does damage, or allows it to be done when it could be prevented, or otherwise ruins and neglects the goods entrusted to him, from indolence idleness, or malice, to the spite and vexation of master and mistress, and in whatever way this can be done purposely (for I do not speak of what happens from oversight and against one's will), you can in a year abscond thirty, forty florins, which if another had taken secretly or carried away, he would be hanged with the rope. But here you [while conscious of such a great theft] may even bid defiance and become insolent, and no one dare call you a thief.

The same I say also of mechanics, workmen, and day-laborers, who all follow their wanton notions, and never know enough ways to overcharge people, while they are lazy and unfaithful in their work. All these are far worse than sneak-thieves, against whom we can guard with locks and bolts, or who, if apprehended, are treated in such a manner that they will not do the same again. But against these no one can guard, no one dare even look awry at them or accuse them of theft, so that one would ten times rather lose from his purse. For here are my neighbors, good friends, my own servants, from whom I expect good [every faithful and diligent service], who defraud me first of all.

Furthermore, in the market and in common trade likewise, this practice is in full swing and force to the greatest extent, where one openly defrauds another with bad merchandise, false measures, weights, coins, and by nimbleness and queer finances or dexterous tricks takes advantage of him; likewise, when one overcharges a person in a trade and wantonly drives a hard bargain, skins and distresses him. And who can recount or think of all these things? To sum up, this is the commonest craft and the largest guild on earth, and if we regard the world throughout all conditions of life, it is nothing else than a vast, wide stall, full of great thieves.

Therefore they are also called swivel-chair robbers, land-and highway-robbers, not pick-locks and sneak-thieves who snatch away the ready cash, but who sit on the chair [at home] and are styled great noblemen, and honorable, pious citizens, and yet rob and steal under a good pretext.

Yes, here we might be silent about the trifling individual thieves if we were to attack the great, powerful arch-thieves with whom lords and princes keep company, who daily plunder not only a city or two, but all Germany. Yea, where should we place the head and supreme protector of all thieves, the Holy Chair at Rome with all its retinue, which has grabbed by theft the wealth of all the world, and holds it to this day?

This is, in short, the course of the world: whoever can steal and rob openly goes free and secure, unmolested by any one, and even demands that he be honored. Meanwhile the little sneak-thieves, who have once trespassed, must bear the shame and punishment to render the former godly and honorable. But let them know that in the sight of God they are the greatest thieves, and that He will punish them as they are worthy and deserve.

Now, since this commandment is so far-reaching [and comprehensive], as just indicated, it is necessary to urge it well and to explain it to the common people, not to let them go on in their wantonness and security, but always to place before their eyes the wrath of God, and inculcate the same. For we have to preach this not to Christians, but chiefly to knaves and scoundrels, to whom it would be more fitting for judges, jailers, or Master Hannes [the executioner] to preach. Therefore let every one know that it is his duty, at the risk of God's displeasure, not only to do no injury to his neighbor, nor to deprive him of gain, nor to perpetrate any act of unfaithfulness or malice in any bargain or trade, but faithfully to preserve his property for him, to secure and promote his advantage, especially when one accepts money, wages, and one's livelihood for such service.

He now who wantonly despises this may indeed pass along and escape the hangman, but he shall not escape the wrath and punishment of God; and when he has long practiced his defiance and arrogance, he shall yet remain a tramp and beggar, and, in addition, have all plagues and misfortune. Now you are going your way [wherever your heart's pleasure calls you] while you ought to preserve the property of your master and mistress, for which service you fill your crop and maw, take your wages like a thief, have people treat you as a nobleman; for there are many that are even insolent towards their masters and mistresses, and are unwilling to do them a favor or service by which to protect them from loss.

But reflect what you will gain when, having come into your own property and being set up in your home (to which God will help with all misfortunes), it [your perfidy] will bob up again and come home to you, and you will find that where you have cheated or done injury to the value of one mite, you will have to pay thirty again.

Such shall be the lot also of mechanics and day-laborers of whom we are now obliged to hear and suffer such intolerable maliciousness, as though they were noblemen in another's possessions, and every one were obliged to give them what they demand. Just let them continue practicing their exactions as long as they can; but God will not forget His commandment, and will reward them according as they have served, and will hang them, not upon a green gallows, but upon a dry one so that all their life they shall neither prosper nor accumulate anything. And indeed, if there were a well-ordered government in the land, such wantonness might soon be checked and prevented, as was the custom in ancient times among the Romans, where such characters were promptly seized by the pate in a way that others took warning.

No more shall all the rest prosper who change the open free market into a carrion-pit of extortion and a den of robbery, where the poor are daily overcharged, new burdens and high prices are imposed, and every one uses the market according to his caprice, and is even defiant and brags as though it were his fair privilege and right to sell his goods for as high a price as he please, and no one had a right to say a word against it. We will indeed look on and let these people skin, pinch, and hoard, but we will trust in God—who will, however, do this of His own accord,— that, after you have been skinning and scraping for a long time, He will pronounce such a blessing on your gains that your grain in the garner, your beer in the cellar, your cattle in the stalls shall perish; yea, where you have cheated and overcharged any one to the amount of a florin, your entire pile shall be consumed with rust, so that you shall never enjoy it.

And indeed, we see and experience this being fulfilled daily before our eyes, that no stolen or dishonestly acquired possession thrives. How many there are who rake and scrape day and night, and yet grow not a farthing richer! And though they gather much, they must suffer so many plagues and misfortunes that they cannot relish it with cheerfulness nor transmit it to their children. But as no one minds it, and we go on as though it did not concern us, God must visit us in a different way and teach us manners by imposing one taxation after another, or billeting a troop of soldiers upon us, who in one hour empty our coffers and purses, and do not quit as long as we have a farthing left, and in addition, by way of thanks, burn and devastate house and home, and outrage and kill wife and children.

And, in short, if you steal much, depend upon it that again as much will be stolen from you; and he who robs and acquires with violence and wrong will submit to one who shall deal after the same fashion with him. For God is master of this art, that since every one robs and steals from the other, He punishes one thief by means of another. Else where should we find enough gallows and ropes?

Now, whoever is willing to be instructed let him know that this is the commandment of God, and that it must not be treated as a jest. For although you despise us, defraud, steal, and rob, we will indeed manage to endure your haughtiness, suffer, and, according to the Lord's Prayer, forgive and show pity; for we know that the godly shall nevertheless have enough, and you injure yourself more than another.

But beware of this: When the poor man comes to you (of whom there are so many now) who must buy with the penny of his daily wages and live upon it, and you are harsh to him, as though every one lived by your favor, and you skin and scrape to the bone, and, besides, with pride and haughtiness turn him off to whom you ought to give for nothing, he will go away wretched and sorrowful, and since he can complain to no one he will cry and call to heaven,—then beware (I say again) as of the devil himself. For such groaning and calling will be no jest, but will have a weight that will prove too heavy for you and all the world. For it will reach Him who takes care of the poor sorrowful hearts, and will not allow them to go unavenged. But if you despise this and become defiant, see whom you have brought upon you: if you succeed and prosper, you may before all the world call God and me a liar.

We have exhorted, warned, and protested enough; he who will not heed or believe it may go on until he learns this by experience Yet it must be impressed upon the young that they may be careful not to follow the old lawless crowd, but keep their eyes fixed upon God's commandment, lest His wrath and punishment come upon them too. It behooves us to do no more than to instruct and reprove with God's Word; but to check such open wantonness there is need of the princes and government, who themselves would have eyes and the courage to establish and maintain order in all manner of trade and commerce, lest the poor be burdened and oppressed nor they themselves be loaded with other men's sins.

Let this suffice as an explanation of what stealing is, that it be not taken too narrowly but made to extend as far as we have to do with our neighbors. And briefly, in a summary, as in the former commandments, it is herewith forbidden, in the first place, to do our neighbor any injury or wrong (in whatever manner supposable, by curtailing, forestalling, and withholding his possessions and property), or even to consent or allow such a thing, but to interpose and prevent it. And, on the other hand, it is commanded that we advance and improve his possessions, and in case he suffers want, that we help, communicate, and lend both to friends and foes.

Whoever now seeks and desires good works will find here more than enough such as are heartily acceptable and pleasing to God, and in addition are favored and crowned with excellent blessings, that we are to be richly compensated for all that we do for our neighbor's good and from friendship; as King Solomon also teaches Prov. 19, 17: He that hath pity upon the poor lendeth unto the Lord; and that which he hath given will He pay him again. Here, then you have a rich Lord, who is certainly sufficient for you, and who will not suffer you to come short in anything or to want; thus you can with a joyful conscience enjoy a hundred times more than you could scrape together with unfaithfulness and wrong. Now, whoever does not desire the blessing will find wrath and misfortune enough.

THE EIGHTH COMMANDMENT.

Thou shalt not bear false witness against thy neighbor.

Over and above our own body, spouse, and temporal possessions, we have yet another treasure, namely, honor and good report [the illustrious testimony of an upright and unsullied name and reputation], with which we cannot dispense. For it is intolerable to live among men in open shame and general contempt. Therefore God wishes the reputation, good name, and upright character of our neighbor to be taken away or diminished as little as his money and possessions, that every one may stand in his integrity before wife, children, servants, and neighbors. And in the first place, we take the plainest meaning of this commandment according to the words (Thou shalt not bear false witness), as pertaining to the public courts of justice, where a poor innocent man is accused and oppressed by false witnesses in order to be punished in his body, property, or honor.

Now, this appears as if it were of little concern to us at present; but with the Jews it was quite a common and ordinary matter. For the people were organized under an excellent and regular government; and where there is still such a government, instances of this sin will not be wanting. The cause of it is that where judges, burgomasters, princes, or others in authority sit in judgment, things never fail to go according to the course of the world; namely, men do not like to offend anybody, flatter, and speak to gain favor, money, prospects, or friendship; and in consequence a poor man and his cause must be oppressed, denounced as wrong, and suffer punishment. And it is a common calamity in the world that in courts of justice there seldom preside godly men.

For to be a judge requires above all things a godly man, and not only a godly, but also a wise, modest, yea, a brave and bold man; likewise, to be a witness requires a fearless and especially a godly man. For a person who is to judge all matters rightly and carry them through with his decision will often offend good friends, relatives, neighbors, and the rich and powerful, who can greatly serve or injure him. Therefore he must be quite blind, have his eyes and ears closed, neither see nor hear, but go straight forward in everything that comes before him, and decide accordingly.

Therefore this commandment is given first of all that every one shall help his neighbor to secure his rights, and not allow them to be hindered or twisted, but shall promote and strictly maintain them, no matter whether he be judge or witness, and let it pertain to whatsoever it will. And especially is a goal set up here for our jurists that they be careful to deal truly and uprightly with every case, allowing right to remain right, and, on the other hand, not perverting anything [by their tricks and technical points turning black into white and making wrong out to be right], nor glossing it over or keeping silent concerning it, irrespective of a person's money, possession, honor, or power. This is one part and the plainest sense of this commandment concerning all that takes place in court.

Next, it extends very much further, if we are to apply it to spiritual jurisdiction or administration; here it is a common occurrence that every one bears false witness against his neighbor. For wherever there are godly preachers and Christians, they must bear the sentence before the world that they are called heretics, apostates, yea, seditious and desperately wicked miscreants. Besides the Word of God must suffer in the most shameful and malicious manner, being persecuted blasphemed, contradicted, perverted and falsely cited and interpreted. But let this pass; for it is the way of the blind world that she condemns and persecutes the truth and the children of God, and yet esteems it no sin.

In the third place, what concerns us all, this commandment forbids all sins of the tongue whereby we may injure or approach too closely to our neighbor. For to bear false witness is nothing else than a work of the tongue. Now, whatever is done with the tongue against a fellow-man God would have prohibited, whether it be false preachers with their doctrine and blasphemy, false judges and witnesses with their verdict, or outside of court by lying and evil-speaking. Here belongs particularly the detestable, shameful vice of speaking behind a person's back and slandering, to which the devil spurs us on and of which there would be much to be said. For it is a common evil plague that every one prefers hearing evil to hearing good of his neighbor; and although we ourselves are so bad that we cannot suffer that any one should say anything bad about us, but every one would much rather that all the world should speak of him in terms of gold, yet we cannot bear that the best is spoken about others.

Therefore, to avoid this vice we should note that no one is allowed publicly to judge and reprove his neighbor, although he may see him sin, unless he have a command to judge and to reprove. For there is a great difference between these two things, judging sin and knowing sin. You may indeed know it, but you are not to judge it. I can indeed see and hear that my neighbor sins, but I have no command to report it to others. Now, if I rush in, judging and passing sentence, I fall into a sin which is greater than his. But if you know it, do nothing else than turn your ears into a grave and cover it, until you are appointed to be judge and to punish by virtue of your office.

Those, then, are called slanderers who are not content with knowing a thing, but proceed to assume jurisdiction, and when they know a slight offense of another, carry it into every corner, and are delighted and tickled that they can stir up another's displeasure [baseness], as swine roll themselves in the dirt and root in it with the snout. This is nothing else than meddling with the judgment and office of God, and pronouncing sentence and punishment with the most severe verdict. For no judge can punish to a higher degree nor go farther than to say: "He is a thief, a murderer, a traitor," etc. Therefore, whoever presumes to say the same of his neighbor goes just as far as the emperor and all governments. For although you do not wield the sword, you employ your poisonous tongue to the shame and hurt of your neighbor.

God therefore would have it prohibited that any one speak evil of another even though he be guilty, and the latter know it right well; much less if he do not know it, and have it only from hearsay. But you say: Shall I not say it if it be the truth? Answer: Why do you not make accusation to regular judges? Ah, I cannot prove it publicly, and hence I might be silenced and turned away in a harsh manner [incur the penalty of a false accusation]. "Ah, indeed, do you smell the roast?" If you do not trust yourself to stand before the proper authorities and to make answer, then hold your tongue. But if you know it, know it for yourself and not for another. For if you tell it to others, although it be true, you will appear as a liar, because you cannot prove it, and you are, besides acting like a knave. For we ought never to deprive any one of his honor or good name unless it be first taken away from him publicly.

False witness, then, is everything which cannot be properly proved. Therefore, what is not manifest upon sufficient evidence no one shall make public or declare for truth; and in short, whatever is secret should be allowed to remain secret, or, at any rate, should be secretly reproved, as we shall hear. Therefore, if you encounter an idle tongue which betrays and slanders some one, contradict such a one promptly to his face, that he may blush thus many a one will hold his tongue who else would bring some poor man into bad repute from which he would not easily extricate himself. For honor and a good name are easily taken away, but not easily restored.

Thus you see that it is summarily forbidden to speak any evil of our neighbor, however the civil government, preachers, father and mother excepted, on the understanding that this commandment does not allow evil to go unpunished. Now, as according to the Fifth Commandment no one is to be injured in body, and yet Master Hannes [the executioner] is excepted, who by virtue of his office does his neighbor no good, but only evil and harm, and nevertheless does not sin against God's commandment, because God has on His own account instituted that office; for He has reserved punishment for His own good pleasure, as He threatens in the First Commandment,—just so also, although no one has a right in his own person to judge and condemn anybody, yet if they to whose office it belongs fail to do it, they sin as well as he who would do so of his own accord, without such office. For here necessity requires one to speak of the evil, to prefer charges, to investigate and testify; and it is not different from the case of a physician who is sometimes compelled to examine and handle the patient whom he is to cure in secret parts. Just so governments, father and mother, brothers and sisters, and other good friends, are under obligation to each other to reprove evil wherever it is needful and profitable.

But the true way in this matter would be to observe the order according to the Gospel, Matt. 18, 15, where Christ says: If thy brother shall trespass against thee, go and tell him his fault between thee and him alone. Here you have a precious and excellent teaching for governing well the tongue, which is to be carefully observed against this detestable misuse. Let this, then, be your rule, that you do not too readily spread evil concerning your neighbor and slander him to others, but admonish him privately that he may amend [his life]. Likewise, also, if some one report to you what this or that one has done, teach him, too, to go and admonish him personally if he have seen it himself; but if not, that he hold his tongue.

The same you can learn also from the daily government of the household. For when the master of the house sees that the servant does not do what he ought, he admonishes him personally. But if he were so foolish as to let the servant sit at home, and went on the streets to complain of him to his neighbors, he would no doubt be told: "You fool, what does that concern us? Why do you not tell it to him?" Behold, that would be acting quite brotherly, so that the evil would be stayed, and your

78

neighbor would retain his honor. As Christ also says in the same place: If he hear thee, thou host gained thy brother. Then you have done a great and excellent work; for do you think it is a little matter to gain a brother? Let all monks and holy orders step forth, with all their works melted together into one mass, and see if they can boast that they have gained a brother.

Further, Christ teaches: But if he will not hear thee, then take with thee one or two more, that in the mouth of two or three witnesses every word may be established. So he whom it concerns is always to be treated with personally, and not to be spoken of without his knowledge. But if that do not avail, then bring it publicly before the community, whether before the civil or the ecclesiastical tribunal. For then you do not stand alone, but you have those witnesses with you by whom you can convict the guilty one, relying on whom the judge can pronounce sentence and punish. This is the right and regular course for checking and reforming a wicked person. But if we gossip about another in all corners and stir the filth, no one will be reformed, and afterwards when we are to stand up and bear witness, we deny having said so. Therefore it would serve such tongues right if their itch for slander were severely punished, as a warning to others. If you were acting for your neighbor's reformation or from love of the truth, you would not sneak about secretly nor shun the day and the light.

All this has been said regarding secret sins. But where the sin is quite public so that the judge and everybody know it you can without any sin avoid him and let him go, because he has brought himself into disgrace, and you may also publicly testify concerning him. For when a matter is public in the light of day, there can be no slandering or false judging or testifying; as, when we now reprove the Pope with his doctrine, which is publicly set forth in books and proclaimed in all the world. For where the sin is public, the reproof also must be public, that every one may learn to guard against it.

Thus we have now the sum and general understanding of this commandment, to wit, that no one do any injury with the tongue to his neighbor, whether friend or foe, nor speak evil of him, no matter whether it be true or false, unless it be done by commandment or for his reformation, but that every one employ his tongue and make it serve for the best of every one else, to cover up his neighbor's sins and infirmities, excuse them, palliate and garnish them with his own reputation. The chief reason for this should be the one which Christ alleges in the Gospel, in which He comprehends all commandments respecting our neighbor, Matt. 7, 12: Whatsoever ye would that men should do to you, do ye even so to them.

Even nature teaches the same thing in our own bodies, as St. Paul says, 1 Cor. 12, 22: Much more, those members of the body which seem to be more feeble are necessary; and those members of the body which we think to be less honorable, upon these we bestow more abundant honor; and our uncomely parts have more abundant comeliness. No one covers his face, eyes, nose, and mouth, for they, being in themselves the most honorable members which we have, do not require it. But the most infirm members, of which we are ashamed, we cover with all diligence; hands, eyes, and the whole body must help to cover and conceal them. Thus also among ourselves should we adorn whatever blemishes and infirmities we find in our neighbor, and serve and help him to promote his honor to the best of our ability, and, on the other hand, prevent whatever may be discreditable to him. And it is especially an excellent and noble virtue for one always to explain advantageously and put the best construction upon all he may hear of his neighbor (if it be not notoriously evil), or at any rate to condone it over and against the poisonous tongues that are busy wherever they can pry out and discover something to blame in a neighbor, and that explain and pervert it in the worst way; as is done now especially with the precious Word of God and its preachers.

There are comprehended therefore in this commandment quite a multitude of good works which please God most highly, and bring abundant good and blessing, if only the blind world and the false saints would recognize them. For there is nothing on or in entire man which can do both greater and more extensive good or harm in spiritual and in temporal matters than the tongue, though it is the least and feeblest member.

THE NINTH AND
TENTH COMMANDMENTS

Thou shalt not covet thy neighbor's house. Thou shalt not covet thy neighbor's wife, nor his man-servant, nor his maid-servant, nor his cattle, nor anything that is his.

These two commandments are given quite exclusively to the Jews; nevertheless, in part they also concern us. For they do not interpret them as referring to unchastity or theft, because these are sufficiently forbidden above. They also thought that they had kept all those when they had done or not done the external act. Therefore God has added these two commandments in order that it be esteemed as sin and forbidden to desire or in any way to aim at getting our neighbor's wife or possessions; and especially because under the Jewish government man-servants and maid-servants were not free as now to serve for wages as long as they pleased, but were their master's property with their body and all they had, as cattle and other possessions. Moreover, every man had power over his wife to put her away publicly by giving her a bill of divorce, and to take another. Therefore they were in constant danger among each other that if one took a fancy to another's wife, he might allege any reason both to dismiss his own wife and to estrange the other's wife from him, that he might obtain her under pretext of right. That was not considered a sin nor disgrace with them; as little as now with hired help, when a proprietor dismisses his man-servant or maid-servant, or takes another's servants from him in any way.

Therefore (I say) they thus interpreted these commandments, and that rightly (although their scope reaches somewhat farther and higher), that no one think or purpose to obtain what belongs to another, such as his wife, servants, house and estate, land meadows, cattle, even with a show of right or by a subterfuge, yet with injury to his neighbor. For above, in the Seventh Commandment, the vice is forbidden where one wrests to himself the possessions of others, or withholds them from his neighbor, which he cannot do by right. But here it is also forbidden to alienate anything from your neighbor, even though you could do so with honor in the eyes of the world, so that no one could accuse or blame you as though you had obtained it wrongfully.

For we are so inclined by nature that no one desires to see another have as much as himself, and each one acquires as much as he can; the other may fare as best he can. And yet we pretend to be godly, know how to adorn ourselves most finely and conceal our rascality, resort to and invent adroit devices and deceitful artifices (such as now are daily most ingeniously contrived) as though they were derived from the law codes; yea, we even dare impertinently to refer to it, and boast of it, and will not have it called rascality, but shrewdness and caution. In this lawyers and jurists assist, who twist and stretch the law to suit it to their cause, stress words and use them for a subterfuge, irrespective of equity or their neighbor's necessity. And, in short, whoever is the most expert and cunning in these affairs finds most help in law, as they themselves say: Vigilantibus iura subveniunt [that is, The laws favor the watchful].

This last commandment therefore is given not for rogues in the eyes of the world, but just for the most pious, who wish to be praised and be called honest and upright people, since they have not offended against the former commandments, as especially the Jews claimed to be, and even now many great noblemen, gentlemen, and princes. For the other common masses belong yet farther down, under the Seventh

Commandment, as those who are not much concerned whether they acquire their possessions with honor and right.

Now, this occurs most frequently in cases that are brought into court, where it is the purpose to get something from our neighbor and to force him out of his own. As (to give examples), when people quarrel and wrangle about a large inheritance, real estate, etc., they avail themselves of, and resort to, whatever has the appearance of right, so dressing and adorning everything that the law must favor their side, and they keep the property with such title that no one can make complaint or lay claim thereto. In like manner, if any one desire to have a castle, city, duchy, or any other great thing, he practices so much financiering through relationships, and by any means he can, that the other is judicially deprived of it, and it is adjudicated to him, and confirmed with deed and seal and declared to have been acquired by princely title and honestly.

Likewise also in common trade where one dexterously slips something out of another's hand, so that he must look after it, or surprises and defrauds him in a matter in which he sees advantage and benefit for himself, so that the latter, perhaps on account of distress or debt, cannot regain or redeem it without injury, and the former gains the half or even more; and yet this must not be considered as acquired by fraud or stolen, but honestly bought. Here they say: First come, first served, and every one must look to his own interest, let another get what he can. And who can be so smart as to think of all the ways in which one can get many things into his possession by such specious pretexts? This the world does not consider wrong [nor is it punished by laws], and will not see that the neighbor is thereby placed at a disadvantage, and must sacrifice what he cannot spare without injury. Yet there is no one who wishes this to be done to him; from which we can easily perceive that such devices and pretexts are false.

Thus it was done formerly also with respect to wives: they knew such devices that if one were pleased with another woman, he personally or through others (as there were many ways and means to be invented) caused her husband to conceive a displeasure toward her, or had her resist him and so conduct herself that he was obliged to dismiss her and leave her to the other. That sort of thing undoubtedly prevailed much under the Law, as also we read in the (Gospel of King Herod that he took his brother's wife while he was yet living, and yet wished to be thought an honorable, pious man, as St. Mark also testifies of him. But such an example, I trust, will not occur among us, because in the New Testament those who are married are forbidden to be divorced, except in such a case where one [shrewdly] by some stratagem takes away a rich bride from another. But it is not a rare thing with us that one estranges or alienates another's man-servant or maid-servant, or entices them away by flattering words.

In whatever way such things happen, we must know that God does not wish that you deprive your neighbor of anything that belongs to him so that he suffer the loss and you gratify your avarice with it, even if you could keep it honorably before the world; for it is a secret and insidious imposition practiced under the hat, as we say, that it may not be observed. For although you go your way as if you had done no one any wrong, you have nevertheless injured your neighbor; and if it is not called stealing and cheating, yet it is called coveting your neighbor's property, that is, aiming at possession of it, enticing it away from him without his will, and being unwilling to see him enjoy what God has granted him. And although the judge and every one must leave you in possession of it, yet God will not leave you therein; for He sees the deceitful heart and the malice of the world, which is sure to take an ell in addition wherever you yield to her a finger's breadth, and at length public wrong and violence follow.

Therefore we allow these commandments to remain in their ordinary meaning, that it is commanded, first, that we do not desire our neighbor's damage, nor even assist, nor give occasion for it, but gladly wish and leave him what he has, and, besides, advance and preserve for him what may be for his profit and service, as we should wish to be treated. Thus these commandments are especially directed against envy and miserable avarice, God wishing to remove all causes and sources whence arises everything by which we do injury to our neighbor, and therefore He expresses it in plain words: Thou shalt not covet, etc. For He would especially have the heart pure, although we shall never attain to that as long as we live here; so that this commandment will remain, like all the rest, one that will constantly accuse us and show how godly we are in the sight of God!

CONCLUSION OF THE
TEN COMMANDMENTS.

Thus we have the Ten Commandments, a compend of divine doctrine, as to what we are to do in order that our whole life may be pleasing to God, and the true fountain and channel from and in which everything must arise and flow that is to be a good work, so that outside of the Ten Commandments no work or thing can be good or pleasing to God, however great or precious it be in the eyes of the world. Let us see now what our great saints can boast of their spiritual orders and their great and grievous works which they have invented and set up, while they let these pass, as though they were far too insignificant, or had long ago been perfectly fulfilled.

I am of opinion indeed, that here one will find his hands full, [and will have enough] to do to observe these, namely, meekness, patience, and love towards enemies, chastity, kindness, etc., and what such virtues imply. But such works are not of value and make no display in the eyes of the world; for they are not peculiar and conceited works and restricted to particular times, places, rites, and customs, but are common, every-day domestic works which one neighbor can practice toward another; therefore they are not of high esteem.

But the other works cause people to open their eyes and ears wide, and men aid to this effect by the great display, expense, and magnificent buildings with which they adorn them, so that everything shines and glitters. There they waft incense, they sing and ring bells, they light tapers and candles, so that nothing else can be seen or heard. For when a priest stands there in a surplice embroidered with gilt, or a layman continues all day upon his knees in church, that is regarded as a most precious work which no one can sufficiently praise. But when a poor girl tends a little child and faithfully does what she is told that is considered nothing; for else what should monks and nuns seek in their cloisters?

But see, is not that a cursed presumption of those desperate saints who dare to invent a higher and better life and estate than the Ten Commandments teach, pretending (as we have said) that this is an ordinary life for the common man, but that theirs is for saints and perfect ones? And the miserable blind people do not see that no man can get so far as to keep one of the Ten Commandments as it should be kept, but both the Apostles' Creed and the Lord's Prayer must come to our aid (as we shall hear), by which that [power and strength to keep the commandments] is sought and prayed for and received continually. Therefore all their boasting amounts to as much as if I boasted and said: To be sure, I have not a penny to make payment with, but I confidently undertake to pay ten florins.

All this I say and urge in order that men might become rid of the sad misuse which has taken such deep root and still cleaves to everybody, and in all estates upon earth become used to looking hither only, and to being concerned about these matters. For it will be a long time before they will produce a doctrine or estates equal to the Ten Commandments, because they are so high that no one can attain to them by human power; and whoever does attain to them is a heavenly, angelic man far above all holiness of the world. Only occupy yourself with them, and try your best, apply all power and ability and you will find so much to do that you will neither seek nor esteem any other work or holiness.

Let this be sufficient concerning the first part of the common Christian doctrine, both for teaching and urging what is necessary. In conclusion, however, we must repeat the text which belongs here, of which we have treated already in the First Commandment, in order that we may learn what pains God requires to the end we may learn to inculcate and practice the Ten Commandments:

For I the Lord, thy God, am a jealous God, visiting the iniquity of the fathers upon the children unto the third and fourth generation of them that hate Me, and showing mercy unto thousands of them that love Me and keep My commandments.

Although (as we have heard above) this appendix was primarily attached to the First Commandment, it was nevertheless [we cannot deny that it was] laid down for the sake of all the commandments, as all of them are to be referred and directed to it. Therefore I have said that this, too, should be presented to and inculcated upon the young, that they may learn and remember it, in order to see what is to urge and compel us to keep these Ten Commandments. And it is to be regarded as though this part were specially added to each, so that it inheres in, and pervades, them all.

Now, there is comprehended in these words (as said before) both an angry word of threatening and a friendly promise to terrify and warn us, and, moreover to induce and encourage us to receive and highly esteem His Word as a matter of divine earnestness, because He Himself declares how much He is concerned about it, and how rigidly He will enforce it, namely, that He will horribly and terribly punish all who despise and transgress His commandments; and again, how richly He will reward, bless, and do all good to those who hold them in high esteem, and gladly do and live according to them. Thus He demands that all our works proceed from a heart which fears and regards God alone, and from such fear avoids everything that is contrary to His will, lest it should move Him to wrath; and, on the other hand, also trusts in Him alone, and from love to Him does all He wishes, because he speaks to us as friendly as a father, and offers us all grace and every good.

Just this is also the meaning and true interpretation of the first and chief commandment, from which all the others must flow and proceed, so that this word: Thou shalt have no other gods before Me, in its simplest meaning states nothing else than this demand: Thou shalt fear, love, and trust in Me as thine only true God. For where there is a heart thus disposed towards God, the same has fulfilled this and all the other commandments. On the other hand, whoever fears and loves anything else in heaven and upon earth will keep neither this nor any. Thus the entire scriptures have everywhere preached and inculcated this commandment, aiming always at these two things: fear of God and trust in Him. And especially the prophet David throughout the Psalms, as when he says [Ps. 147,11]: The Lord taketh pleasure in them that fear Him, in those that hope in His mercy. As if the entire commandment were explained by one verse, as much as to say: The Lord taketh pleasure in those who have no other gods.

Thus the First Commandment is to shine and impart its splendor to all the others. Therefore you must let this declaration run through all the commandments, like a hoop in a wreath, joining the end to the beginning and holding them all together, that it be continually repeated and not forgotten; as, namely, in the Second Commandment, that we fear God and do not take His name in vain for cursing, lying, deceiving, and other modes of leading men astray, or rascality, but make proper and good use of it by calling upon Him in prayer, praise, and thanksgiving, derived from love and trust according to the First Commandment. In like manner such fear, love, and trust is to urge and force us not to despise His Word, but gladly to learn, hear, and esteem it holy, and honor it.

Thus continuing through all the following commandments towards our neighbor likewise, everything is to proceed by virtue of the First Commandment, to wit, that we honor father and mother, masters, and all in authority and be subject and obedient to them, not on their own account, but for God's sake. For you are not to regard or fear father or mother, or from love of them do or omit anything. But see to that which God would have you do, and what He will quite surely demand of you; if you omit that, you have an angry Judge, but in the contrary case a gracious Father.

Again, that you do your neighbor no harm, injury, or violence, nor in any wise encroach upon him as touching his body, wife, property, honor, or rights, as all these things are commanded in their order, even though you have opportunity and cause to do so and no man would reprove you; but that you do good to all men, help them, and promote their interest, howsoever and wherever you can, purely from love of God and in order to please Him, in the confidence that He will abundantly reward you for everything. Thus you see how the First Commandment is the chief source and fountainhead which flows into all the rest, and again, all return to that and depend upon it, so that beginning and end are fastened and bound to each other.

This (I say) it is profitable and necessary always to teach to the young people, to admonish them and to remind them of it, that they may be brought up not only with blows and compulsion, like cattle, but in the fear and reverence of God. For where this is considered and laid to heart that these things are not human trifles, but the commandments of the Divine Majesty, who insists upon them with such earnestness, is angry with, and punishes those who despise them, and, on the other hand, abundantly rewards those who keep them, there will be a spontaneous impulse and a desire gladly to do the will of God. Therefore it is not in vain that it is commanded in the Old Testament to write the Ten Commandments on all walls and corners, yes, even on the garments, not for the sake of merely having them written in these places and making a show of them, as did the Jews, but that we might have our eyes constantly fixed upon them, and have them always in our memory, and that we might practice them in all our actions and ways, and every one make them his daily exercise in all cases, in every business and transaction, as though they were written in every place wherever he would look, yea, wherever he walks or stands. Thus there would be occasion enough, both at home in our own house and abroad with our neighbors, to practice the Ten Commandments, that no one need run far for them.

From this it again appears how highly these Ten Commandments are to be exalted and extolled above all estates, commandments, and works which are taught and practiced aside from them. For here we can boast and say: Let all the wise and saints step forth and produce, if they can, a [single] work like these commandments, upon which God insists with such earnestness, and which He enjoins with His greatest wrath and punishment, and, besides, adds such glorious promises that He will pour out upon us all good things and blessings. Therefore they should be taught above all others, and be esteemed precious and dear, as the highest treasure given by God.

PART SECOND.
OF THE CREED.

Thus far we have heard the first part of Christian doctrine, in which we have seen all that God wishes us to do or to leave undone. Now, there properly follows the Creed, which sets forth to us everything that we must expect and receive from God, and, to state it quite briefly, teaches us to know Him fully. And this is intended to help us do that which according to the Ten Commandments we ought to do. For (as said above) they are set so high that all human ability is far too feeble and weak to [attain to or] keep them. Therefore it is as necessary to learn this part as the former in order that we may know how to attain thereto, whence and whereby to obtain such power. For if we could by our own powers keep the Ten Commandments as they are to be kept, we would need nothing further, neither the Creed nor the Lord's Prayer. But before we explain this advantage and necessity of the Creed, it is sufficient at first for the simple-minded that they learn to comprehend and understand the Creed itself.

In the first place, the Creed has hitherto been divided into twelve articles, although, if all points which are written in the Scriptures and which belong to the Creed were to be distinctly set forth, there would be far more articles, nor could they all be clearly expressed in so few words. But that it may be most easily and clearly understood as it is to be taught to children, we shall briefly sum up the entire Creed in three chief articles, according to the three persons in the Godhead, to whom everything that we believe is related, So that the First Article, of God the Father, explains Creation, the Second Article, of the Son, Redemption, and the Third, of the Holy Ghost, Sanctification. Just as though the Creed were briefly comprehended in so many words: I believe in God the Father, who has created me; I believe in God the Son, who has redeemed me; I believe in the Holy Ghost, who sanctifies me. One God and one faith, but three persons, therefore also three articles or confessions. Let us briefly run over the words.

ARTICLE I.

I believe in God the Father Almighty, Maker of heaven and earth.

This portrays and sets forth most briefly what is the essence, will, activity, and work of God the Father. For since the Ten Commandments have taught that we are to have not more than one God, the question might be asked, What kind of a person is God? What does He do? How can we praise or portray and describe Him, that He may be known? Now, that is taught in this and in the following article, so that the Creed is nothing else than the answer and confession of Christians arranged with respect to the First Commandment. As if you were to ask a little child: My dear, what sort of a God have you? What do you know of Him? he could say: This is my God: first, the Father, who has created heaven and earth; besides this only One I regard nothing else as God; for there is no one else who could create heaven and earth.

But for the learned, and those who are somewhat advanced [have acquired some Scriptural knowledge], these three articles may all be expanded and divided into as many parts as there are words. But now for young scholars let it suffice to indicate the most necessary points, namely, as we have said, that this article refers to the Creation: that we emphasize the words: Creator of heaven and earth But what is the force of this, or what do you mean by these words: I believe in God the Father Almighty, Maker, etc.? Answer: This is what I mean and believe, that I am a creature of God; that is, that He has given and constantly preserves to me my body, soul, and life, members great and small, all my senses, reason, and understanding, and so on, food and drink, clothing and support, wife and children, domestics, house and home, etc. Besides, He causes all creatures to serve for the uses and necessities of life—sun, moon and stars in the firmament, day and night, air, fire, water, earth, and whatever it bears and produces, birds and fishes, beasts, grain, and all kinds of produce, and whatever else there is of bodily and temporal goods, good government, peace, security. Thus we learn from this article that none of us has of himself, nor can preserve, his life nor anything that is here enumerated or can be enumerated, however small and unimportant a thing it might be, for all is comprehended in the word Creator.

Moreover, we also confess that God the Father has not only given us all that we have and see before our eyes, but daily preserves and defends us against all evil and misfortune, averts all sorts of danger and calamity; and that He does all this out of pure love and goodness, without our merit, as a benevolent Father, who cares for us that no evil befall us. But to speak more of this belongs in the other two parts of this article, where we say: Father Almighty Now, since: all that we possess, and, moreover, whatever, in addition, is in heaven and upon the earth, is daily given, preserved, and kept for us by God, it is readily inferred and concluded that it is our duty to love, praise, and thank Him for it without ceasing, and, in short, to serve Him with all these things as He demands and has enjoined in the Ten Commandments.

Here we could say much if we were to expatiate, how few there are that believe this article. For we all pass over it, hear it and say it, but neither see nor consider what the words teach us. For if we believed it with the heart, we would also act accordingly, and not stalk about proudly, act defiantly, and boast as though we had life, riches, power, and honor, etc., of ourselves, so that others must fear and serve us, as is the practice of the wretched, perverse world, which is drowned in blindness, and abuses all the good things and gifts of God only for its own pride, avarice, lust, and luxury, and never once regards God, so as to thank Him or acknowledge Him as Lord and Creator.

Therefore, this article ought to humble and terrify us all, if we believed it. For we sin daily with eyes, ears, hands, body and soul, money and possessions, and with everything we have, especially those who even fight against the Word of God. Yet Christians have this advantage, that they acknowledge themselves in duty bound to serve God for all these things, and to be obedient to Him [which the world knows not how to do].

We ought, therefore, daily to practice this article, impress it upon our mind, and to remember it in all that meets our eyes, and in all good that falls to our lot, and wherever we escape from calamity or danger, that it is God who gives and does all these things, that therein we sense and see His paternal heart and His transcendent love toward us. Thereby the heart would be warmed and kindled to be thankful, and to employ all such good things to the honor and praise of God.

Thus we have most briefly presented the meaning of this article, as much as is at first necessary for the most simple to learn, both as to what we have and receive from God, and what we owe in return, which is a most excellent knowledge, but a far greater treasure. For here we see how the Father has given Himself to us, together with all creatures, and has most richly provided for us in this life, besides that He has overwhelmed us with unspeakable, eternal treasures by His Son and the Holy Ghost, as we shall hear.

ARTICLE II.

And in Jesus Christ, His only Son, our Lord, who was conceived by the Holy Ghost, born of the Virgin Mary; suffered under Pontius Pilate, was crucified, dead, and buried; He descended into hell; the third day He rose again from the dead; He ascended into heaven, and sitteth on the right hand of God the Father Almighty; from thence He shall come to judge the quick and the dead.

Here we learn to know the Second Person of the Godhead, so that we see what we have from God over and above the temporal goods aforementioned; namely, how He has completely poured forth Himself and withheld nothing from us that He has not given us. Now, this article is very rich and broad; but in order to expound it also briefly and in a childlike way, we shall take up one word and sum up in that the entire article, namely (as we have said), that we may here learn how we have been redeemed; and we shall base this on these words: In Jesus Christ, our Lord.

If now you are asked, What do you believe in the Second Article of Jesus Christ? answer briefly: I believe that Jesus Christ, true Son of God, has become my Lord. But what is it to become Lord? It is this, that He has redeemed me from sin, from the devil, from death, and all evil. For before I had no Lord nor King, but was captive under the power of the devil, condemned to death, enmeshed in sin and blindness.

For when we had been created by God the Father, and had received from Him all manner of good, the devil came and led us into disobedience, sin, death, and all evil, so that we fell under His wrath and displeasure and were doomed to eternal damnation, as we had merited and deserved. There was no counsel, help, or comfort until this only and eternal Son of God in His unfathomable goodness had compassion upon our misery and wretchedness, and came from heaven to help us. Those tyrants and jailers, then, are all expelled now, and in their place has come Jesus Christ, Lord of life, righteousness, every blessing, and salvation, and has delivered us poor lost men from the jaws of hell, has won us, made us free, and brought us again into the favor and grace of the Father, and has taken us as His own property under His shelter and protection, that He may govern us by His righteousness, wisdom, power, life, and blessedness.

Let this then, be the sum of this article that the little word Lord signifies simply as much as Redeemer, i.e., He who has brought us from Satan to God, from death to life, from sin to righteousness, and who preserves us in the same. But all the points which follow in order in this article serve no other end than to explain and express this redemption, how and whereby it was accomplished, that is, how much it cost Him, and what He spent and risked that He might win us and bring us under His dominion, namely, that He became man, conceived and born without [any stain of] sin, of the Holy Ghost and of the Virgin Mary, that He might overcome sin; moreover, that He suffered, died and was buried, that He might make satisfaction for me and pay what I owe, not with silver nor gold, but with His own precious blood. And all this, in order to become my Lord; for He did none of these for Himself, nor had He any need of it. And after that He rose again from the dead, swallowed up and devoured death, and finally ascended into heaven and assumed the government at the Father's right hand, so that the devil and all powers must be subject to Him and lie at His feet, until finally, at the last day, He will completely part and separate us from the wicked world, the devil, death, sin, etc.

But to explain all these single points separately belongs not to brief sermons for children, but rather to the ampler sermons that extend throughout the entire year, especially at those times which are appointed for the purpose of treating at length of each article—of the birth, sufferings, resurrection, ascension of Christ, etc.

Ay, the entire Gospel which we preach is based on this, that we properly understand this article as that upon which our salvation and all our happiness rest, and which is so rich and comprehensive that we never can learn it fully.

ARTICLE III.

I believe in the Holy Ghost; the holy Christian Church, the communion of saints; the forgiveness of sins; the resurrection of the body; and the life everlasting. Amen.

This article (as I have said) I cannot relate better than to Sanctification, that through the same the Holy Ghost, with His office, is declared and depicted, namely, that He makes holy. Therefore we must take our stand upon the word Holy Ghost, because it is so precise and comprehensive that we cannot find another. For there are, besides, many kinds of spirits mentioned in the Holy Scriptures, as, the spirit of man, heavenly spirits, and evil spirits. But the Spirit of God alone is called Holy Ghost, that is, He who has sanctified and still sanctifies us. For as the Father is called Creator, the Son Redeemer, so the Holy Ghost, from His work, must be called Sanctifier, or One that makes holy. But how is such sanctifying done? Answer: Just as the Son obtains dominion, whereby He wins us, through His birth, death, resurrection, etc., so also the Holy Ghost effects our sanctification by the following parts, namely, by the communion of saints or the Christian Church, the forgiveness of sins, the resurrection of the body, and the life everlasting; that is, He first leads us into His holy congregation, and places us in the bosom of the Church, whereby He preaches to us and brings us to Christ.

For neither you nor I could ever know anything of Christ, or believe on Him, and obtain Him for our Lord, unless it were offered to us and granted to our hearts by the Holy Ghost through the preaching of the

Gospel. The work is done and accomplished; for Christ has acquired and gained the treasure for us by His suffering, death, resurrection, etc. But if the work remained concealed so that no one knew of it, then it would be in vain and lost. That this treasure, therefore, might not lie buried, but be appropriated and enjoyed, God has caused the Word to go forth and be proclaimed, in which He gives the Holy Ghost to bring this treasure home and appropriate it to us. Therefore sanctifying is nothing else than bringing us to Christ to receive this good, to which we could not attain of ourselves.

Learn, then, to understand this article most clearly. If you are asked: What do you mean by the words: I believe in the Holy Ghost? you can answer: I believe that the Holy Ghost makes me holy, as His name implies. But whereby does He accomplish this, or what are His method and means to this end? Answer: By the Christian Church, the forgiveness of sins, the resurrection of the body, and the life everlasting. For, in the first place, He has a peculiar congregation in the world, which is the mother that begets and bears every Christian through the Word of God, which He reveals and preaches, [and through which] He illumines and enkindles hearts, that they understand, accept it, cling to it, and persevere in it.

For where He does not cause it to be preached and made alive in the heart, so that it is understood, it is lost, as was the case under the Papacy, where faith was entirely put under the bench, and no one recognized Christ as his Lord or the Holy Ghost as his Sanctifier, that is, no one believed that Christ is our Lord in the sense that He has acquired this treasure for us, without our works and merit, and made us acceptable to the Father. What, then, was lacking? This, that the Holy Ghost was not there to reveal it and cause it to be preached; but men and evil spirits were there, who taught us to obtain grace and be saved by our works. Therefore it is not a Christian Church either; for where Christ is not preached, there is no Holy Ghost who creates, calls, and gathers the Christian Church, without which no one can come to Christ the Lord. Let this suffice concerning the sum of this article. But because the parts which are here enumerated are not quite clear to the simple, we shall run over them also.

The Creed denominates the holy Christian Church, communionem sanctorum, a communion of saints; for both expressions, taken together, are identical. But formerly the one [the second] expression was not there, and it has been poorly and unintelligibly translated into German eine Gemeinschaft der Heiligen, a communion of saints. If it is to be rendered plainly, it must be expressed quite differently in the German idiom; for the word ecclesia properly means in German eine Versammlung, an assembly. But we are accustomed to the word church, by which the simple do not understand an assembled multitude, but the consecrated house or building, although the house ought not to be called a church, except only for the reason that the multitude assembles there. For we who assemble there make and choose for ourselves a particular place, and give a name to the house according to the assembly.

Thus the word Kirche (church) means really nothing else than a common assembly and is not German by idiom, but Greek (as is also the word ecclesia); for in their own language they call it kyria, as in Latin it is called curia. Therefore in genuine German, in our mother-tongue, it ought to be called a Christian congregation or assembly (eine christliche Gemeinde oder Sammlung), or, best of all and most clearly, holy Christendom (eine heilige Christenheit).

So also the word communio, which is added, ought not to be rendered communion (Gemeinschaft), but congregation (Gemeinde). And it is nothing else than an interpretation or explanation by which some one meant to explain what the Christian Church is. This our people, who understood neither Latin nor German, have rendered Gemeinschaft der Heiligen (communion of saints), although no German language speaks thus, nor understands it thus. But to speak correct German, it ought to be eine Gemeinde der Heiligen (a congregation of saints), that is, a congregation made up purely of saints, or, to speak yet more plainly, eine heilige Gemeinde, a holy congregation. I say this in order that the words

Gemeinschaft der Heiligen (communion of saints) may be understood, because the expression has become so established by custom that it cannot well be eradicated, and it is treated almost as heresy if one should attempt to change a word.

But this is the meaning and substance of this addition: I believe that there is upon earth a little holy group and congregation of pure saints, under one head, even Christ, called together by the Holy Ghost in one faith, one mind, and understanding, with manifold gifts, yet agreeing in love, without sects or schisms. I am also a part and member of the same a sharer and joint owner of all the goods it possesses, brought to it and incorporated into it by the Holy Ghost by having heard and continuing to hear the Word of God, which is the beginning of entering it. For formerly, before we had attained to this, we were altogether of the devil, knowing nothing of God and of Christ. Thus, until the last day, the Holy Ghost abides with the holy congregation or Christendom, by means of which He fetches us to Christ and which He employs to teach and preach to us the Word, whereby He works and promotes sanctification, causing it [this community] daily to grow and become strong in the faith and its fruits which He produces.

We further believe that in this Christian Church we have forgiveness of sin, which is wrought through the holy Sacraments and Absolution, moreover, through all manner of consolatory promises of the entire Gospel. Therefore, whatever is to be preached concerning the Sacraments belongs here, and, in short, the whole Gospel and all the offices of Christianity, which also must be preached and taught without ceasing. For although the grace of God is secured through Christ, and sanctification is wrought by the Holy Ghost through the Word of God in the unity of the Christian Church, yet on account of our flesh which we bear about with us we are never without sin.

Everything, therefore, in the Christian Church is ordered to the end that we shall daily obtain there nothing but the forgiveness of sin through the Word and signs, to comfort and encourage our consciences as long as we live here. Thus, although we have sins, the [grace of the] Holy Ghost does not allow them to injure us, because we are in the Christian Church, where there is nothing but [continuous, uninterrupted] forgiveness of sin, both in that God forgives us, and in that we forgive, bear with, and help each other.

But outside of this Christian Church, where the Gospel is not, there is no forgiveness, as also there can be no holiness [sanctification]. Therefore all who seek and wish to merit holiness [sanctification], not through the Gospel and forgiveness of sin, but by their works, have expelled and severed themselves [from this Church].

Meanwhile, however, while sanctification has begun and is growing daily, we expect that our flesh will be destroyed and buried with all its uncleanness, and will come forth gloriously, and arise to entire and perfect holiness in a new eternal life. For now we are only half pure and holy, so that the Holy Ghost has ever [some reason why] to continue His work in us through the Word, and daily to dispense forgiveness, until we attain to that life where there will be no more forgiveness, but only perfectly pure and holy people, full of godliness and righteousness, removed and free from sin, death, and all evil, in a new, immortal, and glorified body.

Behold, all this is to be the office and work of the Holy Ghost, that He begin and daily increase holiness upon earth by means of these two things, the Christian Church and the forgiveness of sin. But in our dissolution He will accomplish it altogether in an instant, and will forever preserve us therein by the last two parts.

But the term Auferstehung des Fleisches (resurrection of the flesh) here employed is not according to good German idiom. For when we Germans hear the word Fleisch (flesh), we think no farther than of the shambles. But in good German idiom we would say Auferstehung des Leibes, or Leichnams (resurrection of the body). However, it is not a matter of much moment, if we only understand the words aright.

This, now, is the article which must ever be and remain in operation. For creation we have received; redemption, too, is finished. But the

Holy Ghost carries on His work without ceasing to the last day. And for that purpose He has appointed a congregation upon earth by which He speaks and does everything. For He has not yet brought together all His Christian Church nor dispensed forgiveness. Therefore we believe in Him who through the Word daily brings us into the fellowship of this Christian Church, and through the same Word and the forgiveness of sins bestows, increases, and strengthens faith in order that when He has accomplished it all, and we abide therein, and die to the world and to all evil, He may finally make us perfectly and forever holy; which now we expect in faith through the Word.

Behold, here you have the entire divine essence, will, and work depicted most exquisitely in quite short and yet rich words wherein consists all our wisdom, which surpasses and exceeds the wisdom, mind, and reason of all men. For although the whole world with all diligence has endeavored to ascertain what God is, what He has in mind and does, yet has she never been able to attain to [the knowledge and understanding of] any of these things. But here we have everything in richest measure; for here in all three articles He has Himself revealed and opened the deepest abyss of his paternal heart and of His pure unutterable love. For He has created us for this very object, that He might redeem and sanctify us; and in addition to giving and imparting to us everything in heaven and upon earth, He has given to us even His Son and the Holy Ghost, by whom to bring us to Himself. For (as explained above) we could never attain to the knowledge of the grace and favor of the Father except through the Lord Christ, who is a mirror of the paternal heart, outside of whom we see nothing but an angry and terrible Judge. But of Christ we could know nothing either, unless it had been revealed by the Holy Ghost.

These articles of the Creed, therefore, divide and separate us Christians from all other people upon earth. For all outside of Christianity, whether heathen, Turks, Jews, or false Christians and hypocrites, although they believe in, and worship, only one true God, yet know not what His mind towards them is, and cannot expect any love or blessing from Him;

therefore they abide in eternal wrath and damnation. For they have not the Lord Christ, and, besides, are not illumined and favored by any gifts of the Holy Ghost.

From this you perceive that the Creed is a doctrine quite different from the Ten Commandments; for the latter teaches indeed what we ought to do, but the former tells what God does for us and gives to us. Moreover, apart from this, the Ten Commandments are written in the hearts of all men; the Creed, however, no human wisdom can comprehend, but it must be taught by the Holy Ghost alone. The latter doctrine [of the Law], therefore makes no Christian, for the wrath and displeasure of God abide upon us still, because we cannot keep what God demands of us; but this [namely, the doctrine of faith] brings pure grace, and makes us godly and acceptable to God. For by this knowledge we obtain love and delight in all the commandments of God, because here we see that God gives Himself entire to us, with all that He has and is able to do, to aid and direct us in keeping the Ten Commandments—the Father, all creatures; the Son, His entire work; and the Holy Ghost, all His gifts.

Let this suffice concerning the Creed to lay a foundation for the simple, that they may not be burdened, so that, if they understand the substance of it, they themselves may afterwards strive to acquire more, and to refer to these parts whatever they learn in the Scriptures, and may ever grow and increase in richer understanding. For as long as we live here, we shall daily have enough to do to preach and to learn this.

PART THIRD.
OF PRAYER.

THE LORD'S PRAYER.

We have now heard what we must do and believe, in which things the best and happiest life consists. Now follows the third part, how we ought to pray. For since we are so situated that no man can perfectly keep the Ten Commandments, even though he have begun to believe, and since the devil with all his power together with the world and our own flesh, resists our endeavors, nothing is so necessary as that we should continually resort to the ear of God, call upon Him, and pray to Him, that He would give, preserve, and increase in us faith and the fulfillment of the Ten Commandments, and that He would remove everything that is in our way and opposes us therein. But that we might know what and how to pray, our Lord Christ has Himself taught us both the mode and the words, as we shall see.

But before we explain the Lord's Prayer part by part, it is most necessary first to exhort and incite people to prayer, as Christ and the apostles also have done. And the first matter is to know that it is our duty to pray because of God's commandment. For thus we heard in the Second Commandment: Thou shalt not take the name of the lord, thy God, in vain, that we are there required to praise that holy name, and call upon it in every need, or to pray. For to call upon the name of God is nothing else than to pray. Prayer is therefore as strictly and earnestly commanded as all other commandments: to have no other God, not to kill, not to steal, etc. Let no one think that it is all the same whether he pray or not, as vulgar people do, who grope in such delusion and ask Why should I pray? Who knows whether God heeds or will hear my prayer? If I do not pray, some one else will. And thus they fall into the habit of never praying, and frame a pretext, as though we taught that there is no duty or need of prayer, because we reject false and hypocritical prayers.

But this is true indeed that such prayers as have been offered hitherto when men were babbling and bawling in the churches were no prayers. For such external matters, when they are properly observed, may be a good exercise for young children, scholars, and simple persons, and may be called singing or reading, but not really praying. But praying, as the Second Commandment teaches, is to call upon God in every need. This He requires of us, and has not left it to our choice. But it is our duty and obligation to pray if we would be Christians, as much as it is our duty and obligation to obey our parents and the government; for by calling upon it and praying the name of God is honored and profitably employed. This you must note above all things, that thereby you may silence and repel such thoughts as would keep and deter us from prayer. For just as it would be idle for a son to say to his father, "Of what advantage is my obedience? I will go and do what I can; it is all the same"; but there stands the commandment, Thou shalt and must do it, so also here it is not left to my will to do it or leave it undone, but prayer shall and must be offered at the risk of God's wrath and displeasure.

This is therefore to be understood and noted before everything else, in order that thereby we may silence and repel the thoughts which would keep and deter us from praying, as though it were not of much consequence if we do not pray, or as though it were commanded those who are holier and in better favor with God than we; as, indeed, the human heart is by nature so despondent that it always flees from God and imagines that He does not wish or desire our prayer, because we are sinners and have merited nothing but wrath. Against such thoughts (I say) we should regard this commandment and turn to God, that we may not by such disobedience excite His anger still more. For by this commandment He gives us plainly to understand that He will not cast us from Him nor chase us away, although we are sinners, but rather draw us to Himself, so that we might humble ourselves before Him, bewail this misery and plight of ours, and pray for grace and help. Therefore we read in the Scriptures that He is angry also with those who were smitten for their sin, because they did not return to Him and by their prayers assuage His wrath and seek His grace.

Now, from the fact that it is so solemnly commanded to pray, you are to conclude and think, that no one should by any means despise his prayer, but rather set great store by it, and always seek an illustration from the other commandments. A child should by no means despise his obedience to father and mother, but should always think: This work is a work of obedience, and what I do I do with no other intention than that I may walk in the obedience and commandment of God, on which I can settle and stand firm, and esteem it a great thing, not on account of my worthiness, but on account of the commandment. So here also, what and for what we pray we should regard as demanded by God and done in obedience to Him, and should reflect thus: On my account it would amount to nothing; but it shall avail, for the reason that God has commanded it. Therefore everybody, no matter what he has to say in prayer, should always come before God in obedience to this commandment.

We pray, therefore, and exhort every one most diligently to take this to heart and by no means to despise our prayer. For hitherto it has been taught thus in the devil's name that no one regarded these things, and men supposed it to be sufficient to have done the work, whether God would hear it or not. But that is staking prayer on a risk, and murmuring it at a venture, and therefore it is a lost prayer. For we allow such thoughts as these to lead us astray and deter us: I am not holy or worthy enough; if I were as godly and holy as St. Peter or St. Paul, then I would pray. But put such thoughts far away, for just the same commandment which applied to St. Paul applies also to me; and the Second Commandment is given as much on my account as on his account, so that he can boast of no better or holier commandment.

Therefore you should say: My prayer is as precious, holy, and pleasing to God as that of St. Paul or of the most holy saints. This is the reason: For I will gladly grant that he is holier in his person, but not on account of the commandment; since God does not regard prayer on account of the person, but on account of His word and obedience thereto. For on the commandment on which all the saints rest their prayer I, too, rest mine. Moreover I pray for the same thing for which they all pray and ever have prayed; besides, I have just as great a need of it as those great saints, yea, even a greater one than they.

Let this be the first and most important point, that all our prayers must be based and rest upon obedience to God, irrespective of our person, whether we be sinners or saints, worthy or unworthy. And we must know that God will not have it treated as a jest, but be angry, and punish all who do not pray, as surely as He punishes all other disobedience; next, that He will not suffer our prayers to be in vain or lost. For if He did not intend to answer your prayer, He would not bid you pray and add such a severe commandment to it.

In the second place, we should be the more urged and incited to pray because God has also added a promise, and declared that it shall surely be done to us as we pray, as He says Ps. 50, 15: Call upon Me in the day of trouble: I will deliver thee. And Christ in the Gospel of St. Matthew, 7, 7: Ask, and it shall be given you. For every one that asketh receiveth. Such promises ought certainly to encourage and kindle our hearts to pray with pleasure and delight, since He testifies with His [own] word that our prayer is heartily pleasing to Him, moreover, that it shall assuredly be heard and granted, in order that we may not despise it or think lightly of it, and pray at a venture.

This you can hold up to Him and say: Here I come, dear Father, and pray, not of my own purpose nor upon my own worthiness, but at Thy commandment and promise, which cannot fail or deceive me. Whoever, therefore, does not believe this promise must know again that he excites

God to anger as a person who most highly dishonors Him and reproaches Him with falsehood.

Besides this, we should be incited and drawn to prayer because in addition to this commandment and promise God anticipates us, and Himself arranges the words and form of prayer for us, and places them upon our lips as to how and what we should pray, that we may see how heartily He pities us in our distress, and may never doubt that such prayer is pleasing to Him and shall certainly be answered; which [the Lord's Prayer] is a great advantage indeed over all other prayers that we might compose ourselves. For in them the conscience would ever be in doubt and say: I have prayed, but who knows how it pleases Him, or whether I have hit upon the right proportions and form? Hence there is no nobler prayer to be found upon earth than the Lord's Prayer which we daily pray because it has this excellent testimony, that God loves to hear it, which we ought not to surrender for all the riches of the world.

And it has been prescribed also for this reason that we should see and consider the distress which ought to urge and compel us to pray without ceasing. For whoever would pray must have something to present, state, and name which he desires; if not, it cannot be called a prayer.

Therefore we have rightly rejected the prayers of monks and priests, who howl and growl day and night like fiends; but none of them think of praying for a hair's breadth of anything. And if we would assemble all the churches, together with all ecclesiastics, they would be obliged to confess that they have never from the heart prayed for even a drop of wine. For none of them has ever purposed to pray from obedience to God and faith in His promise, nor has any one regarded any distress, but (when they had done their best) they thought no further than this, to do a good work, whereby they might repay God, as being unwilling to take anything from Him, but wishing only to give Him something.

But where there is to be a true prayer there must be earnestness. Men must feel their distress, and such distress as presses them and compels them to call and cry out then prayer will be made spontaneously, as it ought to be, and men will require no teaching how to prepare for it and to attain to the proper devotion. But the distress which ought to concern us most, both as regards ourselves and every one, you will find abundantly set forth in the Lord's Prayer. Therefore it is to serve also to remind us of the same, that we contemplate it and lay it to heart, lest we become remiss in prayer. For we all have enough that we lack, but the great want is that we do not feel nor see it. Therefore God also requires that you lament and plead such necessities and wants, not because He does not know them, but that you may kindle your heart to stronger and greater desires, and make wide and open your cloak to receive much.

Therefore, every one of us should accustom himself from his youth daily to pray for all his wants, whenever he is sensible of anything affecting his interests or that of other people among whom he may live, as for preachers, the government, neighbors, domestics, and always (as we have said) to hold up to God His commandment and promise, knowing that He will not have them disregarded. This I say because I would like to see these things brought home again to the people that they might learn to pray truly, and not go about coldly and indifferently, whereby they become daily more unfit for prayer; which is just what the devil desires, and for what he works with all his powers. For he is well aware what damage and harm it does him when prayer is in proper practice. For this we must know, that all our shelter and protection rest in prayer alone. For we are far too feeble to cope with the devil and all his power and adherents that set themselves against us, and they might easily crush us under their feet. Therefore we must consider and take up those weapons with which Christians must be armed in order to stand against the devil. For what do you think has hitherto accomplished such great things, has checked or quelled the counsels, purposes, murder, and riot of our enemies, whereby the devil thought to crush us, together with the Gospel, except that the prayer of a few godly men intervened like a wall of iron on our side? They should else have witnessed a far different tragedy, namely, how the devil would have destroyed all Germany in its own blood. But now they may confidently deride it and make a mock of it, however, we shall nevertheless be a match both for themselves and the devil by prayer alone, if we only persevere diligently and not become slack. For whenever a godly Christian prays: Dear Father let Thy will be done, God speaks from on high and says: Yes, dear child, it shall be so, in spite of the devil and all the world.

Let this be said as an exhortation, that men may learn, first of all, to esteem prayer as something great and precious, and to make a proper distinction between babbling and praying for something. For we by no means reject prayer, but the bare, useless howling and murmuring we reject, as Christ Himself also rejects and prohibits long palavers. Now we shall most briefly and clearly treat of the Lord's Prayer. Here there is comprehended in seven successive articles, or petitions, every need which never ceases to relate to us, and each so great that it ought to constrain us to keep praying it all our lives.

THE FIRST PETITION.

Hallowed be Thy name.

This is, indeed, somewhat obscure, and not expressed in good German, for in our mother-tongue we would say: Heavenly Father, help that by all means Thy name may be holy. But what is it to pray that His name may be holy? Is it not holy already? Answer: Yes, it is always holy in its nature, but in our use it is not holy. For God's name was given us when we became Christians and were baptized, so that we are called children of God and have the Sacraments by which He so incorporates us in Himself that everything which is God's must serve for our use.

Here now the great need exists for which we ought to be most concerned, that this name have its proper honor, be esteemed holy and sublime as the greatest treasure and sanctuary that we have; and that as godly children we pray that the name of God, which is already holy in heaven, may also be and remain holy with us upon earth and in all the world.

But how does it become holy among us? Answer, as plainly as it can be said: When both our doctrine and life are godly and Christian. For since in this prayer we call God our Father, it is our duty always to deport and demean ourselves as godly children, that He may not receive shame, but honor and praise from us.

Now the name of God is profaned by us either in words or in works. (For whatever we do upon the earth must be either words or works, speech or act.) In the first place, then, it is profaned when men preach, teach, and speak in the name of God what is false and misleading, so that His name must serve to adorn and to find a market for falsehood. That is, indeed, the greatest profanation and dishonor of the divine name. Furthermore, also when men, by swearing, cursing, conjuring, etc., grossly abuse the holy name as a cloak for their shame. In the second place also by an openly wicked life and works, when those who are called Christians and the people of God are adulterers, drunkards, misers, envious, and slanderers. Here again must the name of God come to shame and be profaned because of us. For just as it is a shame and disgrace to a natural father to have a bad perverse child that opposes him in words and deeds, so that on its account he suffers contempt and reproach, so also it brings dishonor upon God if we who are called by His name and have all manner of goods from Him teach, speak, and live in any other manner except as godly and heavenly children, so that people say of us that we must be not God's, but the devil's children.

Thus you see that in this petition we pray just for that which God demands in the Second Commandment; namely, that His name be not taken in vain to swear, curse, lie, deceive, etc., but be usefully employed to the praise and honor of God. For whoever employs the name of God for any sort of wrong profanes and desecrates this holy name, as aforetime a church was considered desecrated when a murder or any other crime had been committed in it, or when a pyx or relic was desecrated, as being holy in themselves, yet become unholy in use. Thus this point is easy and clear if only the language is understood, that to hallow is the same as in our idiom to praise, magnify, and honor both in word and deed.

Here, now, learn how great need there is of such prayer. For because we see how full the world is of sects and false teachers, who all wear the holy name as a cover and sham for their doctrines of devils, we ought by all means to pray without ceasing, and to cry and call upon God against all such as preach and believe falsely and whatever opposes and persecutes our Gospel and pure doctrine, and would suppress it, as bishops, tyrants, enthusiasts, etc. Likewise also for ourselves who have the Word of God, but are not thankful for it, nor live as we ought according to the same. If now you pray for this with your heart, you can be sure that it pleases God; for He will not hear anything more dear to Him than that His honor and praise is exalted above everything else, and His Word is taught in its purity and is esteemed precious and dear.

THE SECOND PETITION.

Thy kingdom come.

As we prayed in the First Petition concerning the honor and name of God that He would prevent the world from adorning its lies and wickedness with it, but cause it to be esteemed sublime and holy both in doctrine and life, so that He may be praised and magnified in us, so here we pray that His kingdom also may come. But just as the name of God is in itself holy, and we pray nevertheless that it be holy among us, so also His kingdom comes of itself, without our prayer, yet we pray nevertheless that it may come to us, that is, prevail among us and with us, so that we may be a part of those among whom His name is hallowed and His kingdom prospers.

But what is the kingdom of God? Answer: Nothing else than what we learned in the Creed, that God sent His Son Jesus Christ our Lord, into the world to redeem and deliver us from the power of the devil, and to bring us to Himself, and to govern us as a King of righteousness, life and salvation against sin death, and an evil conscience, for which end He has also bestowed His Holy Ghost, who is to bring these things home to us by His holy Word, and to illumine and strengthen us in the faith by His power.

Therefore we pray here in the first place that this may become effective with us, and that His name be so praised through the holy Word of God and a Christian life that both we who have accepted it may abide and daily grow therein, and that it may gain approbation and adherence among other people and proceed with power throughout the world, that many may find entrance into the Kingdom of Grace, be made partakers of redemption, being led thereto by the Holy Ghost, in order that thus we may all together remain forever in the one kingdom now begun.

For the coming of God's Kingdom to us occurs in two ways; first, here in time through the Word and faith; and secondly, in eternity forever through revelation. Now we pray for both these things, that it may come to those who are not yet in it, and, by daily increase, to us who have received the same, and hereafter in eternal life. All this is nothing else than saying: Dear Father, we pray, give us first Thy Word, that the Gospel be preached properly throughout the world; and secondly, that it be received in faith, and work and live in us, so that through the Word and the power of the Holy Ghost Thy kingdom may prevail among us, and the kingdom of the devil be put down, that he may have no right or power over us, until at last it shall be utterly destroyed, and sin, death, and hell shall be exterminated, that we may live forever in perfect righteousness and blessedness.

From this you perceive that we pray here not for a crust of bread or a temporal, perishable good, but for an eternal inestimable treasure and everything that God Himself possesses; which is far too great for any human heart to think of desiring if He had not Himself commanded us to pray for the same. But because He is God, He also claims the honor of giving much more and more abundantly than any one can comprehend,— like an eternal, unfailing fountain, which, the more it pours forth and overflows, the more it continues to give,—and He desires nothing more earnestly of us than that we ask much and great things of Him, and again is angry if we do not ask and pray confidently.

For just as when the richest and most mighty emperor would bid a poor beggar ask whatever he might desire, and were ready to give great imperial presents, and the fool would beg only for a dish of gruel, he would be rightly considered a rogue and a scoundrel who treated the command of his imperial majesty as a jest and sport, and was not worthy of coming into his presence: so also it is a great reproach and dishonor to God if we, to whom He offers and pledges so many unspeakable treasures, despise the same, or have not the confidence to receive them, but scarcely venture to pray for a piece of bread.

All this is the fault of the shameful unbelief which does not look to God for as much good as will satisfy the stomach, much less expects without doubt such eternal treasures of God. Therefore we must strengthen ourselves against it, and let this be our first prayer; then, indeed, we shall have all else in abundance, as Christ teaches [Matt. 6, 33]: Seek ye first the kingdom of God and His righteousness and all these things shall be added unto you. For how could He allow us to suffer want and to be straitened in temporal things when He promises that which is eternal and imperishable?

THE THIRD PETITION.

Thy will be done on earth as it is in heaven.

Thus far we have prayed that God's name be honored by us, and that His kingdom prevail among us; in which two points is comprehended all that pertains to the honor of God and to our salvation, that we receive as our own God and all His riches. But now a need just as great arises, namely, that we firmly keep them, and do not suffer ourselves to be torn therefrom. For as in a good government it is not only necessary that there be those who build and govern well, but also those who make defense, afford protection and maintain it firmly, so here likewise, although we have prayed for the greatest need, for the Gospel, faith, and the Holy Ghost, that He may govern us and redeem us from the power of the devil, we must also pray that His will be done. For there will be happenings quite strange if we are to abide therein, as we shall have to suffer many thrusts and blows on that account from everything that ventures to oppose and prevent the fulfillment of the two petitions that precede.

For no one believes how the devil opposes and resists them, and cannot suffer that any one teach or believe aright. And it hurts him beyond measure to suffer his lies and abominations, that have been honored under the most specious pretexts of the divine name, to be exposed, and to be disgraced himself, and, besides, be driven out of the heart, and suffer such a breach to be made in his kingdom. Therefore he chafes and rages as a fierce enemy with all his power and might, and marshals all his subjects, and, in addition enlists the world and our own flesh as his allies. For our flesh is in itself indolent and inclined to evil, even though we have accepted and believe the Word of God. The world, however, is perverse and wicked; this he incites against us, fans and stirs the fire, that he may hinder and drive us back, cause us to fall, and again bring us under his power. Such is all his will, mind, and thought, for which he strives day and night, and never rests a moment, employing all arts, wiles, ways, and means whichever he can invent.

If we would be Christians, therefore, we must surely expect and reckon upon having the devil with all his angels and the world as our enemies, who will bring every possible misfortune and grief upon us. For where the Word of God is preached, accepted, or believed, and produces fruit, there the holy cross cannot be wanting. And let no one think that he shall have peace; but he must risk what whatever he has upon earth—possessions, honor. house and estate, wife and children, body and life. Now, this hurts our flesh and the old Adam; for the test is to be steadfast and to suffer with patience in whatever way we are assailed, and to let go whatever is taken from us.

Hence there is just as great need, as in all the others, that we pray without ceasing: "Dear Father, Thy will be done, not the will of the devil and of our enemies, nor of anything that would persecute and suppress Thy holy Word or hinder Thy kingdom; and grant that we may bear with patience and overcome whatever is to be endured on that account, lest our poor flesh yield or fall away from weakness or sluggishness."

Behold, thus we have in these three petitions, in the simplest manner, the need which relates to God Himself, yet all for our sakes. For whatever we pray concerns only us, namely, as we have said, that what must be done anyway without us, may also be done in us. For as His name must be hallowed and His kingdom come without our prayer, so also His will must be done and succeed although the devil with all his adherents raise a great tumult, are angry and rage against it, and undertake to exterminate the Gospel utterly. But for our own sakes we must pray that even against their fury His will be done without hindrance also among us, that they may not be able to accomplish anything and we remain firm against all violence and persecution, and submit to such will of God.

Such prayer, then, is to be our protection and defense now, is to repel and put down all that the devil, Pope, bishops, tyrants, and heretics can do against our Gospel. Let them all rage and attempt their utmost, and deliberate and resolve how they may suppress and exterminate us, that their will and counsel may prevail: over and against this one or two Christians with this petition alone shall be our wall against which they shall run and dash themselves to pieces. This consolation and confidence we have, that the will and purpose of the devil and of all our enemies shall and must fail and come to naught, however proud, secure, and powerful they know themselves to be. For if their will were not broken and hindered, the kingdom of God could not abide on earth nor His name be hallowed.

THE FOURTH PETITION.

Give us this day our daily bread.

Here, now, we consider the poor breadbasket, the necessaries of our body and of the temporal life. It is a brief and simple word, but it has a very wide scope. For when you mention and pray for daily bread, you pray for everything that is necessary in order to have and enjoy daily bread and, on the other hand, against everything which interferes with it. Therefore you must open wide and extend your thoughts not only to the oven or the flour-bin but to the distant field and the entire land, which bears and brings to us daily bread and every sort of sustenance. For if God did not cause it to grow, and bless and preserve it in the field, we could never take bread from the oven or have any to set upon the table.

To comprise it briefly, this petition includes everything that belongs to our entire life in the world, because on that account alone do we need daily bread. Now for our life it is not only necessary that our body have food and covering and other necessaries, but also that we spend our days in peace and quiet among the people with whom we live and have intercourse in daily business and conversation and all sorts of doings, in short, whatever pertains both to the domestic and to the neighborly or civil relation and government. For where these two things are hindered [intercepted and disturbed] that they do not prosper as they ought, the necessaries of life also are impeded, so that ultimately life cannot be maintained. And there is, indeed, the greatest need to pray for temporal authority and government, as that by which most of all God preserves to us our daily bread and all the comforts of this life. For though we have received of God all good things in abundance we are not able to retain any of them or use them in security and happiness, if He did not give us a permanent and peaceful government. For where there are dissension, strife, and war, there the daily bread is already taken away, or at least checked.

Therefore it would be very proper to place in the coat-of-arms of every pious prince a loaf of bread instead of a lion, or a wreath of rue, or to stamp it upon the coin, to remind both them and their subjects that by their office we have protection and peace, and that without them we could not eat and retain our daily bread. Therefore they are also worthy of all honor, that we give to them for their office what we ought and can, as to those through whom we enjoy in peace and quietness what we have, because otherwise we would not keep a farthing; and that, in addition, we also pray for them that through them God may bestow on us the more blessing and good.

Let this be a very brief explanation and sketch, showing how far this petition extends through all conditions on earth. Of this any one might indeed make a long prayer, and with many words enumerate all the things that are included therein, as that we pray God to give us food and drink, clothing, house, and home, and health of body; also that He cause the grain and fruits of the field to grow and mature well; furthermore, that He help us at home towards good housekeeping, that He give and preserve to us a godly wife, children, and servants, that He cause our work, trade, or whatever we are engaged in to prosper and succeed, favor us with faithful neighbors and good friends, etc. Likewise, that He give to emperors, kings, and all estates, and especially to the rulers of our country and to all counselors, magistrates, and officers, wisdom, strength, and success that they may govern well and vanquish the Turks and all enemies; to subjects and the common people, obedience, peace, and harmony in their life with one another, and on the other hand, that He would preserve us from all sorts of calamity to body and livelihood, as lightning, hail, fire, flood, poison, pestilence, cattle-plague, war and bloodshed, famine, destructive beasts, wicked men, etc. All this it is well to impress upon the simple, namely, that these things come from God, and must be prayed for by us.

But this petition is especially directed also against our chief enemy, the devil. For all his thought and desire is to deprive us of all that we have from God, or to hinder it; and he is not satisfied to obstruct and destroy spiritual government in leading souls astray by his lies and bringing them under his power, but he also prevents and hinders the stability of all government and honorable, peaceable relations on earth. There he causes so much contention, murder, sedition, and war also lightning and hail to destroy grain and cattle, to poison the air, etc. In short, he is sorry that any one has a morsel of bread from God and eats it in peace; and if it were in his power, and our prayer (next to God) did not prevent him, we would not keep a straw in the field, a farthing in the house, yea, not even our life for an hour, especially those who have the Word of God and would like to be Christians.

Behold, thus God wishes to indicate to us how He cares for us in all our need, and faithfully provides also for our temporal support. and although He abundantly grants and preserves these things even to the wicked and knaves, yet He wishes that we pray for them, in order that we may recognize that we receive them from His hand, and may feel His paternal goodness toward us therein. For when He withdraws His hand, nothing can prosper nor be maintained in the end, as, indeed, we daily see and experience. How much trouble there is now in the world only on account of bad coin, yea, on account of daily oppression and raising of prices in common trade, bargaining and labor on the part of those who wantonly oppress the poor and deprive them of their daily bread! This we must suffer indeed; but let them take care that they do not lose the common intercession, and beware lest this petition in the Lord's Prayer be against them.

THE FIFTH PETITION.

And forgive us our trespasses, as we forgive those who trespass against us.

This part now relates to our poor miserable life, which, although we have and believe the Word of God, and do and submit to His will, and are supported by His gifts and blessings is nevertheless not without sin. For we still stumble daily and transgress because we live in the world among men who do us much harm and give us cause for impatience, anger, revenge, etc. Besides, we have Satan at our back, who sets upon us on every side, and fights (as we have heard) against all the foregoing petitions, so that it is not possible always to stand firm in such a persistent conflict.

Therefore there is here again great need to call upon God and to pray: Dear Father, forgive us our trespasses. Not as though He did not forgive sin without and even before our prayer (for He has given us the Gospel, in which is pure forgiveness before we prayed or ever thought about it). But this is to the intent that we may recognize and accept such forgiveness. For since the flesh in which we daily live is of such a nature that it neither trusts nor believes God, and is ever active in evil lusts and devices, so that we sin daily in word and deed, by commission and omission by which the conscience is thrown into unrest, so that it is afraid of the wrath and displeasure of God, and thus loses the comfort and confidence derived from the Gospel; therefore it is ceaselessly necessary that we run hither and obtain consolation to comfort the conscience again.

But this should serve God's purpose of breaking our pride and keeping us humble. For in case any one should boast of his godliness and despise others, God has reserved this prerogative to Himself, that the person is to consider himself and place this prayer before his eyes, and he will find that he is no better than others, and that in the presence of God all must lower their plumes, and be glad that they can attain forgiveness. And let no one think that as long as we live here he can reach such a position that he will not need such forgiveness. In short, if God does not forgive without ceasing, we are lost.

It is therefore the intent of this petition that God would not regard our sins and hold up to us what we daily deserve, but would deal graciously with us, and forgive, as He has promised, and thus grant us a joyful and confident conscience to stand before Him in prayer. For where the heart is not in right relation towards God, nor can take such confidence, it will nevermore venture to pray. But such a confident and joyful heart can spring from nothing else than the [certain] knowledge of the forgiveness of sin.

But there is here attached a necessary, yet consolatory addition: As we forgive. He has promised that we shall be sure that everything is forgiven and pardoned, yet in the manner that we also forgive our neighbor. For just as we daily sin much against God and yet He forgives everything through grace, so we, too, must ever forgive our neighbor who does us injury, violence, and wrong, shows malice toward us, etc. If, therefore you do not forgive, then do not think that God forgives you; but if you forgive, you have this consolation and assurance, that you are forgiven in heaven, not on account of your forgiving,—for God forgives freely and without condition, out of pure grace, because He has so promised, as the Gospel teaches,—but in order that He may set this up for our confirmation and assurance for a sign alongside of the promise which accords with this prayer, Luke 6, 37: Forgive, and ye shall be forgiven. Therefore Christ also repeats it soon after the Lord's Prayer, and says,

Matt. 6,14: For if ye forgive men their trespasses, your heavenly Father will also forgive you, etc.

This sign is therefore attached to this petition, that, when we pray, we remember the promise and reflect thus: Dear Father, for this reason I come and pray Thee to forgive me, not that I can make satisfaction, or can merit anything by my works, but because Thou hast promised and attached the seal thereto that I should be as sure as though I had absolution pronounced by Thyself. For as much as Baptism and the Lord's Supper appointed as external signs, effect, so much also this sign can effect to confirm our consciences and cause them to rejoice. And it is especially given for this purpose, that we might use and practice it every hour, as a thing that we have with us at all times.

THE SIXTH PETITION.

And lead us not into temptation.

We have now heard enough what toil and labor is required to retain all that for which we pray, and to persevere therein, which, however, is not achieved without infirmities and stumbling. Besides, although we have received forgiveness and a good conscience and are entirely acquitted, yet is our life of such a nature that one stands to-day and to-morrow falls. Therefore, even though we be godly now and stand before God with a good conscience, we must pray again that He would not suffer us to relapse and yield to trials and temptations.

Temptation, however, or (as our Saxons in olden times used to call it) Bekoerunge, is of three kinds, namely, of the flesh, of the world and of the devil. For in the flesh we dwell and carry the old Adam about our neck, who exerts himself and incites us daily to inchastity, laziness, gluttony and drunkenness, avarice and deception, to defraud our neighbor and to overcharge him, and, in short, to all manner of evil lusts which cleave to us by nature, and to which we are incited by the society, example and what we hear and see of other people, which often wound and inflame even an innocent heart.

Next comes the world, which offends us in word and deed, and impels us to anger and impatience. In short, there is nothing but hatred and envy, enmity, violence and wrong, unfaithfulness, vengeance, cursing, raillery slander, pride and haughtiness, with superfluous finery, honor, fame, and power, where no one is willing to be the least, but every one desires to sit at the head and to be seen before all.

Then comes the devil, inciting and provoking in all directions, but especially agitating matters that concern the conscience and spiritual affairs, namely, to induce us to despise and disregard both the Word and works of God to tear us away from faith, hope, and love and bring us into misbelief, false security, and obduracy, or, on the other hand, to despair, denial of God, blasphemy, and innumerable other shocking things. These are indeed snares and nets, yea, real fiery darts which are shot most venomously into the heart, not by flesh and blood, but by the devil.

Great and grievous, indeed, are these dangers and temptations which every Christian must bear, even though each one were alone by himself, so that every hour that we are in this vile life where we are attacked on all sides, chased and hunted down, we are moved to cry out and to pray that God would not suffer us to become weary and faint and to relapse into sin, shame, and unbelief. For otherwise it is impossible to overcome even the least temptation.

This, then, is leading us not into temptation, to wit, when He gives us power and strength to resist, the temptation, however, not being taken away or removed. For while we live in the flesh and have the devil about us, no one can escape temptation and allurements; and it cannot be otherwise than that we must endure trials, yea, be engulfed in them; but we pray for this, that we may not fall and be drowned in them.

To feel temptation is therefore a far different thing from consenting or yielding to it. We must all feel it, although not all in the same manner, but some in a greater degree and more severely than others; as, the young suffer especially from the flesh, afterwards, they that attain to middle life and old age, from the world, but others who are occupied with spiritual matters, that is, strong Christians, from the devil. But such feeling, as long as it is against our will and we would rather be rid of it, can harm no one. For if we did not feel it, it could not be called a temptation. But

135

to consent thereto is when we give it the reins and do not resist or pray against it.

Therefore we Christians must be armed and daily expect to be incessantly attacked, in order that no one may go on in security and heedlessly, as though the devil were far from us, but at all times expect and parry his blows. For though I am now chaste, patient, kind, and in firm faith, the devil will this very hour send such an arrow into my heart that I can scarcely stand. For he is an enemy that never desists nor becomes tired, so that when one temptation ceases, there always arise others and fresh ones.

Accordingly, there is no help or comfort except to run hither and to take hold of the Lord's Prayer, and thus speak to God from the heart: Dear Father, Thou hast bidden me pray; let me not relapse because of temptations. Then you will see that they must desist, and finally acknowledge themselves conquered. Else if you venture to help yourself by your own thoughts and counsel, you will only make the matter worse and give the devil more space. For he has a serpent's head, which if it gain an opening into which he can slip, the whole body will follow without check. But prayer can prevent him and drive him back.

THE SEVENTH AND LAST PETITION.

But deliver us from evil. Amen. In the Greek text this petition reads thus: Deliver or preserve us from the Evil One, or the Malicious One; and it looks as if He were speaking of the devil, as though He would comprehend everything in one so that the entire substance of all our prayer is directed against our chief enemy. For it is he who hinders among us everything that we pray for: the name or honor of God, God's kingdom and will, our daily bread, a cheerful good conscience, etc.

Therefore we finally sum it all up and say: Dear Father pray, help that we be rid of all these calamities. But there is nevertheless also included whatever evil may happen to us under the devil's kingdom—poverty, shame, death, and, in short, all the agonizing misery and heartache of which there is such an unnumbered multitude on the earth. For since the devil is not only a liar, but also a murderer, he constantly seeks our life, and wreaks his anger whenever he can afflict our bodies with misfortune and harm. Hence it comes that he often breaks men's necks or drives them to insanity, drowns some, and incites many to commit suicide, and to many other terrible calamities. Therefore there is nothing for us to do upon earth but to pray against this arch enemy without ceasing. For unless God preserved us, we would not be safe from him even for an hour.

Hence you see again how God wishes us to pray to Him also for all the things which affect our bodily interests, so that we seek and expect help nowhere else except in Him. But this matter He has put last; for if we are to be preserved and delivered from all evil, the name of God must first be hallowed in us, His kingdom must be with us, and His will be done. After that He will finally preserve us from sin and shame, and, besides, from everything that may hurt or injure us.

Thus God has briefly placed before us all the distress which may ever come upon us, so that we might have no excuse whatever for not praying. But all depends upon this, that we learn also to say Amen, that is, that we do not doubt that our prayer is surely heard and [what we pray] shall be done. For this is nothing else than the word of undoubting faith, which does not pray at a venture, but knows that God does not lie to him, since He has promised to grant it. Therefore, where there is no such faith, there cannot be true prayer either.

It is, therefore, a pernicious delusion of those who pray in such a manner that they dare not from the heart say yea and positively conclude that God hears them, but remain in doubt and say, How should I be so bold as to boast that God hears my prayer? For I am but a poor sinner, etc.

The reason for this is, they regard not the promise of God, but their own work and worthiness, whereby they despise God and reproach Him with lying, and therefore they receive nothing. As St. James says [1, 6]: But let him ask in faith, nothing wavering; for he that wavereth is like a wave of the sea, driven with the wind and tossed. For let not that man think that he shall receive anything of the Lord. Behold, such importance God attaches to the fact that we are sure we do not pray in vain, and that we do not in any way despise our prayer.

PART FOURTH.

OF BAPTISM.

We have now finished the three chief parts of the common Christian doctrine. Besides these we have yet to speak of our two Sacraments instituted by Christ, of which also every Christian ought to have at least an ordinary, brief instruction, because without them there can be no Christian; although, alas! hitherto no instruction concerning them has been given. But, in the first place, we take up Baptism, by which we are first received into the Christian Church. However, in order that it may be readily understood we will treat of it in an orderly manner, and keep only to that which it is necessary for us to know. For how it is to be maintained and defended against heretics and sects we will commend to the learned.

In the first place, we must above all things know well the words upon which Baptism is founded, and to which everything refers that is to be said on the subject, namely, where the Lord Christ speaks in the last chapter of Matthew, v. 19:

Go ye therefore and teach all nations, baptizing them in the name of the Father, and of the Son, and of the Holy Ghost.

Likewise in St. Mark, the last chapter, v. 16:

He that believeth and is baptized shall be saved; but he that believeth not shall be damned .

In these words you must note, in the first place, that here stand God's commandment and institution, lest we doubt that Baptism is divine, not devised nor invented by men. For as truly as I can say, No man has spun the Ten Commandments, the Creed, and the Lord's Prayer out of his head, but they are revealed and given by God Himself, so also I can boast that Baptism is no human trifle, but instituted by God Himself, moreover, that it is most solemnly and strictly commanded that we must be baptized or we cannot be saved, lest any one regard it as a trifling matter, like putting on a new red coat. For it is of the greatest importance that we esteem Baptism excellent, glorious, and exalted, for which we contend and fight chiefly, because the world is now so full of sects clamoring that Baptism is an external thing, and that external things are of no benefit. But let it be ever so much an external thing here stand God's Word and command which institute, establish, and confirm Baptism. But what God institutes and commands cannot be a vain, but must be a most precious thing, though in appearance it were of less value than a straw. If hitherto people could consider it a great thing when the Pope with his letters and bulls dispensed indulgences and confirmed altars and churches, solely because of the letters and seals, we ought to esteem Baptism much more highly and more precious, because God has commanded it, and, besides, it is performed in His name. For these are the words, Go ye baptize; however, not in your name, but in the name of God.

For to be baptized in the name of God is to be baptized not by men, but by God Himself. Therefore although it is performed by human hands, it is nevertheless truly God's own work. From this fact every one may himself readily infer that it is a far higher work than any work performed by a man or a saint. For what work greater than the work of God can we do?

But here the devil is busy to delude us with false appearances, and lead us away from the work of God to our own works. For there is a much more splendid appearance when a Carthusian does many great and difficult works and we all think much more of that which we do and merit ourselves. But the Scriptures teach thus: Even though we collect in one mass the works of all the monks, however splendidly they may shine, they would not be as noble and good as if God should pick up a straw. Why? Because the person is nobler and better. Here, then, we must not estimate the person according to the works, but the works according to the person, from whom they must derive their nobility. But insane reason will not regard this, and because Baptism does not shine like the works which we do, it is to be esteemed as nothing.

From this now learn a proper understanding of the subject, and how to answer the question what Baptism is, namely thus, that it is not mere ordinary water, but water comprehended in God's Word and command, and sanctified thereby, so that it is nothing else than a divine water; not that the water in itself is nobler than other water, but that God's Word and command are added.

Therefore it is pure wickedness and blasphemy of the devil that now our new spirits, to mock at Baptism, omit from it God's Word and institution, and look upon it in no other way than as water which is taken from the well, and then blather and say: How is a handful of water to help the soul? Aye, my friend, who does not know that water is water if tearing things asunder is what we are after? But how dare you thus interfere with God's order, and tear away the most precious treasure with which God has connected and enclosed it, and which He will not have separated? For the kernel in the water is God's Word or command and the name of God which is a treasure greater and nobler than heaven and earth.

Comprehend the difference, then, that Baptism is quite another thing than all other water; not on account of the natural quality, but because something more noble is here added; for God Himself stakes His honor His power and might on it. Therefore it is not only natural water, but a divine, heavenly, holy, and blessed water, and in whatever other terms we can praise it,—all on account of the Word, which is a heavenly, holy Word, that no one can sufficiently extol, for it has, and is able to do, all that God is and can do [since it has all the virtue and power of God comprised in it]. Hence also it derives its essence as a Sacrament, as St. Augustine also taught: Accedat verbum ad elementum et fit sacramentum. That is, when the Word is joined to the element or natural substance, it becomes a Sacrament, that is, a holy and divine matter and sign.

Therefore we always teach that the Sacraments and all external things which God ordains and institutes should not be regarded according to the coarse, external mask, as we regard the shell of a nut, but as the Word of God is included therein. For thus we also speak of the parental estate and of civil government. If we propose to regard them in as far as they have noses, eyes, skin, and hair flesh and bones, they look like Turks and heathen, and some one might start up and say: Why should I esteem them more than others? But because the commandment is added: Honor thy father and thy mother, I behold a different man, adorned and clothed with the majesty and glory of God. The commandment (I say) is the chain of gold about his neck, yea, the crown upon his head which shows to me how and why one must honor this flesh and blood.

Thus, and much more even, you must honor Baptism and esteem it glorious on account of the Word, since He Himself has honored it both by words and deeds; moreover, confirmed it with miracles from heaven. For do you think it was a jest that, when Christ was baptized, the heavens were opened and the Holy Ghost descended visibly, and everything was divine glory and majesty?

Therefore I exhort again that these two the water and the Word, by no means be separated from one another and parted. For if the Word is separated from it, the water is the same as that with which the servant cooks, and may indeed be called a bath-keeper's baptism. But when it is added, as God has ordained, it is a Sacrament, and is called Christ-baptism. Let this be the first part regarding the essence and dignity of the holy Sacrament.

In the second place, since we know now what Baptism is, and how it is to be regarded, we must also learn why and for what purpose it is instituted; that is, what it profits, gives and works. And this also we cannot discern better than from the words of Christ above quoted: He that believeth and is baptized shall be saved. Therefore state it most simply thus, that the power, work, profit, fruit, and end of Baptism is this, namely, to save. For no one is baptized in order that he may become a prince, but, as the words declare, that he be saved. But to be saved. we know. is nothing else than to be delivered from sin, death, and the devil, and to enter into the kingdom of Christ, and to live with Him forever.

Here you see again how highly and precious we should esteem Baptism, because in it we obtain such an unspeakable treasure, which also indicates sufficiently that it cannot be ordinary mere water. For mere water could not do such a thing, but the Word does it, and (as said above) the fact that the name of God is comprehended therein. But where the name of God is, there must be also life and salvation, that it may indeed be called a divine, blessed, fruitful, and gracious water; for by the Word such power is imparted to Baptism that it is a laver of regeneration, as St. Paul also calls it, Titus 3, 5.

But as our would-be wise, new spirits assert that faith alone saves, and that works and external things avail nothing, we answer: It is true, indeed, that nothing in us is of any avail but faith, as we shall hear still further. But these blind guides are unwilling to see this, namely, that faith must have something which it believes, that is, of which it takes hold, and upon which it stands and rests. Thus faith clings to the water, and believes that it is Baptism, in which there is pure salvation and life; not through the water (as we have sufficiently stated), but through the fact that it is embodied in the Word and institution of God, and the name of God inheres in it. Now, if I believe this, what else is it than believing in God as in Him who has given and planted His Word into this ordinance, and proposes to us this external thing wherein we may apprehend such a treasure?

Now, they are so mad as to separate faith and that to which faith clings and is bound though it be something external. Yea, it shall and must be something external, that it may be apprehended by the senses, and understood and thereby be brought into the heart, as indeed the entire

Gospel is an external, verbal preaching. In short, what God does and works in us He proposes to work through such external ordinances. Wherever, therefore, He speaks, yea, in whichever direction or by whatever means He speaks, thither faith must look, and to that it must hold. Now here we have the words: He that believeth and is baptized shall be saved. To what else do they refer than to Baptism, that is, to the water comprehended in God's ordinance? Hence it follows that whoever rejects Baptism rejects the Word of God, faith, and Christ, who directs us thither and binds us to Baptism.

In the third place since we have learned the great benefit and power of Baptism, let us see further who is the person that receives what Baptism gives and profits. This is again most beautifully and clearly expressed in the words: He that believeth and is baptized shall be saved. That is, faith alone makes the person worthy to receive profitably the saving, divine water. For, since these blessings are here presented and promised in the words in and with the water, they cannot be received in any other way than by believing them with the heart. Without faith it profits nothing, notwithstanding it is in itself a divine superabundant treasure. Therefore this single word (He that believeth) effects this much that it excludes and repels all works which we can do, in the opinion that we obtain and merit salvation by them. For it is determined that whatever is not faith avails nothing nor receives anything.

But if they say, as they are accustomed: Still Baptism is itself a work, and you say works are of no avail for salvation; what then, becomes of faith? Answer: Yes, our works, indeed, avail nothing for salvation; Baptism, however, is not our work, but God's (for, as was stated, you must put Christ-baptism far away from a bath-keeper's baptism). God's works, however, are saving and necessary for salvation, and do not exclude, but demand, faith; for without faith they could not be apprehended. For by suffering the water to be poured upon you, you have not yet received Baptism in such a manner that it benefits you anything; but it becomes beneficial to you if you have yourself baptized with the thought that this is according to God's command and ordinance, and besides in God's name, in order that you may receive in the water the promised salvation. Now, this the fist cannot do, nor the body; but the heart must believe it.

Thus you see plainly that there is here no work done by us, but a treasure which He gives us, and which faith apprehends; just as the Lord Jesus Christ upon the cross is not a work, but a treasure comprehended in the Word, and offered to us and received by faith. Therefore they do us violence by exclaiming against us as though we preach against faith; while we alone insist upon it as being of such necessity that without it nothing can be received nor enjoyed.

Thus we have these three parts which it is necessary to know concerning this Sacrament especially that the ordinance of God is to be held in all honor, which alone would be sufficient, though it be an entirely external thing like the commandment, Honor thy father and thy mother, which refers to bodily flesh and blood. Therein we regard not the flesh and blood, but the commandment of God in which they are comprehended, and on account of which the flesh is called father and mother; so also, though we had no more than these words, Go ye and baptize, etc., it would be necessary for us to accept and do it as the ordinance of God. Now there is here not only God's commandment and injunction, but also the promise, on account of which it is still far more glorious than whatever else God has commanded and ordained, and is, in short, so full of consolation and grace that heaven and earth cannot comprehend it. But it requires skill to believe this, for the treasure is not wanting, but this is wanting that men apprehend it and hold it firmly.

Therefore every Christian has enough in Baptism to learn and to practice all his life; for he has always enough to do to believe firmly what it promises and brings: victory over death and the devil, forgiveness of sin, the grace of God, the entire Christ, and the Holy Ghost with His gifts. In short, it is so transcendent that if timid nature could realize it, it might well doubt whether it could be true. For consider, if there were somewhere a physician who understood the art of saving men from dying, or, even though they died, of restoring them speedily to life, so that they would thereafter live forever, how the world would pour in money like snow and rain, so that because of the throng of the rich no one could find access! But here in Baptism there is brought free to every one's door such a treasure and medicine as utterly destroys death and preserves all men alive.

Thus we must regard Baptism and make it profitable to ourselves, that when our sins and conscience oppress us, we strengthen ourselves and take comfort and say: Nevertheless I am baptized; but if I am baptized, it is promised me that I shall be saved and have eternal life, both in soul and body. For that is the reason why these two things are done in Baptism namely, that the body, which can apprehend nothing but the water, is sprinkled, and, in addition, the word is spoken for the soul to apprehend. Now, since both, the water and the Word, are one Baptism, therefore body and soul must be saved and live forever: the soul through the Word which it believes, but the body because it is united with the soul and also apprehends Baptism as it is able to apprehend it. We have, therefore, no greater jewel in body and soul, for by it we are made holy and are saved, which no other kind of life, no work upon earth, can attain.

Let this suffice respecting the nature, blessing, and use of Baptism, for it answers the present purpose.

PART FIFTH.

OF THE SACRAMENT OF THE ALTAR.

In the same manner as we have heard regarding Holy Baptism, we must speak also concerning the other Sacrament, namely, these three points: What is it? What are its benefits? and, Who is to receive it? And all these are established by the words by which Christ has instituted it, and which every one who desires to be a Christian and go to the Sacrament should know. For it is not our intention to admit to it and to administer it to those who know not what they seek, or why they come. The words, however, are these:

Our Lord Jesus Christ, the same night in which He was betrayed, took bread; and when He had given thanks, He brake it, and gave it to His disciples, and said, Take, eat; this is My body, which is given for you: this do in remembrance of Me.

After the same manner also He took the cup when He had supped, gave thanks, and gave it to them, saying, Drink ye all of it; this cup is the new testament in My blood, which is shed for you for the remission of sins: this do ye, as oft as ye drink it, in remembrance of Me.

Here also we do not wish to enter into controversy and contend with the traducers and blasphemers of this Sacrament, but to learn first (as we did regarding Baptism) what is of the greatest importance, namely that the chief point is the Word and ordinance or command of God. For it has not been invented nor introduced by any man, but without any one's counsel and deliberation it has been instituted by Christ. Therefore, just as the Ten Commandments, the Lord's Prayer, and the Creed retain their nature and worth although you never keep, pray, or believe them, so also does this venerable Sacrament remain undisturbed, so that nothing is detracted or taken from it, even though we employ and dispense it unworthily. What do you think God cares about what we do or believe, so that on that account He should suffer His ordinance to be changed? Why, in all worldly matters every thing remains as God has created and ordered it, no matter how we employ or use it. This must always be urged, for thereby the prating of nearly all the fanatical spirits can be repelled. For they regard the Sacraments, aside from the Word of God, as something that we do.

Now, what is the Sacrament of the Altar!

Answer: It is the true body and blood of our Lord Jesus Christ, in and under the bread and wine which we Christians are commanded by the Word of Christ to eat and to drink. And as we have said of Baptism that it is not simple water, so here also we say the Sacrament is bread and wine, but not mere bread and wine, such as are ordinarily served at the table, but bread and wine comprehended in, and connected with, the Word of God.

It is the Word (I say) which makes and distinguishes this Sacrament, so that it is not mere bread and wine, but is, and is called, the body and blood of Christ. For it is said: Accedat verbum ad elementum, et At sacramentum. If the Word be joined to the element it becomes a Sacrament. This saying of St. Augustine is so properly and so well put that he has scarcely said anything better. The Word must make a Sacrament of the element, else it remains a mere element. Now, it is not the word or ordinance of a prince or emperor, but of the sublime Majesty, at whose feet all creatures should fall, and affirm it is as He says, and accept it with all reverence fear, and humility.

With this Word you can strengthen your conscience and say: If a hundred thousand devils, together with all fanatics, should rush forward, crying, How can bread and wine be the body and blood of Christ? etc., I

148

know that all spirits and scholars together are not as wise as is the Divine Majesty in His little finger. Now here stands the Word of Christ: Take, eat; this is My body; Drink ye all of it; this is the new testament in My blood, etc. Here we abide, and would like to see those who will constitute themselves His masters, and make it different from what He has spoken. It is true, indeed, that if you take away the Word or regard it without the words, you have nothing but mere bread and wine. But if the words remain with them as they shall and must, then, in virtue of the same, it is truly the body and blood of Christ. For as the lips of Christ say and speak, so it is, as He can never lie or deceive.

Hence it is easy to reply to all manner of questions about which men are troubled at the present time, such as this one: Whether even a wicked priest can minister at, and dispense, the Sacrament, and whatever other questions like this there may be. For here we conclude and say: Even though a knave takes or distributes the Sacrament, he receives the true Sacrament, that is, the true body and blood of Christ, just as truly as he who [receives or] administers it in the most worthy manner. For it is not founded upon the holiness of men, but upon the Word of God. And as no saint upon earth, yea, no angel in heaven, can make bread and wine to be the body and blood of Christ, so also can no one change or alter it, even though it be misused. For the Word by which it became a Sacrament and was instituted does not become false because of the person or his unbelief. For He does not say: If you believe or are worthy, you receive My body and blood, but: Take, eat and drink; this is By body and blood. Likewise: Do this (namely, what I now do, institute, give, and bid you take) . That is as much as to say, No matter whether you are worthy or unworthy, you have here His body and blood by virtue of these words which are added to the bread and wine. Only note and remember this well; for upon these words rest all our foundation, protection, and defense against all errors and deception that have ever come or may yet come.

Thus we have briefly the first point which relates to the essence of this Sacrament. Now examine further the efficacy and benefits on account of which really the Sacrament was instituted; which is also its most necessary part, that we may know what we should seek and obtain there. Now this is plain and clear from the words just mentioned: This is My body and blood, given and shed FOR YOU, for the remission of sins. Briefly that is as much as to say: For this reason we go to the Sacrament because there we receive such a treasure by and in which we obtain forgiveness of sins. Why so? Because the words stand here and give us this; for on this account He bids me eat and drink, that it may be my own and may benefit me, as a sure pledge and token, yea, the very same treasure that is appointed for me against my sins, death, and every calamity.

On this account it is indeed called a food of souls, which nourishes and strengthens the new man. For by Baptism we are first born anew; but (as we said before) there still remains, besides, the old vicious nature of flesh and blood in man, and there are so many hindrances and temptations of the devil and of the world that we often become weary and faint, and sometimes also stumble.

Therefore it is given for a daily pasture and sustenance, that faith may refresh and strengthen itself so as not to fall back in such a battle, but become ever stronger and stronger. For the new life must be so regulated that it continually increase and progress, but it must suffer much opposition. For the devil is such a furious enemy that when he sees that we oppose him and attack the old man, and that he cannot topple us over by force, he prowls and moves about on all sides, tries all devices, and does not desist until he finally wearies us, so that we either renounce our faith or yield hands and feet and become listless or impatient. Now to this end the consolation is here given when the heart feels that the burden is becoming too heavy, that it may here obtain new power and refreshment.

But here our wise spirits contort themselves with their great art and wisdom, crying out and bawling: How can bread and wine forgive sins or strengthen faith? Although they hear and know that we do not say this of bread and wine, because in itself bread is bread, but of such bread and wine as is the body and blood of Christ, and has the words attached to it. That, we say, is verily the treasure, and nothing else, through which such forgiveness is obtained. Now the only way in which it is conveyed and appropriated to us is in the words (Given and shed for you). For herein you have both truths, that it is the body and blood of Christ, and that it is yours as a treasure and gift. Now the body of Christ can never be an unfruitful, vain thing, that effects or profits nothing. Yet however great is the treasure in itself, it must be comprehended in the Word and administered to us, else we should never be able to know or seek it.

Therefore also it is vain talk when they say that the body and blood of Christ are not given and shed for us in the Lord's Supper, hence we could not have forgiveness of sins in the Sacrament. For although the work is accomplished and the forgiveness of sins acquired on the cross, yet it cannot come to us in any other way than through the Word. For what would we otherwise know about it, that such a thing was accomplished or was to be given us if it were not presented by preaching or the oral Word? Whence do they know of it, or how can they apprehend and appropriate to themselves the forgiveness, except they lay hold of and believe the Scriptures and the Gospel? But now the entire Gospel and the article of the Creed: I believe a holy Christian Church, the forgiveness of sin, etc., are by the Word embodied in this Sacrament and presented to us. Why, then, should we allow this treasure to be torn from the Sacrament when they must confess that these are the very words which we hear everywhere in the Gospel, and they cannot say that these words in the Sacrament are of no use, as little as they dare say that the entire Gospel or Word of God, apart from the Sacrament, is of no use?

Thus we have the entire Sacrament, both as to what it is in itself and as to what it brings and profits. Now we must also see who is the person that receives this power and benefit. That is answered briefly, as we said above of Baptism and often elsewhere: Whoever believes it has what the words declare and bring. For they are not spoken or proclaimed to stone and wood, but to those who hear them, to whom He says: Take and eat, etc. And because He offers and promises forgiveness of sin, it cannot be received otherwise than by faith. This faith He Himself demands in the Word when He says: Given and shed for you. As if He said: For this reason I give it, and bid you eat and drink, that you may claim it as yours and enjoy it. Whoever now accepts these words, and believes that what they declare is true, has it. But whoever does not believe it has nothing, as he allows it to be offered to him in vain, and refuses to enjoy such a saving good. The treasure, indeed, is opened and placed at every one's door, yea upon his table, but it is necessary that you also claim it, and confidently view it as the words suggest to you.

This, now, is the entire Christian preparation for receiving this Sacrament worthily. For since this treasure is entirely presented in the words, it cannot be apprehended and appropriated in any other way than with the heart. For such a gift and eternal treasure cannot be seized with the fist. Fasting and prayer, etc., may indeed be an external preparation and discipline for children, that the body may keep and bear itself modestly and reverently towards the body and blood of Christ; yet what is given in and with it the body cannot seize and appropriate. But this is done by the faith of the heart, which discerns this treasure and desires it. This may suffice for what is necessary as a general instruction respecting this Sacrament; for what is further to be said of it belongs to another time.

CONCLUSION

In conclusion, since we have now the true understanding and doctrine of the Sacrament, there is indeed need of some admonition and exhortation, that men may not let so great a treasure which is daily administered and distributed among Christians pass by unheeded, that is, that those who would be Christians make ready to receive this venerable Sacrament often. For we see that men seem weary and lazy with respect to it; and there is a great multitude of such as hear the Gospel, and, because the nonsense of the Pope has been abolished, and we are freed from his laws and coercion, go one, two, three years, or even longer without the Sacrament, as though they were such strong Christians that they have no need of it; and some allow themselves to be prevented and deterred by the pretense that we have taught that no one should approach it except those who feel hunger and thirst, which urge them to it. Some pretend that it is a matter of liberty and not necessary, and that it is sufficient to believe without it; and thus for the most part they go so far that they become quite brutish, and finally despise both the Sacrament and the Word of God.

Now, it is true, as we have said, that no one should by any means be coerced or compelled, lest we institute a new murdering of souls. Nevertheless, it must be known that such people as deprive themselves of, and withdraw from, the Sacrament so long a time are not to be considered Christians. For Christ has not instituted it to be treated as a show, but has commanded His Christians to eat and drink it, and thereby remember Him.

And, indeed, those who are true Christians and esteem the Sacrament precious and holy will urge and impel themselves unto it. Yet that the simple-minded and the weak who also would like to be Christians be the more incited to consider the cause and need which ought to impel them, we will treat somewhat of this point. For as in other matters pertaining to faith, love, and patience, it is not enough to teach and instruct only, but there is need also of daily exhortation, so here also there is need of continuing to preach that men may not become weary and disgusted, since we know and feel how the devil always opposes this and every Christian exercise, and drives and deters therefrom as much as he can.

And we have, in the first place, the clear text in the very words of Christ: Do this in remembrance of Me. These are bidding and commanding words by which all who would be Christians are enjoined to partake of this Sacrament. Therefore, whoever would be a disciple of Christ, with whom He here speaks, must also consider and observe this, not from compulsion, as being forced by men, but in obedience to the Lord Jesus Christ, and to please Him. However, if you say: But the words are added, As oft as ye do it; there He compels no one, but leaves it to our free choice, answer: That is true, yet it is not written that we should never do so. Yea, just because He speaks the words, As oft as ye do it, it is nevertheless implied that we should do it often; and it is added for the reason that He wishes to have the Sacrament free, not limited to special times, like the Passover of the Jews, which they were obliged to eat only once a year, and that just upon the fourteenth day of the first full moon in the evening, and which they must not vary a day. As if He would say by these words: I institute a Passover or Supper for you which you shall enjoy not only once a year, just upon this evening, but often, when and where you will, according to every one's opportunity and necessity, bound to no place or appointed time; although the Pope afterwards perverted it, and again made a Jewish feast of it.

Thus, you perceive, it is not left free in the sense that we may despise it. For that I call despising it if one allow so long a time to elapse and with nothing to hinder him yet never feels a desire for it. If you wish such liberty, you may just as well have the liberty to be no Christian, and neither have to believe nor pray; for the one is just as much the command of Christ as the other. But if you wish to be a Christian, you must from time to time render satisfaction and obedience to this commandment. For this commandment ought ever to move you to examine yourself and to think: See, what sort of a Christian I am! If I were one, I would certainly have some little longing for that which my Lord has commanded [me] to do.

And, indeed, since we act such strangers to it, it is easily seen what sort of Christians we were under the Papacy, namely, that we went from mere compulsion and fear of human commandments, without inclination and love, and never regarded the commandment of Christ. But we neither force nor compel any one; nor need any one do it to serve or please us. But this should induce and constrain you by itself, that He desires it and that it is pleasing to Him. You must not suffer men to coerce you unto faith or any good work. We are doing no more than to say and exhort you as to what you ought to do, not for our sake, but for your own sake. He invites and allures you; if you despise it, you must answer for it yourself.

Now, this is to be the first point, especially for those who are cold and indifferent, that they may reflect upon and rouse themselves. For this is certainly true, as I have found in my own experience, and as every one will find in his own case, that if a person thus withdraw from this Sacrament, he will daily become more and more callous and cold, and will at last disregard it altogether. To avoid this, we must, indeed, examine heart and conscience, and act like a person who desires to be right with God. Now, the more this is done, the more will the heart be warmed and enkindled, that it may not become entirely cold.

But if you say: How if I feel that I am not prepared? Answer: That is also my scruple, especially from the old way under the Pope, in which a person tortured himself to be so perfectly pure that God could not find the least blemish in us. On this account we became so timid that every one was instantly thrown into consternation and said to himself: Alas! you are unworthy! For then nature and reason begin to reckon our unworthiness in comparison with the great and precious good; and then it appears like a dark lantern in contrast with the bright sun, or as filth in comparison with precious stones. Because nature and reason see this, they refuse to approach and tarry until they are prepared so long that one week trails another, and one half year the other. But if you are to regard how good and pure you are, and labor to have no compunctions, you must never approach.

We must, therefore, make a distinction here among men. For those who are wanton and dissolute must be told to stay away; for they are not prepared to receive forgiveness of sin since they do not desire it and do not wish to be godly. But the others, who are not such callous and wicked people, and desire to be godly, must not absent themselves, even though otherwise they be feeble and full of infirmities, as St. Hilary also has said: If any one have not committed sin for which he can rightly be put out of the congregation and esteemed as no Christian, he ought not stay away from the Sacrament, lest he may deprive himself of life. For no one will make such progress that he will not retain many daily infirmities in flesh and blood.

Therefore such people must learn that it is the highest art to know that our Sacrament does not depend upon our worthiness. For we are not baptized because we are worthy and holy, nor do we go to confession because we are pure and without sin, but the contrary because we are poor miserable men and just because we are unworthy; unless it be some one who desires no grace and absolution nor intends to reform.

But whoever would gladly obtain grace and consolation should impel himself, and allow no one to frighten him away, but say: I, indeed, would like to be worthy, but I come, not upon any worthiness, but upon Thy Word, because Thou hast commanded it, as one who would gladly be Thy disciple, no matter what becomes of my worthiness. But this is difficult; for we always have this obstacle and hindrance to encounter, that we look more upon ourselves than upon the Word and lips of Christ. For nature desires so to act that it can stand and rest firmly on itself, otherwise it refuses to make the approach. Let this suffice concerning the first point.

In the second place, there is besides this command also a promise, as we heard above, which ought most strongly to incite and encourage us. For here stand the kind and precious words: This is My body, given for you. This is My blood, shed for you, for the remission of sins. These words, I have said, are not preached to wood and stone, but to me and you; else He might just as well be silent and not institute a Sacrament. Therefore consider, and put yourself into this YOU, that He may not speak to you in vain.

For here He offers to us the entire treasure which He has brought for us from heaven, and to which He invites us also in other places with the greatest kindness, as when He says in St. Matthew 11, 28: Come unto Me, all ye that labor and are heavy laden, and I will give you rest. Now it is surely a sin and a shame that He so cordially and faithfully summons and exhorts us to our highest and greatest good, and we act so distantly with regard to it, and permit so long a time to pass [without partaking of the Sacrament] that we grow quite cold and hardened, so that we have no inclination or love for it. We must never regard the Sacrament as something injurious from which we had better flee but as a pure wholesome, comforting remedy imparting salvation and comfort, which will cure you and give you life both in soul and body. For where the soul has recovered, the body also is relieved. Why, then, is it that we act as if it were a poison, the eating of which would bring death?

To be sure, it is true that those who despise it and live in an unchristian manner receive it to their hurt and damnation; for nothing shall be good or wholesome to them, just as with a sick person who from caprice eats and drinks what is forbidden him by the physician. But those who are sensible of their weakness, desire to be rid of it and long for help, should regard and use it only as a precious antidote against the poison which they have in them. For here in the Sacrament you are to receive from the lips of Christ forgiveness of sin which contains and brings with it the grace of God and the Spirit with all His gifts, protection, shelter, and power against death and the devil and all misfortune.

Thus you have, on the part of God, both the command and the promise of the Lord Jesus Christ. Besides this, on your part, your own distress which is about your neck, and because of which this command, invitation and promise are given, ought to impel you. For He Himself says: They that be whole need not a physician, but they that be sick; that is, those who are weary and heavy-laden with their sins, with the fear of death temptations of the flesh and of the devil. If therefore, you are heavy-laden and feel your weakness, then go joyfully to this Sacrament and obtain refreshment, consolation, and strength. For if you would wait until you are rid of such burdens, that you might come to the Sacrament pure and worthy, you must forever stay away. For in that case He pronounces sentence and says: If you are pure and godly, you have no need of Me, and I, in turn, none of thee. Therefore those alone are called unworthy who neither feel their infirmities nor wish to be considered sinners.

But if you say: What, then, shall I do if I cannot feel such distress or experience hunger and thirst for the Sacrament? Answer: For those who are so minded that they do not realize their condition I know no better counsel than that they put their hand into their bosom to ascertain whether they also have flesh and blood. And if you find that to be the case, then go, for your good, to St. Paul's Epistle to the Galatians, and hear what sort of a fruit your flesh is: Now the works of the flesh (he says [chap. 5, 19ff.]) are manifest, which are these: Adultery fornication uncleanness, lasciviousness, idolatry, witchcraft, hatred, variance, emulations, wrath, strife, seditions, heresies, envyings, murders, drunkenness, revelings, and such like.

Therefore, if you cannot feel it, at least believe the Scriptures, they will not lie to you and they know your flesh better than you yourself. Yea, St. Paul further concludes in Rom. 7, 18: I know that in me, that is, in my flesh, dwelleth no good thing. If St. Paul may speak thus of his flesh, we do not propose to be better nor more holy. But that we do not feel it is so much the worse; for it is a sign that there is a leprous flesh which feels nothing, and yet [the leprosy] rages and keeps spreading. Yet as we have said, if you are quite dead to all sensibility, still believe the Scriptures, which pronounce sentence upon you. And, in short, the less you feel your sins and infirmities, the more reason have you to go to the Sacrament to seek help and a remedy.

In the second place, look about you and see whether you are also in the world, or if you do not know it, ask your neighbors about it. If you are in the world, do not think that there will be lack of sins and misery. For only begin to act as though you would be godly and adhere to the Gospel, and see whether no one will become your enemy, and, moreover, do you harm, wrong, and violence, and likewise give you cause for sin and vice. If you have not experienced it, then let the Scriptures tell you, which everywhere give this praise and testimony to the world.

Besides this, you will also have the devil about you, whom you will not entirely tread under foot, because our Lord Christ Himself could not entirely avoid him. Now, what is the devil? Nothing else than what the Scriptures call him, a liar and murderer. A liar, to lead the heart astray from the Word of God, and to blind it, that you cannot feel your distress or come to Christ. A murderer, who cannot bear to see you live one single hour. If you could see how many knives, darts, and arrows are every moment aimed at you, you would be glad to come to the Sacrament as often as possible. But there is no reason why we walk so securely and heedlessly, except that we neither think nor believe that we are in the flesh, and in this wicked world or in the kingdom of the devil.

Therefore, try this and practice it well, and do but examine yourself, or look about you a little, and only keep to the Scriptures. If even then you still feel nothing, you have so much the more misery to lament both to God and to your brother. Then take advice and have others pray for you, and do not desist until the stone be removed from your heart. Then, indeed, the distress will not fail to become manifest, and you will find that you have sunk twice as deep as any other poor sinner, and are much more in need of the Sacrament against the misery which unfortunately you do not see, so that, with the grace of God, you may feel it more and become the more hungry for the Sacrament, especially since the devil plies his force against you, and lies in wait for you without ceasing, to seize and destroy you, soul and body, so that you are not safe from him one hour. How soon can he have brought you suddenly into misery and distress when you least expect it!

Let this, then, be said for exhortation, not only for those of us who are old and grown, but also for the young people, who ought to be brought up in the Christian doctrine and understanding. For thereby the Ten Commandments, the Creed, and the Lord's Prayer might be the more easily inculcated to our youth, so that they would receive them with pleasure and earnestness, and thus would practice them from their youth and accustom themselves to them. For the old are now well-nigh done for, so that these and other things cannot be attained, unless we train the people who are to come after us and succeed us in our office and work, in order that they also may bring up their children successfully that the Word of God and the Christian Church may be preserved. Therefore let every father of a family know that it is his duty by the injunction and command of God, to teach these things to his children, or have them learn what they ought to know. For since they are baptized and received into the Christian Church, they should also enjoy this communion of the Sacrament, in order that they may serve us and be useful to us; for they must all indeed help us to believe, love, pray, and fight against the devil.

CONCERNING CHRISTIAN LIBERTY

LETTER OF MARTIN LUTHER
TO POPE LEO X.

Among those monstrous evils of this age with which I have now
for three years been waging war, I am sometimes compelled to look to
you and to call you to mind, most blessed father Leo. In truth, since
you alone are everywhere considered as being the cause of my engaging
in war, I cannot at any time fail to remember you; and although I have
been compelled by the causeless raging of your impious flatterers against
me to appeal from your seat to a future council—fearless of the futile
decrees of your predecessors Pius and Julius, who in their foolish tyranny
prohibited such an action—yet I have never been so alienated in feeling
from your Blessedness as not to have sought with all my might, in diligent
prayer and crying to God, all the best gifts for you and for your see. But
those who have hitherto endeavoured to terrify me with the majesty of
your name and authority, I have begun quite to despise and triumph over.
One thing I see remaining which I cannot despise, and this has been the
reason of my writing anew to your Blessedness: namely, that I find that
blame is cast on me, and that it is imputed to me as a great offence, that
in my rashness I am judged to have spared not even your person.

Now, to confess the truth openly, I am conscious that, whenever I
have had to mention your person, I have said nothing of you but what
was honourable and good. If I had done otherwise, I could by no means
have approved my own conduct, but should have supported with all my
power the judgment of those men concerning me, nor would anything
have pleased me better, than to recant such rashness and impiety. I have
called you Daniel in Babylon; and every reader thoroughly knows with

what distinguished zeal I defended your conspicuous innocence against Silvester, who tried to stain it. Indeed, the published opinion of so many great men and the repute of your blameless life are too widely famed and too much reverenced throughout the world to be assailable by any man, of however great name, or by any arts. I am not so foolish as to attack one whom everybody praises; nay, it has been and always will be my desire not to attack even those whom public repute disgraces. I am not delighted at the faults of any man, since I am very conscious myself of the great beam in my own eye, nor can I be the first to cast a stone at the adulteress.

I have indeed inveighed sharply against impious doctrines, and I have not been slack to censure my adversaries on account, not of their bad morals, but of their impiety. And for this I am so far from being sorry that I have brought my mind to despise the judgments of men and to persevere in this vehement zeal, according to the example of Christ, who, in His zeal, calls His adversaries a generation of vipers, blind, hypocrites, and children of the devil. Paul, too, charges the sorcerer with being a child of the devil, full of all subtlety and all malice; and defames certain persons as evil workers, dogs, and deceivers. In the opinion of those delicate-eared persons, nothing could be more bitter or intemperate than Paul's language. What can be more bitter than the words of the prophets? The ears of our generation have been made so delicate by the senseless multitude of flatterers that, as soon as we perceive that anything of ours is not approved of, we cry out that we are being bitterly assailed; and when we can repel the truth by no other pretence, we escape by attributing bitterness, impatience, intemperance, to our adversaries. What would be the use of salt if it were not pungent, or of the edge of the sword if it did not slay? Accursed is the man who does the work of the Lord deceitfully.

Wherefore, most excellent Leo, I beseech you to accept my vindication, made in this letter, and to persuade yourself that I have never thought any evil concerning your person; further, that I am one who desires that eternal blessing may fall to your lot, and that I have no dispute with any man concerning morals, but only concerning the word of truth. In all other things I will yield to any one, but I neither can nor will forsake and deny the word. He who thinks otherwise of me, or has taken in my words in another sense, does not think rightly, and has not taken in the truth.

Your see, however, which is called the Court of Rome, and which neither you nor any man can deny to be more corrupt than any Babylon or Sodom, and quite, as I believe, of a lost, desperate, and hopeless impiety, this I have verily abominated, and have felt indignant that the people of Christ should be cheated under your name and the pretext of the Church of Rome; and so I have resisted, and will resist, as long as the spirit of faith shall live in me. Not that I am striving after impossibilities, or hoping that by my labours alone, against the furious opposition of so many flatterers, any good can be done in that most disordered Babylon; but that I feel myself a debtor to my brethren, and am bound to take thought for them, that fewer of them may be ruined, or that their ruin may be less complete, by the plagues of Rome. For many years now, nothing else has overflowed from Rome into the world—as you are not ignorant—than the laying waste of goods, of bodies, and of souls, and the worst examples of all the worst things. These things are clearer than the light to all men; and the Church of Rome, formerly the most holy of all Churches, has become the most lawless den of thieves, the most shameless of all brothels, the very kingdom of sin, death, and hell; so that not even antichrist, if he were to come, could devise any addition to its wickedness.

Meanwhile you, Leo, are sitting like a lamb in the midst of wolves, like Daniel in the midst of lions, and, with Ezekiel, you dwell among scorpions. What opposition can you alone make to these monstrous evils? Take to yourself three or four of the most learned and best of the cardinals. What are these among so many? You would all perish by poison before you could undertake to decide on a remedy. It is all over with the Court of Rome; the wrath of God has come upon her to the uttermost.

She hates councils; she dreads to be reformed; she cannot restrain the madness of her impiety; she fills up the sentence passed on her mother, of whom it is said, "We would have healed Babylon, but she is not healed; let us forsake her." It had been your duty and that of your cardinals to apply a remedy to these evils, but this gout laughs at the physician's hand, and the chariot does not obey the reins. Under the influence of these feelings, I have always grieved that you, most excellent Leo, who were worthy of a better age, have been made pontiff in this. For the Roman Court is not worthy of you and those like you, but of Satan himself, who in truth is more the ruler in that Babylon than you are.

Oh, would that, having laid aside that glory which your most abandoned enemies declare to be yours, you were living rather in the office of a private priest or on your paternal inheritance! In that glory none are worthy to glory, except the race of Iscariot, the children of perdition. For what happens in your court, Leo, except that, the more wicked and execrable any man is, the more prosperously he can use your name and authority for the ruin of the property and souls of men, for the multiplication of crimes, for the oppression of faith and truth and of the whole Church of God? Oh, Leo! in reality most unfortunate, and sitting on a most perilous throne, I tell you the truth, because I wish you well; for if Bernard felt compassion for his Anastasius at a time when the Roman see, though even then most corrupt, was as yet ruling with better hope than now, why should not we lament, to whom so much further corruption and ruin has been added in three hundred years?

Is it not true that there is nothing under the vast heavens more corrupt, more pestilential, more hateful, than the Court of Rome? She incomparably surpasses the impiety of the Turks, so that in very truth she, who was formerly the gate of heaven, is now a sort of open mouth of hell, and such a mouth as, under the urgent wrath of God, cannot be blocked up; one course alone being left to us wretched men: to call back and save some few, if we can, from that Roman gulf.

166

Behold, Leo, my father, with what purpose and on what principle it is that I have stormed against that seat of pestilence. I am so far from having felt any rage against your person that I even hoped to gain favour with you and to aid you in your welfare by striking actively and vigorously at that your prison, nay, your hell. For whatever the efforts of all minds can contrive against the confusion of that impious Court will be advantageous to you and to your welfare, and to many others with you. Those who do harm to her are doing your office; those who in every way abhor her are glorifying Christ; in short, those are Christians who are not Romans.

But, to say yet more, even this never entered my heart: to inveigh against the Court of Rome or to dispute at all about her. For, seeing all remedies for her health to be desperate, I looked on her with contempt, and, giving her a bill of divorcement, said to her, "He that is unjust, let him be unjust still; and he that is filthy, let him be filthy still," giving myself up to the peaceful and quiet study of sacred literature, that by this I might be of use to the brethren living about me.

While I was making some advance in these studies, Satan opened his eyes and goaded on his servant John Eccius, that notorious adversary of Christ, by the unchecked lust for fame, to drag me unexpectedly into the arena, trying to catch me in one little word concerning the primacy of the Church of Rome, which had fallen from me in passing. That boastful Thraso, foaming and gnashing his teeth, proclaimed that he would dare all things for the glory of God and for the honour of the holy apostolic seat; and, being puffed up respecting your power, which he was about to misuse, he looked forward with all certainty to victory; seeking to promote, not so much the primacy of Peter, as his own pre-eminence among the theologians of this age; for he thought it would contribute in no slight degree to this, if he were to lead Luther in triumph. The result having proved unfortunate for the sophist, an incredible rage torments him; for he feels that whatever discredit to Rome has arisen through me has been caused by the fault of himself alone.

Suffer me, I pray you, most excellent Leo, both to plead my own cause, and to accuse your true enemies. I believe it is known to you in what way Cardinal Cajetan, your imprudent and unfortunate, nay unfaithful, legate, acted towards me. When, on account of my reverence for your name, I had placed myself and all that was mine in his hands, he did not so act as to establish peace, which he could easily have established by one little word, since I at that time promised to be silent and to make an end of my case, if he would command my adversaries to do the same. But that man of pride, not content with this agreement, began to justify my adversaries, to give them free licence, and to order me to recant, a thing which was certainly not in his commission. Thus indeed, when the case was in the best position, it came through his vexatious tyranny into a much worse one. Therefore whatever has followed upon this is the fault not of Luther, but entirely of Cajetan, since he did not suffer me to be silent and remain quiet, which at that time I was entreating for with all my might. What more was it my duty to do?

Next came Charles Miltitz, also a nuncio from your Blessedness. He, though he went up and down with much and varied exertion, and omitted nothing which could tend to restore the position of the cause thrown into confusion by the rashness and pride of Cajetan, had difficulty, even with the help of that very illustrious prince the Elector Frederick, in at last bringing about more than one familiar conference with me. In these I again yielded to your great name, and was prepared to keep silence, and to accept as my judge either the Archbishop of Treves, or the Bishop of Naumburg; and thus it was done and concluded. While this was being done with good hope of success, lo! that other and greater enemy of yours, Eccius, rushed in with his Leipsic disputation, which he had undertaken against Carlstadt, and, having taken up a new question concerning the primacy of the Pope, turned his arms unexpectedly against me, and completely overthrew the plan for peace. Meanwhile Charles Miltitz was waiting, disputations were held, judges were being chosen, but no decision was arrived at. And no wonder! for by the falsehoods, pretences, and arts of Eccius the whole business was brought into such thorough disorder, confusion, and festering soreness, that, whichever way the sentence might lean, a greater conflagration was sure to arise; for he was seeking, not after truth, but after his own credit. In this case too I omitted nothing which it was right that I should do.

I confess that on this occasion no small part of the corruptions of Rome came to light; but, if there was any offence in this, it was the fault of Eccius, who, in taking on him a burden beyond his strength, and in furiously aiming at credit for himself, unveiled to the whole world the disgrace of Rome.

Here is that enemy of yours, Leo, or rather of your Court; by his example alone we may learn that an enemy is not more baneful than a flatterer. For what did he bring about by his flattery, except evils which no king could have brought about? At this day the name of the Court of Rome stinks in the nostrils of the world, the papal authority is growing weak, and its notorious ignorance is evil spoken of. We should hear none of these things, if Eccius had not disturbed the plans of Miltitz and myself for peace. He feels this clearly enough himself in the indignation he shows, too late and in vain, against the publication of my books. He ought to have reflected on this at the time when he was all mad for renown, and was seeking in your cause nothing but his own objects, and that with the greatest peril to you. The foolish man hoped that, from fear of your name, I should yield and keep silence; for I do not think he presumed on his talents and learning. Now, when he sees that I am very confident and speak aloud, he repents too late of his rashness, and sees—if indeed he does see it—that there is One in heaven who resists the proud, and humbles the presumptuous.

Since then we were bringing about by this disputation nothing but the greater confusion of the cause of Rome, Charles Miltitz for the third time addressed the Fathers of the Order, assembled in chapter, and sought their advice for the settlement of the case, as being now in a most troubled and perilous state. Since, by the favour of God, there was no hope of proceeding against me by force, some of the more noted of their number were sent to me, and begged me at least to show respect to your person and to vindicate in a humble letter both your innocence and my own. They said that the affair was not as yet in a position of extreme hopelessness, if Leo X., in his inborn kindliness, would put his hand to it. On this I, who have always offered and wished for peace, in order that I might devote myself to calmer and more useful pursuits, and who for this very purpose have acted with so much spirit and vehemence, in order to put down by the strength and impetuosity of my words, as well as of my feelings, men whom I saw to be very far from equal to myself—I, I say, not only gladly yielded, but even accepted it with joy and gratitude, as the greatest kindness and benefit, if you should think it right to satisfy my hopes.

Thus I come, most blessed Father, and in all abasement beseech you to put to your hand, if it is possible, and impose a curb to those flatterers who are enemies of peace, while they pretend peace. But there is no reason, most blessed Father, why any one should assume that I am to utter a recantation, unless he prefers to involve the case in still greater confusion. Moreover, I cannot bear with laws for the interpretation of the word of God, since the word of God, which teaches liberty in all other things, ought not to be bound. Saving these two things, there is nothing which I am not able, and most heartily willing, to do or to suffer. I hate contention; I will challenge no one; in return I wish not to be challenged; but, being challenged, I will not be dumb in the cause of Christ my Master. For your Blessedness will be able by one short and easy word to call these controversies before you and suppress them, and to impose silence and peace on both sides—a word which I have ever longed to hear.

Therefore, Leo, my Father, beware of listening to those sirens who make you out to be not simply a man, but partly a god, so that you can command and require whatever you will. It will not happen so, nor will you prevail. You are the servant of servants, and more than any other man, in a most pitiable and perilous position. Let not those men deceive you who pretend that you are lord of the world; who will not allow any one to be a Christian without your authority; who babble of your having power over heaven, hell, and purgatory. These men are your enemies and are seeking your soul to destroy it, as Isaiah says, "My people, they that call thee blessed are themselves deceiving thee." They are in error who raise you above councils and the universal Church; they are in error who attribute to you alone the right of interpreting Scripture. All these men are seeking to set up their own impieties in the Church under your name, and alas! Satan has gained much through them in the time of your predecessors.

In brief, trust not in any who exalt you, but in those who humiliate you. For this is the judgment of God: "He hath cast down the mighty from their seat, and hath exalted the humble." See how unlike Christ was to His successors, though all will have it that they are His vicars. I fear that in truth very many of them have been in too serious a sense His vicars, for a vicar represents a prince who is absent. Now if a pontiff rules while Christ is absent and does not dwell in his heart, what else is he but a vicar of Christ? And then what is that Church but a multitude without Christ? What indeed is such a vicar but antichrist and an idol? How much more rightly did the Apostles speak, who call themselves servants of a present Christ, not the vicars of an absent one!

Perhaps I am shamelessly bold in seeming to teach so great a head, by whom all men ought to be taught, and from whom, as those plagues of yours boast, the thrones of judges receive their sentence; but I imitate St. Bernard in his book concerning Considerations addressed to Eugenius, a book which ought to be known by heart by every pontiff. I do this, not from any desire to teach, but as a duty, from that simple and faithful solicitude which teaches us to be anxious for all that is safe for our neighbours, and does not allow considerations of worthiness or unworthiness to be entertained, being intent only on the dangers or advantage of others. For since I know that your Blessedness is driven and tossed by the waves at

Rome, so that the depths of the sea press on you with infinite perils, and that you are labouring under such a condition of misery that you need even the least help from any the least brother, I do not seem to myself to be acting unsuitably if I forget your majesty till I shall have fulfilled the office of charity. I will not flatter in so serious and perilous a matter; and if in this you do not see that I am your friend and most thoroughly your subject, there is One to see and judge.

In fine, that I may not approach you empty-handed, blessed Father, I bring with me this little treatise, published under your name, as a good omen of the establishment of peace and of good hope. By this you may perceive in what pursuits I should prefer and be able to occupy myself to more profit, if I were allowed, or had been hitherto allowed, by your impious flatterers. It is a small matter, if you look to its exterior, but, unless I mistake, it is a summary of the Christian life put together in small compass, if you apprehend its meaning. I, in my poverty, have no other present to make you, nor do you need anything else than to be enriched by a spiritual gift. I commend myself to your Paternity and Blessedness, whom may the Lord Jesus preserve for ever. Amen.

Wittenberg, 6th September, 1520.

CONCERNING CHRISTIAN LIBERTY

Christian faith has appeared to many an easy thing; nay, not a few even reckon it among the social virtues, as it were; and this they do because they have not made proof of it experimentally, and have never tasted of what efficacy it is. For it is not possible for any man to write well about it, or to understand well what is rightly written, who has not at some time tasted of its spirit, under the pressure of tribulation; while he who has tasted of it, even to a very small extent, can never write, speak, think, or hear about it sufficiently. For it is a living fountain, springing up into eternal life, as Christ calls it in John iv.

Now, though I cannot boast of my abundance, and though I know how poorly I am furnished, yet I hope that, after having been vexed by various temptations, I have attained some little drop of faith, and that I can speak of this matter, if not with more elegance, certainly with more solidity, than those literal and too subtle disputants who have hitherto discoursed upon it without understanding their own words. That I may open then an easier way for the ignorant—for these alone I am trying to serve—I first lay down these two propositions, concerning spiritual liberty and servitude:—

A Christian man is the most free lord of all, and subject to none; a Christian man is the most dutiful servant of all, and subject to every one.

Although these statements appear contradictory, yet, when they are found to agree together, they will make excellently for my purpose. They are both the statements of Paul himself, who says, "Though I be free from all men, yet have I made myself servant unto all" (1 Cor. ix. 19), and "Owe no man anything, but to love one another" (Rom. xiii. 8). Now love is by its own nature dutiful and obedient to the beloved object. Thus even Christ, though Lord of all things, was yet made of a woman; made under the law; at once free and a servant; at once in the form of God and in the form of a servant.

Let us examine the subject on a deeper and less simple principle. Man is composed of a twofold nature, a spiritual and a bodily. As regards the spiritual nature, which they name the soul, he is called the spiritual, inward, new man; as regards the bodily nature, which they name the flesh, he is called the fleshly, outward, old man. The Apostle speaks of this: "Though our outward man perish, yet the inward man is renewed day by day" (2 Cor. iv. 16). The result of this diversity is that in the Scriptures opposing statements are made concerning the same man, the fact being that in the same man these two men are opposed to one another; the flesh lusting against the spirit, and the spirit against the flesh (Gal. v. 17).

We first approach the subject of the inward man, that we may see by what means a man becomes justified, free, and a true Christian; that is, a spiritual, new, and inward man. It is certain that absolutely none among outward things, under whatever name they may be reckoned, has any influence in producing Christian righteousness or liberty, nor, on the other hand, unrighteousness or slavery. This can be shown by an easy argument.

What can it profit the soul that the body should be in good condition, free, and full of life; that it should eat, drink, and act according to its pleasure; when even the most impious slaves of every kind of vice are prosperous in these matters? Again, what harm can ill-health, bondage, hunger, thirst, or any other outward evil, do to the soul, when even the most pious of men and the freest in the purity of their conscience, are harassed by these things? Neither of these states of things has to do with the liberty or the slavery of the soul.

And so it will profit nothing that the body should be adorned with sacred vestments, or dwell in holy places, or be occupied in sacred offices,

174

or pray, fast, and abstain from certain meats, or do whatever works can be done through the body and in the body. Something widely different will be necessary for the justification and liberty of the soul, since the things I have spoken of can be done by any impious person, and only hypocrites are produced by devotion to these things. On the other hand, it will not at all injure the soul that the body should be clothed in profane raiment, should dwell in profane places, should eat and drink in the ordinary fashion, should not pray aloud, and should leave undone all the things above mentioned, which may be done by hypocrites.

And, to cast everything aside, even speculation, meditations, and whatever things can be performed by the exertions of the soul itself, are of no profit. One thing, and one alone, is necessary for life, justification, and Christian liberty; and that is the most holy word of God, the Gospel of Christ, as He says, "I am the resurrection and the life; he that believeth in Me shall not die eternally" (John xi. 25), and also, "If the Son shall make you free, ye shall be free indeed" (John viii. 36), and, "Man shall not live by bread alone, but by every word that proceedeth out of the mouth of God" (Matt. iv. 4).

Let us therefore hold it for certain and firmly established that the soul can do without everything except the word of God, without which none at all of its wants are provided for. But, having the word, it is rich and wants for nothing, since that is the word of life, of truth, of light, of peace, of justification, of salvation, of joy, of liberty, of wisdom, of virtue, of grace, of glory, and of every good thing. It is on this account that the prophet in a whole Psalm (Psalm cxix.), and in many other places, sighs for and calls upon the word of God with so many groanings and words.

Again, there is no more cruel stroke of the wrath of God than when He sends a famine of hearing His words (Amos viii. 11), just as there is no greater favour from Him than the sending forth of His word, as it is said, "He sent His word and healed them, and delivered them from their destructions" (Psalm cvii. 20). Christ was sent for no other office than that of the word; and the order of Apostles, that of bishops, and that of the whole body of the clergy, have been called and instituted for no object but the ministry of the word.

But you will ask, What is this word, and by what means is it to be used, since there are so many words of God? I answer, The Apostle Paul (Rom. i.) explains what it is, namely the Gospel of God, concerning His Son, incarnate, suffering, risen, and glorified, through the Spirit, the Sanctifier. To preach Christ is to feed the soul, to justify it, to set it free, and to save it, if it believes the preaching. For faith alone and the efficacious use of the word of God, bring salvation. "If thou shalt confess with thy mouth the Lord Jesus, and shalt believe in thine heart that God hath raised Him from the dead, thou shalt be saved" (Rom. x. 9); and again, "Christ is the end of the law for righteousness to every one that believeth" (Rom. x. 4), and "The just shall live by faith" (Rom. i. 17). For the word of God cannot be received and honoured by any works, but by faith alone. Hence it is clear that as the soul needs the word alone for life and justification, so it is justified by faith alone, and not by any works. For if it could be justified by any other means, it would have no need of the word, nor consequently of faith.

But this faith cannot consist at all with works; that is, if you imagine that you can be justified by those works, whatever they are, along with it. For this would be to halt between two opinions, to worship Baal, and to kiss the hand to him, which is a very great iniquity, as Job says. Therefore, when you begin to believe, you learn at the same time that all that is in you is utterly guilty, sinful, and damnable, according to that saying, "All have sinned, and come short of the glory of God" (Rom. iii. 23), and also: "There is none righteous, no, not one; they are all gone out of the way; they are together become unprofitable: there is none that doeth good, no, not one" (Rom. iii. 10-12). When you have learnt this, you will know that Christ is necessary for you, since He has suffered and risen again for you, that, believing on Him, you might by this faith become another man, all your sins being remitted, and you being justified by the merits of another, namely of Christ alone.

Since then this faith can reign only in the inward man, as it is said, "With the heart man believeth unto righteousness" (Rom. x. 10); and since it alone justifies, it is evident that by no outward work or labour can the inward man be at all justified, made free, and saved; and that no works whatever have any relation to him. And so, on the other hand, it is solely by impiety and incredulity of heart that he becomes guilty and a slave of sin, deserving condemnation, not by any outward sin or work. Therefore the first care of every Christian ought to be to lay aside all reliance on works, and strengthen his faith alone more and more, and by it grow in the knowledge, not of works, but of Christ Jesus, who has suffered and risen again for him, as Peter teaches (1 Peter v.) when he makes no other work to be a Christian one. Thus Christ, when the Jews asked Him what they should do that they might work the works of God, rejected the multitude of works, with which He saw that they were puffed up, and commanded them one thing only, saying, "This is the work of God: that ye believe on Him whom He hath sent, for Him hath God the Father sealed" (John vi. 27, 29).

Hence a right faith in Christ is an incomparable treasure, carrying with it universal salvation and preserving from all evil, as it is said, "He that believeth and is baptised shall be saved; but he that believeth not shall be damned" (Mark xvi. 16). Isaiah, looking to this treasure, predicted, "The consumption decreed shall overflow with righteousness. For the Lord God of hosts shall make a consumption, even determined (verbum abbreviatum et consummans), in the midst of the land" (Isa. x. 22, 23). As if he said, "Faith, which is the brief and complete fulfilling of the law, will fill those who believe with such righteousness that they will need nothing else for justification." Thus, too, Paul says, "For with the heart man believeth unto righteousness" (Rom. x. 10).

But you ask how it can be the fact that faith alone justifies, and affords without works so great a treasure of good things, when so many works, ceremonies, and laws are prescribed to us in the Scriptures? I answer, Before all things bear in mind what I have said: that faith alone without works justifies, sets free, and saves, as I shall show more clearly below.

Meanwhile it is to be noted that the whole Scripture of God is divided into two parts, precepts and promises. The precepts certainly teach us what is good, but what they teach is not forthwith done. For they show us what we ought to do, but do not give us the power to do it. They were ordained, however, for the purpose of showing man to himself, that through them he may learn his own impotence for good and may despair of his own strength. For this reason they are called the Old Testament, and are so.

For example, "Thou shalt not covet," is a precept by which we are all convicted of sin, since no man can help coveting, whatever efforts to the contrary he may make. In order therefore that he may fulfil the precept, and not covet, he is constrained to despair of himself and to seek elsewhere and through another the help which he cannot find in himself; as it is said, "O Israel, thou hast destroyed thyself; but in Me is thine help" (Hosea xiii. 9). Now what is done by this one precept is done by all; for all are equally impossible of fulfilment by us.

Now when a man has through the precepts been taught his own impotence, and become anxious by what means he may satisfy the law—for the law must be satisfied, so that no jot or tittle of it may pass away, otherwise he must be hopelessly condemned—then, being truly humbled and brought to nothing in his own eyes, he finds in himself no resource for justification and salvation.

Then comes in that other part of Scripture, the promises of God, which declare the glory of God, and say, "If you wish to fulfil the law, and, as the law requires, not to covet, lo! believe in Christ, in whom are promised to you grace, justification, peace, and liberty." All these things you shall have, if you believe, and shall be without them if you do not believe. For what is impossible for you by all the works of the law, which are many and yet useless, you shall fulfil in an easy and summary way through faith, because God the Father has made everything to depend on faith, so that whosoever has it has all things, and he who has it not has nothing. "For God hath concluded them all in unbelief, that He might have mercy upon all" (Rom. xi. 32). Thus the promises of God give that which the precepts exact, and fulfil what the law commands; so that all is of God alone, both the precepts and their fulfilment. He alone commands; He alone also fulfils. Hence the promises of God belong to the New Testament; nay, are the New Testament.

Now, since these promises of God are words of holiness, truth, righteousness, liberty, and peace, and are full of universal goodness, the soul, which cleaves to them with a firm faith, is so united to them, nay, thoroughly absorbed by them, that it not only partakes in, but is penetrated and saturated by, all their virtues. For if the touch of Christ was healing, how much more does that most tender spiritual touch, nay, absorption of the word, communicate to the soul all that belongs to the word! In this way therefore the soul, through faith alone, without works, is from the word of God justified, sanctified, endued with truth, peace, and liberty, and filled full with every good thing, and is truly made the child of God, as it is said, "To them gave He power to become the sons of God, even to them that believe on His name" (John i. 12).

From all this it is easy to understand why faith has such great power, and why no good works, nor even all good works put together, can compare with it, since no work can cleave to the word of God or be in the soul. Faith alone and the word reign in it; and such as is the word, such is the soul made by it, just as iron exposed to fire glows like fire, on account of its union with the fire. It is clear then that to a Christian man his faith suffices for everything, and that he has no need of works for justification. But if he has no need of works, neither has he need of the law; and if he has no need of the law, he is certainly free from the law, and the saying is true, "The law is not made for a righteous man" (1 Tim. i. 9). This is that Christian liberty, our faith, the effect of which is, not that we should be careless or lead a bad life, but that no one should need the law or works for justification and salvation.

Let us consider this as the first virtue of faith; and let us look also to the second. This also is an office of faith: that it honours with the utmost veneration and the highest reputation Him in whom it believes, inasmuch as it holds Him to be truthful and worthy of belief. For there is no honour like that reputation of truth and righteousness with which we honour Him in whom we believe. What higher credit can we attribute to any one than truth and righteousness, and absolute goodness? On the other hand, it is the greatest insult to brand any one with the reputation of falsehood and unrighteousness, or to suspect him of these, as we do when we disbelieve him.

Thus the soul, in firmly believing the promises of God, holds Him to be true and righteous; and it can attribute to God no higher glory than the credit of being so. The highest worship of God is to ascribe to Him truth, righteousness, and whatever qualities we must ascribe to one in whom we believe. In doing this the soul shows itself prepared to do His whole will; in doing this it hallows His name, and gives itself up to be dealt with as it may please God. For it cleaves to His promises, and never doubts that He is true, just, and wise, and will do, dispose, and provide for all things in the best way. Is not such a soul, in this its faith, most obedient to God in all things? What commandment does there remain which has not been amply fulfilled by such an obedience? What fulfilment can be more full than universal obedience? Now this is not accomplished by works, but by faith alone.

On the other hand, what greater rebellion, impiety, or insult to God can there be, than not to believe His promises? What else is this, than either to make God a liar, or to doubt His truth—that is, to attribute truth to ourselves, but to God falsehood and levity? In doing this, is not a man denying God and setting himself up as an idol in his own heart? What then can works, done in such a state of impiety, profit us, were they even angelic or apostolic works? Rightly hath God shut up all, not in wrath nor in lust, but in unbelief, in order that those who pretend that they are fulfilling the law by works of purity and benevolence (which are social and human virtues) may not presume that they will therefore be saved, but, being included in the sin of unbelief, may either seek mercy, or be justly condemned.

But when God sees that truth is ascribed to Him, and that in the faith of our hearts He is honoured with all the honour of which He is worthy, then in return He honours us on account of that faith, attributing to us truth and righteousness. For faith does truth and righteousness in rendering to God what is His; and therefore in return God gives glory to our righteousness. It is true and righteous that God is true and righteous; and to confess this and ascribe these attributes to Him, this it is to be true and righteous. Thus He says, "Them that honour Me I will honour, and they that despise Me shall be lightly esteemed" (1 Sam. ii. 30). And so Paul says that Abraham's faith was imputed to him for righteousness, because by it he gave glory to God; and that to us also, for the same reason, it shall be imputed for righteousness, if we believe (Rom. iv.).

The third incomparable grace of faith is this: that it unites the soul 3 to Christ, as the wife to the husband, by which mystery, as the Apostle teaches, Christ and the soul are made one flesh. Now if they are one flesh, and if a true marriage—nay, by far the most perfect of all marriages—is accomplished between them (for human marriages are but feeble types of this one great marriage), then it follows that all they have becomes theirs in common, as well good things as evil things; so that whatsoever Christ possesses, that the believing soul may take to itself and boast of as its own, and whatever belongs to the soul, that Christ claims as His.

If we compare these possessions, we shall see how inestimable is the gain. Christ is full of grace, life, and salvation; the soul is full of sin, death, and condemnation. Let faith step in, and then sin, death, and hell will belong to Christ, and grace, life, and salvation to the soul. For, if He is a Husband, He must needs take to Himself that which is His wife's, and at the same time, impart to His wife that which is His. For, in giving

181

her His own body and Himself, how can He but give her all that is His? And, in taking to Himself the body of His wife, how can He but take to Himself all that is hers?

In this is displayed the delightful sight, not only of communion, but of a prosperous warfare, of victory, salvation, and redemption. For, since Christ is God and man, and is such a Person as neither has sinned, nor dies, nor is condemned, nay, cannot sin, die, or be condemned, and since His righteousness, life, and salvation are invincible, eternal, and almighty,—when I say, such a Person, by the wedding-ring of faith, takes a share in the sins, death, and hell of His wife, nay, makes them His own, and deals with them no otherwise than as if they were His, and as if He Himself had sinned; and when He suffers, dies, and descends to hell, that He may overcome all things, and since sin, death, and hell cannot swallow Him up, they must needs be swallowed up by Him in stupendous conflict. For His righteousness rises above the sins of all men; His life is more powerful than all death; His salvation is more unconquerable than all hell.

Thus the believing soul, by the pledge of its faith in Christ, becomes free from all sin, fearless of death, safe from hell, and endowed with the eternal righteousness, life, and salvation of its Husband Christ. Thus He presents to Himself a glorious bride, without spot or wrinkle, cleansing her with the washing of water by the word; that is, by faith in the word of life, righteousness, and salvation. Thus He betrothes her unto Himself "in faithfulness, in righteousness, and in judgment, and in loving-kindness, and in mercies" (Hosea ii. 19, 20).

Who then can value highly enough these royal nuptials? Who can comprehend the riches of the glory of this grace? Christ, that rich and pious Husband, takes as a wife a needy and impious harlot, redeeming her from all her evils and supplying her with all His good things. It is impossible now that her sins should destroy her, since they have been laid upon Christ and swallowed up in Him, and since she has in her Husband Christ a righteousness which she may claim as her own, and which she can set up with confidence against all her sins, against death and hell, saying, "If I have sinned, my Christ, in whom I believe, has not sinned; all mine is His, and all His is mine," as it is written, "My beloved is mine, and I am His" (Cant. ii. 16). This is what Paul says: "Thanks be to God, which giveth us the victory through our Lord Jesus Christ," victory over sin and death, as he says, "The sting of death is sin, and the strength of sin is the law" (1 Cor. xv. 56, 57).

From all this you will again understand why so much importance is attributed to faith, so that it alone can fulfil the law and justify without any works. For you see that the First Commandment, which says, "Thou shalt worship one God only," is fulfilled by faith alone. If you were nothing but good works from the soles of your feet to the crown of your head, you would not be worshipping God, nor fulfilling the First Commandment, since it is impossible to worship God without ascribing to Him the glory of truth and of universal goodness, as it ought in truth to be ascribed. Now this is not done by works, but only by faith of heart. It is not by working, but by believing, that we glorify God, and confess Him to be true. On this ground faith alone is the righteousness of a Christian man, and the fulfilling of all the commandments. For to him who fulfils the first the task of fulfilling all the rest is easy.

Works, since they are irrational things, cannot glorify God, although they may be done to the glory of God, if faith be present. But at present we are inquiring, not into the quality of the works done, but into him who does them, who glorifies God, and brings forth good works. This is faith of heart, the head and the substance of all our righteousness. Hence that is a blind and perilous doctrine which teaches that the commandments are fulfilled by works. The commandments must have been fulfilled previous to any good works, and good works follow their fulfillment, as we shall see.

But, that we may have a wider view of that grace which our inner man has in Christ, we must know that in the Old Testament God sanctified to Himself every first-born male. The birthright was of great value, giving a superiority over the rest by the double honour of priesthood and kingship. For the first-born brother was priest and lord of all the rest.

Under this figure was foreshown Christ, the true and only First-born of God the Father and of the Virgin Mary, and a true King and Priest, not in a fleshly and earthly sense. For His kingdom is not of this world; it is in heavenly and spiritual things that He reigns and acts as Priest; and these are righteousness, truth, wisdom, peace, salvation, etc. Not but that all things, even those of earth and hell, are subject to Him—for otherwise how could He defend and save us from them?—but it is not in these, nor by these, that His kingdom stands.

So, too, His priesthood does not consist in the outward display of vestments and gestures, as did the human priesthood of Aaron and our ecclesiastical priesthood at this day, but in spiritual things, wherein, in His invisible office, He intercedes for us with God in heaven, and there offers Himself, and performs all the duties of a priest, as Paul describes Him to the Hebrews under the figure of Melchizedek. Nor does He only pray and intercede for us; He also teaches us inwardly in the spirit with the living teachings of His Spirit. Now these are the two special offices of a priest, as is figured to us in the case of fleshly priests by visible prayers and sermons.

As Christ by His birthright has obtained these two dignities, so He imparts and communicates them to every believer in Him, under that law of matrimony of which we have spoken above, by which all that is the husband's is also the wife's. Hence all we who believe on Christ are kings and priests in Christ, as it is said, "Ye are a chosen generation, a royal priesthood, a holy nation, a peculiar people, that ye should show forth the praises of Him who hath called you out of darkness into His marvellous light" (1 Peter ii. 9).

These two things stand thus. First, as regards kingship, every Christian is by faith so exalted above all things that, in spiritual power, he is completely lord of all things, so that nothing whatever can do him any hurt; yea, all things are subject to him, and are compelled to be subservient to his

184

salvation. Thus Paul says, "All things work together for good to them who are the called" (Rom. viii. 28), and also, "Whether life, or death, or things present, or things to come, all are yours; and ye are Christ's" (1 Cor. iii. 22, 23).

Not that in the sense of corporeal power any one among Christians has been appointed to possess and rule all things, according to the mad and senseless idea of certain ecclesiastics. That is the office of kings, princes, and men upon earth. In the experience of life we see that we are subjected to all things, and suffer many things, even death. Yea, the more of a Christian any man is, to so many the more evils, sufferings, and deaths is he subject, as we see in the first place in Christ the First-born, and in all His holy brethren.

This is a spiritual power, which rules in the midst of enemies, and is powerful in the midst of distresses. And this is nothing else than that strength is made perfect in my weakness, and that I can turn all things to the profit of my salvation; so that even the cross and death are compelled to serve me and to work together for my salvation. This is a lofty and eminent dignity, a true and almighty dominion, a spiritual empire, in which there is nothing so good, nothing so bad, as not to work together for my good, if only I believe. And yet there is nothing of which I have need—for faith alone suffices for my salvation—unless that in it faith may exercise the power and empire of its liberty. This is the inestimable power and liberty of Christians.

Nor are we only kings and the freest of all men, but also priests for ever, a dignity far higher than kingship, because by that priesthood we are worthy to appear before God, to pray for others, and to teach one another mutually the things which are of God. For these are the duties of priests, and they cannot possibly be permitted to any unbeliever. Christ has obtained for us this favour, if we believe in Him: that just as we are His brethren and co-heirs and fellow-kings with Him, so we should be also fellow-priests with Him, and venture with confidence, through the spirit of faith, to come into the presence of God, and cry, "Abba,

Father!" and to pray for one another, and to do all things which we see done and figured in the visible and corporeal office of priesthood. But to an unbelieving person nothing renders service or work for good. He himself is in servitude to all things, and all things turn out for evil to him, because he uses all things in an impious way for his own advantage, and not for the glory of God. And thus he is not a priest, but a profane person, whose prayers are turned into sin, nor does he ever appear in the presence of God, because God does not hear sinners.

Who then can comprehend the loftiness of that Christian dignity which, by its royal power, rules over all things, even over death, life, and sin, and, by its priestly glory, is all-powerful with God, since God does what He Himself seeks and wishes, as it is written, "He will fulfil the desire of them that fear Him; He also will hear their cry, and will save them"? (Psalm cxlv. 19). This glory certainly cannot be attained by any works, but by faith only.

From these considerations any one may clearly see how a Christian man is free from all things; so that he needs no works in order to be justified and saved, but receives these gifts in abundance from faith alone. Nay, were he so foolish as to pretend to be justified, set free, saved, and made a Christian, by means of any good work, he would immediately lose faith, with all its benefits. Such folly is prettily represented in the fable where a dog, running along in the water and carrying in his mouth a real piece of meat, is deceived by the reflection of the meat in the water, and, in trying with open mouth to seize it, loses the meat and its image at the same time.

Here you will ask, "If all who are in the Church are priests, by what character are those whom we now call priests to be distinguished from the laity?" I reply, By the use of these words, "priest," "clergy," "spiritual person," "ecclesiastic," an injustice has been done, since they have been transferred from the remaining body of Christians to those few who are now, by hurtful custom, called ecclesiastics. For Holy Scripture makes no distinction between them, except that those who are now boastfully

186

called popes, bishops, and lords, it calls ministers, servants, and stewards, who are to serve the rest in the ministry of the word, for teaching the faith of Christ and the liberty of believers. For though it is true that we are all equally priests, yet we cannot, nor, if we could, ought we all to, minister and teach publicly. Thus Paul says, "Let a man so account of us as of the ministers of Christ and stewards of the mysteries of God" (1 Cor. iv. 1).

This bad system has now issued in such a pompous display of power and such a terrible tyranny that no earthly government can be compared to it, as if the laity were something else than Christians. Through this perversion of things it has happened that the knowledge of Christian grace, of faith, of liberty, and altogether of Christ, has utterly perished, and has been succeeded by an intolerable bondage to human works and laws; and, according to the Lamentations of Jeremiah, we have become the slaves of the vilest men on earth, who abuse our misery to all the disgraceful and ignominious purposes of their own will.

Returning to the subject which we had begun, I think it is made clear by these considerations that it is not sufficient, nor a Christian course, to preach the works, life, and words of Christ in a historic manner, as facts which it suffices to know as an example how to frame our life, as do those who are now held the best preachers, and much less so to keep silence altogether on these things and to teach in their stead the laws of men and the decrees of the Fathers. There are now not a few persons who preach and read about Christ with the object of moving the human affections to sympathise with Christ, to indignation against the Jews, and other childish and womanish absurdities of that kind.

Now preaching ought to have the object of promoting faith in Him, so that He may not only be Christ, but a Christ for you and for me, and that what is said of Him, and what He is called, may work in us. And this faith is produced and is maintained by preaching why Christ came, what He has brought us and given to us, and to what profit and advantage He is to be received. This is done when the Christian liberty which we have from Christ Himself is rightly taught, and we are shown in what manner all we Christians are kings and priests, and how we are lords of all things, and may be confident that whatever we do in the presence of God is pleasing and acceptable to Him.

Whose heart would not rejoice in its inmost core at hearing these things? Whose heart, on receiving so great a consolation, would not become sweet with the love of Christ, a love to which it can never attain by any laws or works? Who can injure such a heart, or make it afraid? If the consciousness of sin or the horror of death rush in upon it, it is prepared to hope in the Lord, and is fearless of such evils, and undisturbed, until it shall look down upon its enemies. For it believes that the righteousness of Christ is its own, and that its sin is no longer its own, but that of Christ; but, on account of its faith in Christ, all its sin must needs be swallowed up from before the face of the righteousness of Christ, as I have said above. It learns, too, with the Apostle, to scoff at death and sin, and to say, "O death, where is thy sting? O grave, where is thy victory? The sting of death is sin, and the strength of sin is the law. But thanks be to God, which giveth us the victory through our Lord Jesus Christ" (1 Cor. xv. 55-57). For death is swallowed up in victory, not only the victory of Christ, but ours also, since by faith it becomes ours, and in it we too conquer.

Let it suffice to say this concerning the inner man and its liberty, and concerning that righteousness of faith which needs neither laws nor good works; nay, they are even hurtful to it, if any one pretends to be justified by them.

And now let us turn to the other part: to the outward man. Here we shall give an answer to all those who, taking offence at the word of faith and at what I have asserted, say, "If faith does everything, and by itself suffices for justification, why then are good works commanded? Are we then to take our ease and do no works, content with faith?" Not so, impious men, I reply; not so. That would indeed really be the case, if we were thoroughly and completely inner and spiritual persons; but that will not happen until the last day, when the dead shall be raised. As long as we live in the flesh, we are but beginning and making advances in that which shall be completed in a future life. On this account the Apostle calls that which we have in this life the firstfruits of the Spirit (Rom. viii. 23). In future we shall have the tenths, and the fullness of the Spirit. To this part belongs the fact I have stated before: that the Christian is the servant of all and subject to all. For in that part in which he is free he does no works, but in that in which he is a servant he does all works. Let us see on what principle this is so.

Although, as I have said, inwardly, and according to the spirit, a man is amply enough justified by faith, having all that he requires to have, except that this very faith and abundance ought to increase from day to day, even till the future life, still he remains in this mortal life upon earth, in which it is necessary that he should rule his own body and have intercourse with men. Here then works begin; here he must not take his ease; here he must give heed to exercise his body by fastings, watchings, labour, and other regular discipline, so that it may be subdued to the spirit, and obey and conform itself to the inner man and faith, and not rebel against them nor hinder them, as is its nature to do if it is not kept under. For the inner man, being conformed to God and created after the image of God through faith, rejoices and delights itself in Christ, in whom such blessings have been conferred on it, and hence has only this task before it: to serve God with joy and for nought in free love.

But in doing this he comes into collision with that contrary will in his own flesh, which is striving to serve the world and to seek its own gratification. This the spirit of faith cannot and will not bear, but applies itself with cheerfulness and zeal to keep it down and restrain it, as Paul says, "I delight in the law of God after the inward man; but I see another law in my members, warring against the law of my mind and bringing me into captivity to the law of sin" (Rom. vii. 22, 23), and again, "I keep under my body, and bring it unto subjection, lest that by any means, when I have preached to others, I myself should be a castaway" (1 Cor. ix. 27), and "They that are Christ's have crucified the flesh, with the affections and lusts" (Gal. v. 24).

These works, however, must not be done with any notion that by them a man can be justified before God—for faith, which alone is righteousness before God, will not bear with this false notion—but solely with this purpose: that the body may be brought into subjection, and be purified from its evil lusts, so that our eyes may be turned only to purging away those lusts. For when the soul has been cleansed by faith and made to love God, it would have all things to be cleansed in like manner, and especially its own body, so that all things might unite with it in the love and praise of God. Thus it comes that, from the requirements of his own body, a man cannot take his ease, but is compelled on its account to do many good works, that he may bring it into subjection. Yet these works are not the means of his justification before God; he does them out of disinterested love to the service of God; looking to no other end than to do what is well-pleasing to Him whom he desires to obey most dutifully in all things.

On this principle every man may easily instruct himself in what measure, and with what distinctions, he ought to chasten his own body. He will fast, watch, and labour, just as much as he sees to suffice for keeping down the wantonness and concupiscence of the body. But those who pretend to be justified by works are looking, not to the mortification of their lusts, but only to the works themselves; thinking that, if they can accomplish as many works and as great ones as possible, all is well with them, and they are justified. Sometimes they even injure their brain, and extinguish nature, or at least make it useless. This is enormous folly, and ignorance of Christian life and faith, when a man seeks, without faith, to be justified and saved by works.

To make what we have said more easily understood, let us set it forth under a figure. The works of a Christian man, who is justified and saved by his faith out of the pure and unbought mercy of God, ought to be regarded in the same light as would have been those of Adam and Eve

190

in paradise and of all their posterity if they had not sinned. Of them it is said, "The Lord God took the man and put him into the garden of Eden to dress it and to keep it" (Gen. ii. 15). Now Adam had been created by God just and righteous, so that he could not have needed to be justified and made righteous by keeping the garden and working in it; but, that he might not be unemployed, God gave him the business of keeping and cultivating paradise. These would have indeed been works of perfect freedom, being done for no object but that of pleasing God, and not in order to obtain justification, which he already had to the full, and which would have been innate in us all.

So it is with the works of a believer. Being by his faith replaced afresh in paradise and created anew, he does not need works for his justification, but that he may not be idle, but may exercise his own body and preserve it. His works are to be done freely, with the sole object of pleasing God. Only we are not yet fully created anew in perfect faith and love; these require to be increased, not, however, through works, but through themselves.

A bishop, when he consecrates a church, confirms children, or performs any other duty of his office, is not consecrated as bishop by these works; nay, unless he had been previously consecrated as bishop, not one of those works would have any validity; they would be foolish, childish, and ridiculous. Thus a Christian, being consecrated by his faith, does good works; but he is not by these works made a more sacred person, or more a Christian. That is the effect of faith alone; nay, unless he were previously a believer and a Christian, none of his works would have any value at all; they would really be impious and damnable sins.

True, then, are these two sayings: "Good works do not make a good man, but a good man does good works"; "Bad works do not make a bad man, but a bad man does bad works." Thus it is always necessary that the substance or person should be good before any good works can be done, and that good works should follow and proceed from a good person. As Christ says, "A good tree cannot bring forth evil fruit, neither can a corrupt tree bring forth good fruit" (Matt. vii. 18). Now it is clear that the fruit does not bear the tree, nor does the tree grow on the fruit; but, on the contrary, the trees bear the fruit, and the fruit grows on the trees.

As then trees must exist before their fruit, and as the fruit does not make the tree either good or bad, but on the contrary, a tree of either kind produces fruit of the same kind, so must first the person of the man be good or bad before he can do either a good or a bad work; and his works do not make him bad or good, but he himself makes his works either bad or good.

We may see the same thing in all handicrafts. A bad or good house does not make a bad or good builder, but a good or bad builder makes a good or bad house. And in general no work makes the workman such as it is itself; but the workman makes the work such as he is himself. Such is the case, too, with the works of men. Such as the man himself is, whether in faith or in unbelief, such is his work: good if it be done in faith; bad if in unbelief. But the converse is not true that, such as the work is, such the man becomes in faith or in unbelief. For as works do not make a believing man, so neither do they make a justified man; but faith, as it makes a man a believer and justified, so also it makes his works good.

Since then works justify no man, but a man must be justified before he can do any good work, it is most evident that it is faith alone which, by the mere mercy of God through Christ, and by means of His word, can worthily and sufficiently justify and save the person; and that a Christian man needs no work, no law, for his salvation; for by faith he is free from all law, and in perfect freedom does gratuitously all that he does, seeking nothing either of profit or of salvation—since by the grace of God he is already saved and rich in all things through his faith—but solely that which is well-pleasing to God.

So, too, no good work can profit an unbeliever to justification and salvation; and, on the other hand, no evil work makes him an evil and condemned person, but that unbelief, which makes the person and the tree bad, makes his works evil and condemned. Wherefore, when any man is made good or bad, this does not arise from his works, but from his faith or unbelief, as the wise man says, "The beginning of sin is to fall away from God"; that is, not to believe. Paul says, "He that cometh to God must believe" (Heb. xi. 6); and Christ says the same thing: "Either make the tree good and his fruit good; or else make the tree corrupt, and his fruit corrupt" (Matt. xii. 33),—as much as to say, He who wishes to have good fruit will begin with the tree, and plant a good one; even so he who wishes to do good works must begin, not by working, but by believing, since it is this which makes the person good. For nothing makes the person good but faith, nor bad but unbelief.

It is certainly true that, in the sight of men, a man becomes good or evil by his works; but here "becoming" means that it is thus shown and recognised who is good or evil, as Christ says, "By their fruits ye shall know them" (Matt. vii. 20). But all this stops at appearances and externals; and in this matter very many deceive themselves, when they presume to write and teach that we are to be justified by good works, and meanwhile make no mention even of faith, walking in their own ways, ever deceived and deceiving, going from bad to worse, blind leaders of the blind, wearying themselves with many works, and yet never attaining to true righteousness, of whom Paul says, "Having a form of godliness, but denying the power thereof, ever learning and never able to come to the knowledge of the truth" (2 Tim. iii. 5, 7).

He then who does not wish to go astray, with these blind ones, must look further than to the works of the law or the doctrine of works; nay, must turn away his sight from works, and look to the person, and to the manner in which it may be justified. Now it is justified and saved, not by works or laws, but by the word of God—that is, by the promise of His grace—so that the glory may be to the Divine majesty, which has saved us who believe, not by works of righteousness which we have done, but according to His mercy, by the word of His grace.

From all this it is easy to perceive on what principle good works are to be cast aside or embraced, and by what rule all teachings put forth concerning works are to be understood. For if works are brought forward as grounds of justification, and are done under the false persuasion that we can pretend to be justified by them, they lay on us the yoke of necessity, and extinguish liberty along with faith, and by this very addition to their use they become no longer good, but really worthy of condemnation. For such works are not free, but blaspheme the grace of God, to which alone it belongs to justify and save through faith. Works cannot accomplish this, and yet, with impious presumption, through our folly, they take it on themselves to do so; and thus break in with violence upon the office and glory of grace.

We do not then reject good works; nay, we embrace them and teach them in the highest degree. It is not on their own account that we condemn them, but on account of this impious addition to them and the perverse notion of seeking justification by them. These things cause them to be only good in outward show, but in reality not good, since by them men are deceived and deceive others, like ravening wolves in sheep's clothing.

Now this leviathan, this perverted notion about works, is invincible when sincere faith is wanting. For those sanctified doers of works cannot but hold it till faith, which destroys it, comes and reigns in the heart. Nature cannot expel it by her own power; nay, cannot even see it for what it is, but considers it as a most holy will. And when custom steps in besides, and strengthens this pravity of nature, as has happened by means of impious teachers, then the evil is incurable, and leads astray multitudes to irreparable ruin. Therefore, though it is good to preach and write about penitence, confession, and satisfaction, yet if we stop there, and do not go on to teach faith, such teaching is without doubt deceitful and devilish. For Christ, speaking by His servant John, not only said, "Repent ye," but added, "for the kingdom of heaven is at hand" (Matt. iii. 2).

For not one word of God only, but both, should be preached; new and old things should be brought out of the treasury, as well the voice of the law as the word of grace. The voice of the law should be brought forward, that men may be terrified and brought to a knowledge of their sins, and thence be converted to penitence and to a better manner of life. But we must not stop here; that would be to wound only and not to bind up, to strike and not to heal, to kill and not to make alive, to bring down to hell and not to bring back, to humble and not to exalt. Therefore the word of grace and of the promised remission of sin must also be preached, in order to teach and set up faith, since without that word contrition, penitence, and all other duties, are performed and taught in vain.

There still remain, it is true, preachers of repentance and grace, but they do not explain the law and the promises of God to such an end, and in such a spirit, that men may learn whence repentance and grace are to come. For repentance comes from the law of God, but faith or grace from the promises of God, as it is said, "Faith cometh by hearing, and hearing by the word of God" (Rom. x. 17), whence it comes that a man, when humbled and brought to the knowledge of himself by the threatenings and terrors of the law, is consoled and raised up by faith in the Divine promise. Thus "weeping may endure for a night, but joy cometh in the morning" (Psalm xxx. 5). Thus much we say concerning works in general, and also concerning those which the Christian practises with regard to his own body.

Lastly, we will speak also of those works which he performs towards his neighbour. For man does not live for himself alone in this mortal body, in order to work on its account, but also for all men on earth; nay, he lives only for others, and not for himself. For it is to this end that he brings his own body into subjection, that he may be able to serve others more sincerely and more freely, as Paul says, "None of us liveth to himself, and no man dieth to himself. For whether we live, we live unto the Lord; and whether we die, we die unto the Lord" (Rom. xiv. 7,

195

8). Thus it is impossible that he should take his ease in this life, and not work for the good of his neighbours, since he must needs speak, act, and converse among men, just as Christ was made in the likeness of men and found in fashion as a man, and had His conversation among men.

Yet a Christian has need of none of these things for justification and salvation, but in all his works he ought to entertain this view and look only to this object—that he may serve and be useful to others in all that he does; having nothing before his eyes but the necessities and the advantage of his neighbour. Thus the Apostle commands us to work with our own hands, that we may have to give to those that need. He might have said, that we may support ourselves; but he tells us to give to those that need. It is the part of a Christian to take care of his own body for the very purpose that, by its soundness and well-being, he may be enabled to labour, and to acquire and preserve property, for the aid of those who are in want, that thus the stronger member may serve the weaker member, and we may be children of God, thoughtful and busy one for another, bearing one another's burdens, and so fulfilling the law of Christ.

Here is the truly Christian life, here is faith really working by love, when a man applies himself with joy and love to the works of that freest servitude in which he serves others voluntarily and for nought, himself abundantly satisfied in the fulness and riches of his own faith.

Thus, when Paul had taught the Philippians how they had been made rich by that faith in Christ in which they had obtained all things, he teaches them further in these words: "If there be therefore any consolation in Christ, if any comfort of love, if any fellowship of the Spirit, if any bowels and mercies, fulfil ye my joy, that ye be like-minded, having the same love, being of one accord, of one mind. Let nothing be done through strife or vainglory; but in lowliness of mind let each esteem other better than themselves. Look not every man on his own things, but every man also on the things of others" (Phil. ii. 1-4).

In this we see clearly that the Apostle lays down this rule for a Christian life: that all our works should be directed to the advantage of others, since every Christian has such abundance through his faith that all his other works and his whole life remain over and above wherewith to serve and benefit his neighbour of spontaneous goodwill.

To this end he brings forward Christ as an example, saying, "Let this mind be in you, which was also in Christ Jesus, who, being in the form of God, thought it not robbery to be equal with God, but made Himself of no reputation, and took upon Him the form of a servant, and was made in the likeness of men; and being found in fashion as a man, He humbled Himself, and became obedient unto death" (Phil. ii. 5-8). This most wholesome saying of the Apostle has been darkened to us by men who, totally misunderstanding the expressions "form of God," "form of a servant," "fashion," "likeness of men," have transferred them to the natures of Godhead and manhood. Paul's meaning is this: Christ, when He was full of the form of God and abounded in all good things, so that He had no need of works or sufferings to be just and saved—for all these things He had from the very beginning—yet was not puffed up with these things, and did not raise Himself above us and arrogate to Himself power over us, though He might lawfully have done so, but, on the contrary, so acted in labouring, working, suffering, and dying, as to be like the rest of men, and no otherwise than a man in fashion and in conduct, as if He were in want of all things and had nothing of the form of God; and yet all this He did for our sakes, that He might serve us, and that all the works He should do under that form of a servant might become ours.

Thus a Christian, like Christ his Head, being full and in abundance through his faith, ought to be content with this form of God, obtained by faith; except that, as I have said, he ought to increase this faith till it be perfected. For this faith is his life, justification, and salvation, preserving his person itself and making it pleasing to God, and bestowing on him all that Christ has, as I have said above, and as Paul affirms: "The life which

197

I now live in the flesh I live by the faith of the Son of God" (Gal. ii. 20). Though he is thus free from all works, yet he ought to empty himself of this liberty, take on him the form of a servant, be made in the likeness of men, be found in fashion as a man, serve, help, and in every way act towards his neighbour as he sees that God through Christ has acted and is acting towards him. All this he should do freely, and with regard to nothing but the good pleasure of God, and he should reason thus:—

Lo! my God, without merit on my part, of His pure and free mercy, has given to me, an unworthy, condemned, and contemptible creature all the riches of justification and salvation in Christ, so that I no longer am in want of anything, except of faith to believe that this is so. For such a Father, then, who has overwhelmed me with these inestimable riches of His, why should I not freely, cheerfully, and with my whole heart, and from voluntary zeal, do all that I know will be pleasing to Him and acceptable in His sight? I will therefore give myself as a sort of Christ, to my neighbour, as Christ has given Himself to me; and will do nothing in this life except what I see will be needful, advantageous, and wholesome for my neighbour, since by faith I abound in all good things in Christ.

Thus from faith flow forth love and joy in the Lord, and from love a cheerful, willing, free spirit, disposed to serve our neighbour voluntarily, without taking any account of gratitude or ingratitude, praise or blame, gain or loss. Its object is not to lay men under obligations, nor does it distinguish between friends and enemies, or look to gratitude or ingratitude, but most freely and willingly spends itself and its goods, whether it loses them through ingratitude, or gains goodwill. For thus did its Father, distributing all things to all men abundantly and freely, making His sun to rise upon the just and the unjust. Thus, too, the child does and endures nothing except from the free joy with which it delights through Christ in God, the Giver of such great gifts.

You see, then, that, if we recognize those great and precious gifts, as Peter says, which have been given to us, love is quickly diffused in our hearts through the Spirit, and by love we are made free, joyful, all-powerful, active workers, victors over all our tribulations, servants to our neighbour, and nevertheless lords of all things. But, for those who do not recognise the good things given to them through Christ, Christ has been born in vain; such persons walk by works, and will never attain the taste and feeling of these great things. Therefore just as our neighbour is in want, and has need of our abundance, so we too in the sight of God were in want, and had need of His mercy. And as our heavenly Father has freely helped us in Christ, so ought we freely to help our neighbour by our body and works, and each should become to other a sort of Christ, so that we may be mutually Christs, and that the same Christ may be in all of us; that is, that we may be truly Christians.

Who then can comprehend the riches and glory of the Christian life? It can do all things, has all things, and is in want of nothing; is lord over sin, death, and hell, and at the same time is the obedient and useful servant of all. But alas! it is at this day unknown throughout the world; it is neither preached nor sought after, so that we are quite ignorant about our own name, why we are and are called Christians. We are certainly called so from Christ, who is not absent, but dwells among us—provided, that is, that we believe in Him and are reciprocally and mutually one the Christ of the other, doing to our neighbour as Christ does to us. But now, in the doctrine of men, we are taught only to seek after merits, rewards, and things which are already ours, and we have made of Christ a taskmaster far more severe than Moses.

The Blessed Virgin beyond all others, affords us an example of the same faith, in that she was purified according to the law of Moses, and like all other women, though she was bound by no such law and had no need of purification. Still she submitted to the law voluntarily and of free love, making herself like the rest of women, that she might not offend or throw contempt on them. She was not justified by doing this; but, being already justified, she did it freely and gratuitously. Thus ought our works too to be done, and not in order to be justified by them; for, being first justified by faith, we ought to do all our works freely and cheerfully for the sake of others.

St. Paul circumcised his disciple Timothy, not because he needed circumcision for his justification, but that he might not offend or contemn those Jews, weak in the faith, who had not yet been able to comprehend the liberty of faith. On the other hand, when they contemned liberty and urged that circumcision was necessary for justification, he resisted them, and would not allow Titus to be circumcised. For, as he would not offend or contemn any one's weakness in faith, but yielded for the time to their will, so, again, he would not have the liberty of faith offended or contemned by hardened self-justifiers, but walked in a middle path, sparing the weak for the time, and always resisting the hardened, that he might convert all to the liberty of faith. On the same principle we ought to act, receiving those that are weak in the faith, but boldly resisting these hardened teachers of works, of whom we shall hereafter speak at more length.

Christ also, when His disciples were asked for the tribute money, asked of Peter whether the children of a king were not free from taxes. Peter agreed to this; yet Jesus commanded him to go to the sea, saying, "Lest we should offend them, go thou to the sea, and cast a hook, and take up the fish that first cometh up; and when thou hast opened his mouth thou shalt find a piece of money; that take, and give unto them for Me and thee" (Matt. xvii. 27).

This example is very much to our purpose; for here Christ calls Himself and His disciples free men and children of a King, in want of nothing; and yet He voluntarily submits and pays the tax. Just as far, then, as this work was necessary or useful to Christ for justification or salvation, so far do all His other works or those of His disciples avail for justification. They are really free and subsequent to justification, and only done to serve others and set them an example.

Such are the works which Paul inculcated, that Christians should be subject to principalities and powers and ready to every good work

(Titus iii. 1), not that they may be justified by these things—for they are already justified by faith—but that in liberty of spirit they may thus be the servants of others and subject to powers, obeying their will out of gratuitous love.

Such, too, ought to have been the works of all colleges, monasteries, and priests; every one doing the works of his own profession and state of life, not in order to be justified by them, but in order to bring his own body into subjection, as an example to others, who themselves also need to keep under their bodies, and also in order to accommodate himself to the will of others, out of free love. But we must always guard most carefully against any vain confidence or presumption of being justified, gaining merit, or being saved by these works, this being the part of faith alone, as I have so often said.

Any man possessing this knowledge may easily keep clear of danger among those innumerable commands and precepts of the Pope, of bishops, of monasteries, of churches, of princes, and of magistrates, which some foolish pastors urge on us as being necessary for justification and salvation, calling them precepts of the Church, when they are not so at all. For the Christian freeman will speak thus: I will fast, I will pray, I will do this or that which is commanded me by men, not as having any need of these things for justification or salvation, but that I may thus comply with the will of the Pope, of the bishop, of such a community or such a magistrate, or of my neighbour as an example to him; for this cause I will do and suffer all things, just as Christ did and suffered much more for me, though He needed not at all to do so on His own account, and made Himself for my sake under the law, when He was not under the law. And although tyrants may do me violence or wrong in requiring obedience to these things, yet it will not hurt me to do them, so long as they are not done against God.

From all this every man will be able to attain a sure judgment and faithful discrimination between all works and laws, and to know who are blind and foolish pastors, and who are true and good ones. For whatsoever work is not directed to the sole end either of keeping under the body, or of doing service to our neighbour—provided he require nothing contrary to the will of God—is no good or Christian work. Hence I greatly fear that at this day few or no colleges, monasteries, altars, or ecclesiastical functions are Christian ones; and the same may be said of fasts and special prayers to certain saints. I fear that in all these nothing is being sought but what is already ours; while we fancy that by these things our sins are purged away and salvation is attained, and thus utterly do away with Christian liberty. This comes from ignorance of Christian faith and liberty.

This ignorance and this crushing of liberty are diligently promoted by the teaching of very many blind pastors, who stir up and urge the people to a zeal for these things, praising them and puffing them up with their indulgences, but never teaching faith. Now I would advise you, if you have any wish to pray, to fast, or to make foundations in churches, as they call it, to take care not to do so with the object of gaining any advantage, either temporal or eternal. You will thus wrong your faith, which alone bestows all things on you, and the increase of which, either by working or by suffering, is alone to be cared for. What you give, give freely and without price, that others may prosper and have increase from you and your goodness. Thus you will be a truly good man and a Christian. For what to you are your goods and your works, which are done over and above for the subjection of the body, since you have abundance for yourself through your faith, in which God has given you all things?

We give this rule: the good things which we have from God ought to flow from one to another and become common to all, so that every one of us may, as it were, put on his neighbour, and so behave towards him as if he were himself in his place. They flowed and do flow from Christ to us; He put us on, and acted for us as if He Himself were what we are. From us they flow to those who have need of them; so that my faith and righteousness ought to be laid down before God as a covering and intercession for the sins of my neighbour, which I am to take on myself, and so labour and endure servitude in them, as if they were my own; for thus has Christ done for us. This is true love and the genuine truth of Christian life. But only there is it true and genuine where there is true and genuine faith. Hence the Apostle attributes to charity this quality: that she seeketh not her own.

We conclude therefore that a Christian man does not live in himself, but in Christ and in his neighbour, or else is no Christian: in Christ by faith; in his neighbour by love. By faith he is carried upwards above himself to God, and by love he sinks back below himself to his neighbour, still always-abiding in God and His love, as Christ says, "Verily I say unto you, Hereafter ye shall see heaven open, and the angels of God ascending and descending upon the Son of man" (John i. 51).

Thus much concerning liberty, which, as you see, is a true and spiritual liberty, making our hearts free from all sins, laws, and commandments, as Paul says, "The law is not made for a righteous man" (1 Tim. i. 9), and one which surpasses all other external liberties, as far as heaven is above earth. May Christ make us to understand and preserve this liberty. Amen.

Finally, for the sake of those to whom nothing can be stated so well but that they misunderstand and distort it, we must add a word, in case they can understand even that. There are very many persons who, when they hear of this liberty of faith, straightway turn it into an occasion of licence. They think that everything is now lawful for them, and do not choose to show themselves free men and Christians in any other way than by their contempt and reprehension of ceremonies, of traditions, of human laws; as if they were Christians merely because they refuse to fast on stated days, or eat flesh when others fast, or omit the customary prayers; scoffing at the precepts of men, but utterly passing over all the rest that belongs to the Christian religion. On the other hand, they are most pertinaciously resisted by those who strive after salvation solely by their observance of and reverence for ceremonies, as if they would be saved merely because they fast on stated days, or abstain from flesh, or make formal prayers; talking loudly of the precepts of the Church and of the Fathers, and not caring a straw about those things which belong to our genuine faith. Both these parties are plainly culpable, in that, while they neglect matters which are of weight and necessary for salvation, they contend noisily about such as are without weight and not necessary.

How much more rightly does the Apostle Paul teach us to walk in the middle path, condemning either extreme and saying, "Let not him that eateth despise him that eateth not; and let not him which eateth not judge him that eateth" (Rom. xiv. 3)! You see here how the Apostle blames those who, not from religious feeling, but in mere contempt, neglect and rail at ceremonial observances, and teaches them not to despise, since this "knowledge puffeth up." Again, he teaches the pertinacious upholders of these things not to judge their opponents. For neither party observes towards the other that charity which edifieth. In this matter we must listen to Scripture, which teaches us to turn aside neither to the right hand nor to the left, but to follow those right precepts of the Lord which rejoice the heart. For just as a man is not righteous merely because he serves and is devoted to works and ceremonial rites, so neither will he be accounted righteous merely because he neglects and despises them.

It is not from works that we are set free by the faith of Christ, but from the belief in works, that is from foolishly presuming to seek justification through works. Faith redeems our consciences, makes them upright, and preserves them, since by it we recognise the truth that justification does not depend on our works, although good works neither can nor ought to be absent, just as we cannot exist without food and drink and all the functions of this mortal body. Still it is not on them that our justification is based, but on faith; and yet they ought not on that account to be despised or neglected. Thus in this world we are compelled by the needs of this bodily life; but we are not hereby justified. "My kingdom is not hence, nor of this world," says Christ; but He does not say, "My kingdom is not here, nor in this world." Paul, too, says, "Though we walk in the flesh, we do not war after the flesh" (2 Cor. x. 3), and "The life which I now live in the flesh I live by the faith of the Son of God" (Gal. ii. 20). Thus our doings, life, and being, in works and ceremonies, are done from the necessities of this life, and with the motive of governing our bodies; but yet we are not justified by these things, but by the faith of the Son of God.

The Christian must therefore walk in the middle path, and set these two classes of men before his eyes. He may meet with hardened and obstinate ceremonialists, who, like deaf adders, refuse to listen to the truth of liberty, and cry up, enjoin, and urge on us their ceremonies, as if they could justify us without faith. Such were the Jews of old, who would not understand, that they might act well. These men we must resist, do just the contrary to what they do, and be bold to give them offence, lest by this impious notion of theirs they should deceive many along with themselves. Before the eyes of these men it is expedient to eat flesh, to break fasts, and to do in behalf of the liberty of faith things which they hold to be the greatest sins. We must say of them, "Let them alone; they be blind leaders of the blind" (Matt. xv. 14). In this way Paul also would not have Titus circumcised, though these men urged it; and Christ defended the Apostles, who had plucked ears of corn on the Sabbath day; and many like instances.

Or else we may meet with simple-minded and ignorant persons, weak in the faith, as the Apostle calls them, who are as yet unable to apprehend that liberty of faith, even if willing to do so. These we must spare, lest they should be offended. We must bear with their infirmity, till they shall be more fully instructed. For since these men do not act thus from hardened malice, but only from weakness of faith, therefore, in order to avoid giving them offence, we must keep fasts and do other things which they consider necessary. This is required of us by charity, which injures no one, but serves all men. It is not the fault of these persons that they are weak, but that of their pastors, who by the snares and weapons of their own traditions have brought them into bondage and wounded their souls when they ought to have been set free and healed by the teaching of faith and liberty. Thus the Apostle says, "If meat make my brother to offend, I will eat no flesh while the world standeth" (1 Cor. viii. 13); and again, "I know, and am persuaded by the Lord Jesus, that there is nothing unclean of itself; but to him that esteemeth anything to be unclean, to him it is unclean. It is evil for that man who eateth with offence" (Rom. xiv. 14, 20).

Thus, though we ought boldly to resist those teachers of tradition, and though the laws of the pontiffs, by which they make aggressions on the people of God, deserve sharp reproof, yet we must spare the timid crowd, who are held captive by the laws of those impious tyrants, till they are set free. Fight vigorously against the wolves, but on behalf of the sheep, not against the sheep. And this you may do by inveighing against the laws and lawgivers, and yet at the same time observing these laws with the weak, lest they be offended, until they shall themselves recognise the tyranny, and understand their own liberty. If you wish to use your liberty, do it secretly, as Paul says, "Hast thou faith? have it to thyself before God" (Rom. xiv. 22). But take care not to use it in the presence of the weak. On the other hand, in the presence of tyrants and obstinate opposers, use your liberty in their despite, and with the utmost pertinacity, that they too may understand that they are tyrants, and their laws useless for justification, nay that they had no right to establish such laws.

Since then we cannot live in this world without ceremonies and works, since the hot and inexperienced period of youth has need of being restrained and protected by such bonds, and since every one is bound to keep under his own body by attention to these things, therefore the minister of Christ must be prudent and faithful in so ruling and teaching the people of Christ, in all these matters, that no root of bitterness may spring up among them, and so many be defiled, as Paul warned the Hebrews; that is, that they may not lose the faith, and begin to be defiled by a belief in works as the means of justification. This is a thing which easily happens, and defiles very many, unless faith be constantly inculcated along with works. It is impossible to avoid this evil, when faith is passed over in silence, and only the ordinances of men are taught, as has been done hitherto by the pestilent, impious, and soul-destroying traditions of our pontiffs and opinions of our theologians. An infinite number of souls have been drawn down to hell by these snares, so that you may recognise the work of antichrist.

In brief, as poverty is imperilled amid riches, honesty amid business, humility amid honours, abstinence amid feasting, purity amid pleasures, so is justification by faith imperilled among ceremonies. Solomon says, "Can a man take fire in his bosom, and his clothes not be burned?" (Prov. vi. 27). And yet as we must live among riches, business, honours, pleasures, feastings, so must we among ceremonies, that is among perils. Just as infant boys have the greatest need of being cherished in the bosoms and by the care of girls, that they may not die, and yet, when they are grown, there is peril to their salvation in living among girls, so inexperienced and fervid young men require to be kept in and restrained by the barriers of ceremonies, even were they of iron, lest their weak minds should rush headlong into vice. And yet it would be death to them to persevere in believing that they can be justified by these things. They must rather be taught that they have been thus imprisoned, not with the purpose of their being justified or gaining merit in this way, but in order that they might avoid wrong-doing, and be more easily instructed in that righteousness which is by faith, a thing which the headlong character of youth would not bear unless it were put under restraint.

Hence in the Christian life ceremonies are to be no otherwise looked upon than as builders and workmen look upon those preparations for building or working which are not made with any view of being permanent or anything in themselves, but only because without them there could be no building and no work. When the structure is completed, they are laid aside. Here you see that we do not contemn these preparations, but set the highest value on them; a belief in them we do contemn, because no one thinks that they constitute a real and permanent structure. If any one were so manifestly out of his senses as to have no other object in life but that of setting up these preparations with all possible expense, diligence, and perseverance, while he never thought of the structure itself, but pleased himself and made his boast of these useless preparations and props, should we not all pity his madness and think that, at the cost thus thrown away, some great building might have been raised?

Thus, too, we do not contemn works and ceremonies—nay, we set the highest value on them; but we contemn the belief in works, which no one should consider to constitute true righteousness, as do those hypocrites who employ and throw away their whole life in the pursuit of works, and yet never attain to that for the sake of which the works are done. As the Apostle says, they are "ever learning and never able to come to the knowledge of the truth" (2 Tim. iii. 7). They appear to wish to build, they make preparations, and yet they never do build; and thus they continue in a show of godliness, but never attain to its power.

Meanwhile they please themselves with this zealous pursuit, and even dare to judge all others, whom they do not see adorned with such a glittering display of works; while, if they had been imbued with faith, they might have done great things for their own and others' salvation, at the same cost which they now waste in abuse of the gifts of God. But since human nature and natural reason, as they call it, are naturally superstitious, and quick to believe that justification can be attained by any laws or works proposed to them, and since nature is also exercised and confirmed in the same view by the practice of all earthly lawgivers, she can never of her own power free herself from this bondage to works, and come to a recognition of the liberty of faith.

We have therefore need to pray that God will lead us and make us taught of God, that is, ready to learn from God; and will Himself, as He has promised, write His law in our hearts; otherwise there is no hope for us. For unless He himself teach us inwardly this wisdom hidden in a mystery, nature cannot but condemn it and judge it to be heretical. She takes offence at it, and it seems folly to her, just as we see that it happened of old in the case of the prophets and Apostles, and just as blind and impious pontiffs, with their flatterers, do now in my case and that of those who are like me, upon whom, together with ourselves, may God at length have mercy, and lift up the light of His countenance upon them, that we may know His way upon earth and His saving health among all nations, who is blessed for evermore. Amen. In the year of the Lord MDXX.

THE SMALCALD ARTICLES.

Articles of Christian Doctrine which were to have been presented on our part to the Council, if any had been assembled at Mantua or elsewhere, indicating what we could accept or yield, and what we could not.

Translated by F. Bente and W. H. T. Dau

PREFACE OF DR. MARTIN LUTHER.

Since Pope Paul III convoked a Council last year, to assemble at Mantua about Whitsuntide, and afterwards transferred it from Mantua, so that it is not yet known where he will or can fix it, and we on our part either had to expect that we would be summoned also to the Council or [to fear that we would] be condemned unsummoned, I was directed to compile and collect the articles of our doctrine [in order that it might be plain] in case of deliberation as to what and how far we would be both willing and able to yield to the Papists, and in what points we intended to persevere and abide to the end.

I have accordingly compiled these articles and presented them to our side. They have also been accepted and unanimously confessed by our side, and it has been resolved that, in case the Pope with his adherents should ever be so bold as seriously and in good faith, without lying and cheating, to hold a truly free [legitimate] Christian Council (as, indeed, he would be in duty bound to do), they be publicly delivered in order to set forth the Confession of our Faith.

But though the Romish court is so dreadfully afraid of a free Christian Council, and shuns the light so shamefully, that it has [entirely] removed, even from those who are on its side, the hope that it will ever permit a free Council, much less that it will itself hold one, whereat, as is just, they [many Papists] are greatly offended and have no little trouble on that account [are disgusted with this negligence of the Pope], since they notice thereby that the Pope would rather see all Christendom perish and all souls damned than suffer either himself or his adherents to be reformed even a little, and his [their] tyranny to be limited, nevertheless

I have determined meanwhile to publish these articles in plain print, so that, should I die before there would be a Council (as I fully expect and hope, because the knaves who flee the light and shun the day take such wretched pains to delay and hinder the Council), those who live and remain after me may have my testimony and confession to produce, in addition to the Confession which I have issued previously, whereby up to this time I have abided, and, by God's grace, will abide.

For what shall I say? How shall I complain? I am still living, writing, preaching, and lecturing daily; [and] yet there are found such spiteful men, not only among the adversaries, but also false brethren that profess to be on our side, as dare to cite my writings and doctrine directly against myself, and let me look on and listen, although they know well that I teach otherwise, and as wish to adorn their venom with my labor, and under my name to [deceive and] mislead the poor people. [Good God!] Alas! what first will happen when I am dead?

Indeed, I ought to reply to everything while I am still living. But, again, how can I alone stop all the mouths of the devil? especially of those (as they all are poisoned) who will not hear or notice what we write, but solely exercise themselves with all diligence how they may most shamefully pervert and corrupt our word in every letter. These I let the devil answer, or at last Gods wrath, as they deserve. I often think of the good Gerson who doubts whether anything good should be [written and] published. If it is not done, many souls are neglected who could be delivered: but if it is done, the devil is there with malignant, villainous tongues without number which envenom and pervert everything, so that nevertheless the fruit [the usefulness of the writings] is prevented. Yet what they gain thereby is manifest. For while they have lied so shamefully against us and by means of lies wished to retain the people, God has constantly advanced His work, and been making their following ever smaller and ours greater, and by their lies has caused and still causes them to be brought to shame.

214

I must tell a story. There was a doctor sent here to Wittenberg from France, who said publicly before us that his king was sure and more than sure, that among us there is no church, no magistrate, no married life, but all live promiscuously as cattle, and each one does as he pleases. Imagine now, how will those who by their writings have instilled such gross lies into the king and other countries as the pure truth, look at us on that day before the judgment-seat of Christ? Christ, the Lord and Judge of us all, knows well that they lie and have [always] lied, His sentence they in turn, must hear; that I know certainly. God convert to repentance those who can be converted! Regarding the rest it will be said, Woe, and, alas! eternally.

But to return to the subject. I verily desire to see a truly Christian Council [assembled some time], in order that many matters and persons might be helped. Not that we need It, for our churches are now, through God's grace, so enlightened and equipped with the pure Word and right use of the Sacraments, with knowledge of the various callings and of right works, that we on our part ask for no Council, and on such points have nothing better to hope or expect from a Council. But we see in the bishoprics everywhere so many parishes vacant and desolate that one's heart would break, and yet neither the bishops nor canons care how the poor people live or die, for whom nevertheless Christ has died, and who are not permitted to hear Him speak with them as the true Shepherd with His sheep. This causes me to shudder and fear that at some time He may send a council of angels upon Germany utterly destroying us, like Sodom and Gomorrah, because we so wantonly mock Him with the Council.

Besides such necessary ecclesiastical affairs, there would be also in the political estate innumerable matters of great importance to improve. There is the disagreement between the princes and the states; usury and avarice have burst in like a flood, and have become lawful [are defended with a show of right]; wantonness, lewdness, extravagance in dress, gluttony, gambling, idle display, with all kinds of bad habits and wickedness, insubordination of subjects, of domestics and laborers of every trade, also the exactions [and most exorbitant selling prices] of the peasants (and who can enumerate all?) have so increased that they cannot be rectified by ten Councils and twenty Diets. If such chief matters of the spiritual and worldly estates as are contrary to God would be considered in the Council, they would have all hands so full that the child's play and absurdity of long gowns [official insignia], large tonsures, broad cinctures [or sashes], bishops' or cardinals' hats or maces, and like jugglery would in the mean time be forgotten. If we first had performed God's command and order in the spiritual and secular estate we would find time enough to reform food, clothing, tonsures, and surplices. But if we want to swallow such camels, and, instead, strain at gnats, let the beams stand and judge the motes, we also might indeed be satisfied with the Council.

Therefore I have presented few articles; for we have without this so many commands of God to observe in the Church, the state and the family that we can never fulfil them. What, then, is the use, or what does it profit that many decrees and statutes thereon are made in the Council, especially when these chief matters commanded of God are neither regarded nor observed? Just as though He were bound to honor our jugglery as a reward of our treading His solemn commandments under foot. But our sins weigh upon us and cause God not to be gracious to us; for we do not repent, and, besides, wish to defend every abomination.

O Lord Jesus Christ, do Thou Thyself convoke a Council, and deliver Thy servants by Thy glorious advent! The Pope and his adherents are done for; they will have none of Thee. Do Thou, then, help us, who are poor and needy, who sigh to Thee, and beseech Thee earnestly, according to the grace which Thou hast given us, through Thy Holy Ghost who liveth and reigneth with Thee and the Father, blessed forever. Amen.

THE FIRST PART

Treats of the Sublime Articles Concerning the Divine Majesty, as:

I. That Father, Son, and Holy Ghost, three distinct persons in one divine essence and nature, are one God, who has created heaven and earth.

II. That the Father is begotten of no one; the Son of the Father; the Holy Ghost proceeds from Father and Son. III. That not the Father nor the Holy Ghost but the Son became man.

IV. That the Son became man in this manner, that He was conceived, without the cooperation of man, by the Holy Ghost, and was born of the pure, holy [and always] Virgin Mary. Afterwards He suffered, died, was buried, descended to hell, rose from the dead, ascended to heaven, sits at the right hand of God, will come to judge the quick and the dead, etc. as the Creed of the Apostles, as well as that of St. Athanasius, and the Catechism in common use for children, teach.

Concerning these articles there is no contention or dispute, since we on both sides confess them. Therefore it is not necessary now to treat further of them.

THE SECOND PART

Treats of the Articles which Refer to the Office and Work of Jesus Christ, or Our Redemption.

The first and chief article is this,

That Jesus Christ, our God and Lord, died for our sins, and was raised again for our justification, Rom. 4, 25.

And He alone is the Lamb of God which taketh away the sins of the world, John 1, 29; and God has laid upon Him the iniquities of us all, Is. 53, 6.

Likewise: All have sinned and are justified without merit [freely, and without their own works or merits] by His grace, through the redemption that is in Christ Jesus, in His blood, Rom. 3, 23 f.

Now, since it is necessary to believe this, and it cannot be otherwise acquired or apprehended by any work, law, or merit, it is clear and certain that this faith alone justifies us as St. Paul says, Rom. 3, 28: For we conclude that a man is justified by faith, without the deeds of the Law. Likewise v. 26: That He might be just, and the Justifier of him which believeth in Christ.

Of this article nothing can be yielded or surrendered [nor can anything be granted or permitted contrary to the same], even though heaven and earth, and whatever will not abide, should sink to ruin. For there is none other name under heaven, given among men whereby we must be saved, says Peter, Acts 4, 12. And with His stripes we are healed, Is. 53, 5. And upon this article all things depend which we teach and practice in opposition to the Pope, the devil, and the [whole] world. Therefore, we must be sure concerning this doctrine, and not doubt; for otherwise all is lost, and the Pope and devil and all things gain the victory and suit over us.

Article II: Of the Mass.

That the Mass in the Papacy must be the greatest and most horrible abomination, as it directly and powerfully conflicts with this chief article, and yet above and before all other popish idolatries it has been the chief and most specious. For it has been held that this sacrifice or work of the Mass, even though it be rendered by a wicked [and abandoned] scoundrel, frees men from sins, both in this life and also in purgatory, while only the Lamb of God shall and must do this, as has been said above. Of this article nothing is to be surrendered or conceded, because the first article does not allow it.

If, perchance, there were reasonable Papists we might speak moderately and in a friendly way, thus: first, why they so rigidly uphold the Mass. For it is but a pure invention of men, and has not been commanded by God; and every invention of man we may [safely] discard, as Christ declares, Matt. 15, 9: In vain do they worship Me, teaching for doctrines the commandments of men.

Secondly. It is an unnecessary thing, which can be omitted without sin and danger.

Thirdly. The Sacrament can be received in a better and more blessed way [more acceptable to God], (yea, the only blessed way), according to the institution of Christ. Why, then, do they drive the world to woe and [extreme] misery on account of a fictitious, unnecessary matter, which can be well obtained in another and more blessed way?

Let [care be taken that] it be publicly preached to the people that the Mass as men's twaddle [commentitious affair or human figment] can be omitted without sin, and that no one will be condemned who does not observe it, but that he can be saved in a better way without the Mass. I wager [Thus it will come to pass] that the Mass will then collapse of itself, not only among the insane [rude] common people, but also among all pious, Christian, reasonable, God-fearing hearts; and that the more, when they would hear that the Mass is a [very] dangerous thing, fabricated and invented without the will and Word of God.

Fourthly. Since such innumerable and unspeakable abuses have arisen in the whole world from the buying and selling of masses, the Mass should by right be relinquished, if for no other purpose than to prevent abuses, even though in itself it had something advantageous and good. How much more ought we to relinquish it, so as to prevent [escape] forever these horrible abuses, since it is altogether unnecessary, useless, and dangerous, and we can obtain everything by a more necessary, profitable, and certain way without the Mass.

Fifthly. But since the Mass is nothing else and can be nothing else (as the Canon and all books declare), than a work of men (even of wicked scoundrels), by which one attempts to reconcile himself and others to God, and to obtain and merit the remission of sins and grace (for thus the Mass is observed when it is observed at the very best; otherwise what purpose would it serve ?), for this very reason it must and should [certainly] be condemned and rejected. For this directly conflicts with the chief article, which says that it is not a wicked or a godly hireling of the Mass with his own work, but the Lamb of God and the Son of God, that taketh away our sins.

But if any one should advance the pretext that as an act of devotion he wishes to administer the Sacrament, or Communion, to himself, he is not in earnest [he would commit a great mistake, and would not be speaking seriously and sincerely]. For if he wishes to commune in sincerity, the surest and best way for him is in the Sacrament administered according to Christ's institution. But that one administer communion to himself is a human notion, uncertain, unnecessary, yea, even prohibited. And he does not know what he is doing, because without the Word of God he obeys a false human opinion and invention. So, too, it is not right (even though the matter were otherwise correct) for one to use the common Sacrament of [belonging to] the Church according to his own private devotion, and without God s Word and apart from the communion of the Church to trifle therewith.

This article concerning the Mass will be the whole business of the Council. [The Council will perspire most over, and be occupied with this article concerning the Mass.] For if it were [although it would be] possible for them to concede to us all the other articles, yet they could not concede this. As Campegius said at Augsburg that he would be torn to pieces before he would relinquish the Mass, so, by the help of God, I, too, would suffer myself to be reduced to ashes before I would allow a hireling of the Mass, be he good or bad, to be made equal to Christ Jesus, my Lord and Savior, or to be exalted above Him. Thus we are and remain eternally separated and opposed to one another. They feel well enough that when the Mass falls, the Papacy lies in ruins. Before they will permit this to occur, they will put us all to death if they can.

In addition to all this, this dragon's tail, [I mean] the Mass, has begotten a numerous vermin-brood of manifold idolatries.

First, purgatory. Here they carried their trade into purgatory by masses for souls, and vigils, and weekly, monthly, and yearly celebrations of obsequies, and finally by the Common Week and All Souls Day, by soul-baths so that the Mass is used almost alone for the dead, although Christ has instituted the Sacrament alone for the living. Therefore purgatory, and every solemnity, rite, and commerce connected with it, is to be regarded as nothing but a specter of the devil. For it conflicts with the chief article [which teaches] that only Christ, and not the works of men, are to help [set free] souls. Not to mention the fact that nothing has been [divinely] commanded or enjoined upon us concerning the dead. Therefore all this may be safely omitted, even if it were no error and idolatry.

The Papists quote here Augustine and some of the Fathers who are said to have written concerning purgatory, and they think that we do not understand for what purpose and to what end they spoke as they did. St. Augustine does not write that there is a purgatory nor has he a testimony of Scripture to constrain him thereto, but he leaves it in doubt whether there is one, and says that his mother asked to be remembered at the altar or Sacrament. Now, all this is indeed nothing but the devotion of men, and that, too, of individuals, and does not establish an article of faith, which is the prerogative of God alone.

Our Papists, however, cite such statements [opinions] of men in order that men should believe in their horrible, blasphemous, and cursed traffic in masses for souls in purgatory [or in sacrifices for the dead and oblations], etc. But they will never prove these things from Augustine. Now, when they have abolished the traffic in masses for purgatory, of which Augustine never dreamt, we will then discuss with them whether the expressions of Augustine without Scripture [being without the warrant of the Word] are to be admitted, and whether the dead should be remembered at the Eucharist. For it will not do to frame articles of faith from the works or words of the holy Fathers; otherwise their kind of fare, of garments, of house, etc., would have to become an article of faith, as was done with relies. [We have, however, another rule, namely] The rule is: The Word of God shall establish articles of faith, and no one else, not even an angel.

Secondly. From this it has followed that evil spirits have perpetrated much knavery [exercised their malice] by appearing as the souls of the departed, and with unspeakable [horrible] lies and tricks demanded masses, vigils, pilgrimages, and other alms. All of which we had to receive as articles of faith, and to live accordingly; and the Pope confirmed these things, as also the Mass and all other abominations. Here, too, there is no [cannot and must not be any] yielding or surrendering.

Thirdly. [Hence arose] the pilgrimages. Here, too, masses, the remission of sins and the grace of God were sought, for the Mass controlled everything. Now it is indeed certain that such pilgrimages, without the Word of God, have not been commanded us, neither are they necessary, since we can have these things [the soul can be cared for] in a better way, and can omit these pilgrimages without any sin and danger. Why therefore do they leave at home [desert] their own parish [their called ministers, their parishes], the Word of God, wives, children, etc., who are ordained and [attention to whom is necessary and has been] commanded, and run after these unnecessary, uncertain, pernicious will-o'-the-wisps of the devil [and errors]? Unless the devil was riding [made insane] the Pope, causing him to praise and establish these practices, whereby the people again and again revolted from Christ to their own works, and became idolaters, which is worst of all; moreover, it is neither necessary nor commanded, but is senseless and doubtful, and besides harmful. Hence here, too, there can be no yielding or surrendering [to yield or concede anything here is not lawful], etc. And let this be preached, that such pilgrimages are not necessary, but dangerous; and then see what will become of them. [For thus they will perish of their own accord.]

Fourthly. Fraternities [or societies], in which cloisters, chapters, vicars have assigned and communicated (by a legal contract and sale) all masses and good works, etc., both for the living and the dead. This is not only altogether a human bauble, without the Word of God, entirely unnecessary and not commanded, but also contrary to the chief article, Of Redemption. Therefore it is in no way to be tolerated.

Fifthly. The relics, in which there are found so many falsehoods and tomfooleries concerning the bones of dogs and horses, that even the devil has laughed at such rascalities, ought long ago to have been condemned, even though there were some good in them; and so much the more because they are without the Word of God; being neither commanded nor counseled, they are an entirely unnecessary and useless thing. But the worst is that [they have imagined that] these relics had to work indulgence

223

and the forgiveness of sins [and have revered them] as a good work and service of God, like the Mass, etc.

Sixthly. Here belong the precious indulgences granted (but only for money) both to the living and the dead, by which the miserable [sacrilegious and accursed] Judas, or Pope, has sold the merit of Christ, together with the superfluous merits of all saints and of the entire Church, etc. All these things [and every single one of them] are not to be borne, and are not only without the Word of God, without necessity, not commanded, but are against the chief article. For the merit of Christ is [apprehended and] obtained not by our works or pence, but from grace through faith, without money and merit; and is offered [and presented] not through the power of the Pope, but through the preaching of God's Word.

Of the Invocation of Saints.

The invocation of saints is also one of the abuses of Antichrist conflicting with the chief article, and destroys the knowledge of Christ. Neither is it commanded nor counseled, nor has it any example [or testimony] in Scripture, and even though it were a precious thing, as it is not [while, on the contrary, it is a most harmful thing], in Christ we have everything a thousandfold better [and surer, so that we are not in need of calling upon the saints] .

And although the angels in heaven pray for us (as Christ Himself also does), as also do the saints on earth, and perhaps also in heaven, yet it does not follow thence that we should invoke and adore the angels and saints, and fast, hold festivals, celebrate Mass in their honor, make offerings, and establish churches, altars, divine worship, and in still other ways serve them, and regard them as helpers in need [as patrons and intercessors], and divide among them all kinds of help, and ascribe to each one a particular form of assistance, as the Papists teach and do. For this is idolatry, and such honor belongs alone to God. For as a Christian and saint upon earth you can pray for me, not only in one, but in many necessities. But for this reason I am not obliged to adore and invoke you, and celebrate festivals, fast, make oblations, hold masses for your honor [and worship], and put my faith in you for my salvation. I can in other ways indeed honor, love, and thank you in Christ. If now such idolatrous honor were withdrawn from angels and departed saints, the remaining honor would be without harm and would quickly be forgotten. For when advantage and assistance, both bodily and spiritual, are no more to be expected, the saints will not be troubled [the worship of the saints will soon vanish], neither in their graves nor in heaven. For without a reward or out of pure love no one will much remember, or esteem, or honor them [bestow on them divine honor].

In short, the Mass itself and anything that proceeds from it, and anything that is attached to it, we cannot tolerate, but must condemn, in order that we may retain the holy Sacrament pure and certain, according to the institution of Christ, employed and received through faith.

Article III: Of Chapters and Cloisters.

That chapters and cloisters [colleges of canons and communistic dwellings], which were formerly founded with the good intention [of our forefathers] to educate learned men and chaste [and modest] women, ought again to be turned to such use, in order that pastors, preachers, and other ministers of the churches may be had, and likewise other necessary persons [fitted] for [the political administration of] the secular government [or for the commonwealth] in cities and countries, and well-educated, maidens for mothers and housekeepers, etc.

If they will not serve this purpose, it is better that they be abandoned or razed, rather than [continued and], with their blasphemous services invented by men, regarded as something better than the ordinary Christian life and the offices and callings ordained by God. For all this also is contrary to the first chief article concerning the redemption made through Jesus Christ. Add to this that (like all other human inventions) these have neither been commanded; they are needless and useless, and, besides, afford occasion for dangerous and vain labor [dangerous annoyances and fruitless worship], such services as the prophets call Aven, i.e., pain and labor.

Article IV: Of the Papacy.

That the Pope is not, according to divine law or according to the Word of God the head of all Christendom (for this [name] belongs to One only, whose name is Jesus Christ), but is only the bishop and pastor of the Church at Rome, and of those who voluntarily or through a human creature (that is, a political magistrate) have attached themselves to him, to be Christians, not under him as a lord, but with him as brethren [colleagues] and comrades, as the ancient councils and the age of St. Cyprian show.

But to-day none of the bishops dare to address the Pope as brother as was done at that time [in the age of Cyprian]; but they must call him most gracious lord, even though they be kings or emperors. This [Such arrogance] we will not, cannot, must not take upon our conscience [with a good conscience approve]. Let him, however, who will do it, do so without us [at his own risk].

Hence it follows that all things which the Pope, from a power so false, mischievous, blasphemous, and arrogant, has done and undertaken. have been and still are purely diabolical affairs and transactions (with the exception of such things as pertain to the secular government, where God often permits much good to be effected for a people, even through a tyrant and [faithless] scoundrel) for the ruin of the entire holy [catholic or] Christian Church (so far as it is in his power) and for the destruction of the first and chief article concerning the redemption made through Jesus Christ.

For all his bulls and books are extant, in which he roars like a lion (as the angel in Rev. 12 depicts him, [crying out] that no Christian can

226

be saved unless he obeys him and is subject to him in all things that he wishes, that he says, and that he does. All of which amounts to nothing less than saying: Although you believe in Christ, and have in Him [alone] everything that is necessary to salvation, yet it is nothing and all in vain unless you regard [have and worship] me as your god, and be subject and obedient to me. And yet it is manifest that the holy Church has been without the Pope for at least more than five hundred years, and that even to the present day the churches of the Greeks and of many other languages neither have been nor are yet under the Pope. Besides, as often remarked, it is a human figment which is not commanded, and is unnecessary and useless; for the holy Christian [or catholic] Church can exist very well without such a head, and it would certainly have remained better [purer, and its career would have been more prosperous] if such a head had not been raised up by the devil. And the Papacy is also of no use in the Church, because it exercises no Christian office; and therefore it is necessary for the Church to continue and to exist without the Pope.

And supposing that the Pope would yield this point, so as not to be supreme by divine right or from Gods command, but that we must have [there must be elected] a [certain] head, to whom all the rest adhere [as their support] in order that the [concord and] unity of Christians may be preserved against sects and heretics, and that such a head were chosen by men, and that it were placed within the choice and power of men to change or remove this head, just as the Council of Constance adopted nearly this course with reference to the Popes, deposing three and electing a fourth; supposing, I say, that the Pope and See at Rome would yield and accept this (which, nevertheless, is impossible; for thus he would have to suffer his entire realm and estate to be overthrown and destroyed, with all his rights and books, a thing which, to speak in few words, he cannot do), nevertheless, even in this way Christianity would not be helped, but many more sects would arise than before.

For since men would have to be subject to this head, not from God's command, but from their personal good pleasure, it would easily and in

227

a short time be despised, and at last retain no member; neither would it have to be forever confined to Rome or any other place, but it might be wherever and in whatever church God would grant a man fit for the [taking upon him such a great] office. Oh, the complicated and confused state of affairs [perplexity] that would result!

Therefore the Church can never be better governed and preserved than if we all live under one head, Christ, and all the bishops equal in office (although they be unequal in gifts), be diligently joined in unity of doctrine, faith, Sacraments, prayer, and works of love, etc., as St. Jerome writes that the priests at Alexandria together and in common governed the churches, as did also the apostles, and afterwards all bishops throughout all Christendom, until the Pope raised his head above all.

This teaching shows forcefully that the Pope is the very Antichrist, who has exalted himself above, and opposed himself against Christ because he will not permit Christians to be saved without his power, which, nevertheless, is nothing, and is neither ordained nor commanded by God. This is, properly speaking to exalt himself above all that is called God as Paul says, 2 Thess. 2, 4. Even the Turks or the Tartars, great enemies of Christians as they are, do not do this, but they allow whoever wishes to believe in Christ, and take bodily tribute and obedience from Christians.

The Pope, however, prohibits this faith, saying that to be saved a person must obey him. This we are unwilling to do, even though on this account we must die in God s name. This all proceeds from the fact that the Pope has wished to be called the supreme head of the Christian Church by divine right. Accordingly he had to make himself equal and superior to Christ, and had to cause himself to be proclaimed the head and then the lord of the Church, and finally of the whole world, and simply God on earth, until he has dared to issue commands even to the angels in heaven. And when we distinguish the Pope s teaching from, or measure and hold it against, Holy Scripture, it is found [it appears plainly] that the Pope s teaching, where it is best, has been taken from the imperial

228

and heathen law and treats of political matters and decisions or rights, as the Decretals show; furthermore, it teaches of ceremonies concerning churches, garments, food, persons and [similar] puerile, theatrical and comical things without measure, but in all these things nothing at all of Christ, faith, and the commandments of God. Lastly, it is nothing else than the devil himself, because above and against God he urges [and disseminates] his [papal] falsehoods concerning masses, purgatory, the monastic life, one's own works and [fictitious] divine worship (for this is the very Papacy [upon each of which the Papacy is altogether founded and is standing]), and condemns, murders and tortures all Christians who do not exalt and honor these abominations [of the Pope] above all things. Therefore, just as little as we can worship the devil himself as Lord and God, we can endure his apostle, the Pope, or Antichrist, in his rule as head or lord. For to lie and to kill, and to destroy body and soul eternally, that is wherein his papal government really consists, as I have very clearly shown in many books.

In these four articles they will have enough to condemn in the Council. For they cannot and will not concede us even the least point in one of these articles. Of this we should be certain, and animate ourselves with [be forewarned and made firm in] the hope that Christ, our Lord, has attacked His adversary, and he will press the attack home [pursue and destroy him] both by His Spirit and coming. Amen.

For in the Council we will stand not before the Emperor or the political magistrate, as at Augsburg (where the Emperor published a most gracious edict, and caused matters to be heard kindly [and dispassionately]), but [we will appear] before the Pope and devil himself, who intends to listen to nothing, but merely [when the case has been publicly announced] to condemn, to murder and to force us to idolatry. Therefore we ought not here to kiss his feet, or to say: Thou art my gracious lord, but as the angel in Zechariah 3, 2 said to Satan: The Lord rebuke thee, O Satan.

THE THIRD PART OF THE ARTICLES.

Concerning the following articles we may [will be able to] treat with learned and reasonable men, or among ourselves. The Pope and his [the Papal] government do not care much about these. For with them conscience is nothing, but money, [glory] honors, power are [to them] everything.

I. Of Sin.

Here we must confess, as Paul says in Rom. 5, 11, that sin originated [and entered the world] from one man Adam, by whose disobedience all men were made sinners, [and] subject to death and the devil. This is called original or capital sin.

The fruits of this sin are afterwards the evil deeds which are forbidden in the Ten Commandments, such as [distrust] unbelief, false faith, idolatry, to be without the fear of God, presumption [recklessness], despair, blindness [or complete loss of sight], and, in short not to know or regard God; furthermore to lie, to swear by [to abuse] God's name [to swear falsely], not to pray, not to call upon God, not to regard [to despise or neglect] God's Word, to be disobedient to parents, to murder, to be unchaste, to steal, to deceive, etc.

This hereditary sin is so deep and [horrible] a corruption of nature that no reason can understand it, but it must be [learned and] believed from the revelation of Scriptures, Ps. 51, 5; Rom. 6, 12 ff.; Ex. 33, 3; Gen. 3, 7 ff. Hence, it is nothing but error and blindness in regard to this article what the scholastic doctors have taught, namely:

230

That since the fall of Adam the natural powers of man have remained entire and incorrupt, and that man by nature has a right reason and a good will; which things the philosophers teach.

Again that man has a free will to do good and omit evil, and, conversely, to omit good and do evil.

Again, that man by his natural powers can observe and keep [do] all the commands of God.

Again, that, by his natural powers, man can love God above all things and his neighbor as himself.

Again, if a man does as much as is in him, God certainly grants him His grace.

Again, if he wishes to go to the Sacrament, there is no need of a good intention to do good, but it is sufficient if he has not a wicked purpose to commit sin; so entirely good is his nature and so efficacious the Sacrament.

[Again,] that it is not founded upon Scripture that for a good work the Holy Ghost with His grace is necessary.

Such and many similar things have arisen from want of understanding and ignorance as regards both this sin and Christ, our Savior and they are truly heathen dogmas, which we cannot endure. For if this teaching were right [approved], then Christ has died in vain, since there is in man no defect nor sin for which he should have died; or He would have died only for the body, not for the soul, inasmuch as the soul is [entirely] sound, and the body only is subject to death.

II. Of the Law

Here we hold that the Law was given by God, first, to restrain sin by threats and the dread of punishment, and by the promise and offer of grace and benefit. But all this miscarried on account of the wickedness which sin has wrought in man. For thereby a part [some] were rendered worse, those, namely, who are hostile to [hate] the Law, because it forbids what they like to do, and enjoins what they do not like to do. Therefore, wherever they can escape [if they were not restrained by] punishment, they [would] do more against the Law than before. These, then, are the rude and wicked [unbridled and secure] men, who do evil wherever they [notice that they] have the opportunity.

The rest become blind and arrogant [are smitten with arrogance and blindness], and [insolently] conceive the opinion that they observe and can observe the Law by their own powers, as has been said above concerning the scholastic theologians; thence come the hypocrites and [self-righteous or] false saints.

But the chief office or force of the Law is that it reveal original sin with all its fruits, and show man how very low his nature has fallen, and has become [fundamentally and] utterly corrupted; as the Law must tell man that he has no God nor regards [cares for] God, and worships other gods, a matter which before and without the Law he would not have believed. In this way he becomes terrified, is humbled, desponds, despairs, and anxiously desires aid, but sees no escape; he begins to be an enemy of [enraged at] God, and to murmur, etc. This is what Paul says, Rom. 4, 15: The Law worketh wrath. And Rom. 5, 20: Sin is increased by the Law. [The Law entered that the offense might abound.]

III. Of Repentance.

This office [of the Law] the New Testament retains and urges, as St. Paul, Rom. 1, 18 does, saying: The wrath of God is revealed from heaven against all ungodliness and unrighteousness of men. Again, 3, 19: All the world is guilty before God. No man is righteous before Him. And Christ says, John 16, 8: The Holy Ghost will reprove the world of sin.

This, then, is the thunderbolt of God by which He strikes in a heap [hurls to the ground] both manifest sinners and false saints [hypocrites], and suffers no one to be in the right [declares no one righteous], but drives them all together to terror and despair. This is the hammer, as

Jeremiah says, 23, 29: Is not My Word like a hammer that breaketh the rock in pieces? This is not activa contritio or manufactured repentance, but passiva contritio [torture of conscience], true sorrow of heart, suffering and sensation of death.

This, then, is what it means to begin true repentance; and here man must hear such a sentence as this: You are all of no account, whether you be manifest sinners or saints [in your own opinion]; you all must become different and do otherwise than you now are and are doing [no matter what sort of people you are], whether you are as great, wise, powerful, and holy as you may. Here no one is [righteous, holy], godly, etc.

But to this office the New Testament immediately adds the consolatory promise of grace through the Gospel, which must be believed, as Christ declares, Mark 1,15: Repent and believe the Gospel, i.e., become different and do otherwise, and believe My promise. And John, preceding Him, is called a preacher of repentance, however, for the remission of sins, i.e., John was to accuse all, and convict them of being sinners, that they might know what they were before God, and might acknowledge that they were lost men, and might thus be prepared for the Lord, to receive grace, and to expect and accept from Him the remission of sins. Thus also Christ Himself says, Luke 24, 47: Repentance and remission of sins must be preached in My name among all nations.

But whenever the Law alone, without the Gospel being added exercises this its office there is [nothing else than] death and hell, and man must despair, like Saul and Judas; as St. Paul, Rom. 7, 10, says: Through sin the Law killeth. On the other hand, the Gospel brings consolation and remission not only in one way, but through the word and Sacraments, and the like, as we shall hear afterward in order that [thus] there is with the Lord plenteous redemption, as Ps. 130, 7 says against the dreadful captivity of sin.

However, we must now contrast the false repentance of the sophists with true repentance, in order that both may be the better understood.

Of the False Repentance of the Papists.

It was impossible that they should teach correctly concerning repentance, since they did not [rightly] know the real sins [the real sin]. For, as has been shown above, they do not believe aright concerning original sin, but say that the natural powers of man have remained [entirely] unimpaired and incorrupt; that reason can teach aright, and the will can in accordance therewith do aright [perform those things which are taught], that God certainly bestows His grace when a man does as much as is in him, according to his free will.

It had to follow thence [from this dogma] that they did [must do] penance only for actual sins such as wicked thoughts to which a person yields (for wicked emotion [concupiscence, vicious feelings, and inclinations], lust and improper dispositions [according to them] are not sins), and for wicked words and wicked deeds, which free will could readily have omitted.

And of such repentance they fix three parts contrition, confession, and satisfaction, with this [magnificent] consolation and promise added: If man truly repent, [feel remorse,] confess, render satisfaction, he thereby would have merited forgiveness, and paid for his sins before God [atoned for his sins and obtained a plenary redemption]. Thus in repentance they instructed men to repose confidence in their own works. Hence the expression originated, which was employed in the pulpit when public absolution was announced to the people: Prolong O God, my life, until I shall make satisfaction for my sins and amend my life.

There was here [profound silence and] no mention of Christ nor faith; but men hoped by their own works to overcome and blot out sins before God. And with this intention we became priests and monks, that we might array ourselves against sin.

As to contrition, this is the way it was done: Since no one could remember all his sins (especially as committed through an entire year), they inserted this provision, namely, that if an unknown sin should be

234

remembered later [if the remembrance of a concealed sin should perhaps return], this also must be repented of and confessed etc. Meanwhile they were [the person was] commended to the grace of God.

Moreover, since no one could know how great the contrition ought to be in order to be sufficient before God, they gave this consolation: He who could not have contrition, at least ought to have attrition, which I may call half a contrition or the beginning of contrition, for they have themselves understood neither of these terms nor do they understand them now, as little as I. Such attrition was reckoned as contrition when a person went to confession.

And when it happened that any one said that he could not have contrition nor lament his sins (as might have occurred in illicit love or the desire for revenge, etc.), they asked whether he did not wish or desire to have contrition [lament]. When one would reply Yes (for who, save the devil himself, would here say No?), they accepted this as contrition, and forgave him his sins on account of this good work of his [which they adorned with the name of contrition]. Here they cited the example of St. Bernard, etc.

Here we see how blind reason, in matters pertaining to God, gropes about, and, according to its own imagination, seeks for consolation in its own works, and cannot think of [entirely forgets] Christ and faith. But if it be [clearly] viewed in the light, this contrition is a manufactured and fictitious thought [or imagination], derived from man's own powers, without faith and without the knowledge of Christ. And in it the poor sinner, when he reflected upon his own lust and desire for revenge, would sometimes [perhaps] have laughed rather than wept [either laughed or wept, rather than to think of something else], except such as either had been truly struck by [the lightning of] the Law, or had been vainly vexed by the devil with a sorrowful spirit. Otherwise [with the exception of these persons] such contrition was certainly mere hypocrisy, and did not mortify the lust for sins [flames of sin]; for they had to grieve, while they would rather have continued to sin, if it had been free to them.

As regards confession, the procedure was this: Every one had [was enjoined] to enumerate all his sins (which is an impossible thing). This was a great torment. From such as he had forgotten [But if any one had forgotten some sins] he would be absolved on the condition that, if they would occur to him, he must still confess them. In this way he could never know whether he had made a sufficiently pure confession [perfectly and correctly], or when confessing would ever have an end. Yet he was pointed to his own works, and comforted thus: The more fully [sincerely and frankly] one confesses, and the more he humiliates himself and debases himself before the priest, the sooner and better he renders satisfaction for his sins; for such humility certainly would earn grace before God.

Here, too, there was no faith nor Christ, and the virtue of the absolution was not declared to him, but upon his enumeration of sins and his self-abasement depended his consolation. What torture, rascality, and idolatry such confession has produced is more than can be related.

As to satisfaction, this is by far the most involved [perplexing] part of all. For no man could know how much to render for a single sin, not to say how much for all. Here they have resorted to the device of imposing a small satisfaction, which could indeed be rendered, as five Paternosters, a day's fast, etc.; for the rest [that was lacking] of the [in their] repentance they were directed to purgatory.

Here, too, there was nothing but anguish and [extreme] misery. [For] some thought that they would never get out of purgatory, because, according to the old canons seven years' repentance is required for a single mortal sin. Nevertheless, confidence was placed upon our work of satisfaction, and if the satisfaction could have been perfect, confidence would have been placed in it entirely, and neither faith nor Christ would have been of use. But this confidence was impossible. For although any one had done penance in that way for a hundred years, he would still not have known whether he had finished his penance. That meant forever to do penance and never to come to repentance.

Here now the Holy See at Rome, coming to the aid of the poor Church, invented indulgences, whereby it forgave and remitted [expiation or] satisfaction, first, for a single instance, for seven years, for a hundred years and distributed them among the cardinals and bishops, so that one could grant indulgence for a hundred years and another for a hundred days. But he reserved to himself alone the power to remit the entire satisfaction.

Now, since this began to yield money, and the traffic in bulls became profitable he devised the golden jubilee year [a truly goldbearing year], and fixed it at Rome. He called this the remission of all punishment and guilt. Then the people came running, because every one would fain have been freed from this grievous, unbearable burden. This meant to find [dig up] and raise the treasures of the earth. Immediately the Pope pressed still further, and multiplied the golden years one upon another. But the more he devoured money, the wider grew his maw.

Later, therefore, he issued them [those golden years of his] by his legates [everywhere] to the countries, until all churches and houses were full of the Golden Year. At last he also made an inroad into purgatory among the dead, first, by founding masses and vigils, afterwards, by indulgences and the Golden Year, and finally souls became so cheap that he released one for a farthing.

But all this, too, was of no avail. For although the Pope taught men to depend upon, and trust in, these indulgences [for salvation], yet he rendered the [whole] matter again uncertain. For in his bulls he declares: Whoever would share in the indulgences or a Golden Year must be contrite, and have confessed, and pay money. Now, we have heard above that this contrition and confession are with them uncertain and hypocrisy. Likewise, also no one knew what soul was in purgatory, and if some were therein, no one knew which had properly repented and confessed. Thus he took the precious money [the Pope snatched up the holy pence], and comforted them meanwhile with [led them to confidence in] his power

237

and indulgence, and [then again led them away from that and] directed them again to their uncertain work.

If, now [although], there were some who did not believe [acknowledge] themselves guilty of such actual sins in [committed by] thoughts, words, and works,—as I, and such as I, in monasteries and chapters [fraternities or colleges of priests], wished to be monks and priests, and by fasting, watching, praying, saying Mass, coarse garments, and hard beds, etc., fought against [strove to resist] evil thoughts, and in full earnest and with force wanted to be holy, and yet the hereditary, inborn evil sometimes did in sleep what it is wont to do (as also St. Augustine and Jerome among others confess),—still each one held the other in esteem, so that some, according to our teaching, were regarded as holy, without sin and full of good works, so much so that with this mind we would communicate and sell our good works to others, as being superfluous to us for heaven. This is indeed true, and seals, letters, and instances [that this happened] are at hand.

[When there were such, I say] These did not need repentance. For of what would they repent, since they had not indulged wicked thoughts? What would they confess [concerning words not uttered], since they had avoided words? For what should they render satisfaction, since they were so guiltless of any deed that they could even sell their superfluous righteousness to other poor sinners? Such saints were also the Pharisees and scribes in the time of Christ.

Here comes the fiery angel, St. John [Rev. 10], the true preacher of [true] repentance, and with one [thunderclap and] bolt hurls both [those selling and those buying works] on one heap, and says: Repent! Matt. 3, 2. Now, the former [the poor wretches] imagine: Why, we have repented! The latter [the rest] say: We need no repentance. John says: Repent ye, both of you, for ye are false penitents; so are these [the rest] false saints [or hypocrites], and all of you on either side need the forgiveness of sins, because neither of you know what true sin is not to say anything about your duty to repent of it and shun it. For no one of you is good; you are full of unbelief, stupidity, and ignorance of God and God's will. For here He is present of whose fulness have all we received, and grace for grace, John 1, 16, and without Him no man can be just before God. Therefore, if you wish to repent, repent aright-your penance will not accomplish anything [is nothing]. And you hypocrites, who do not need repentance, you serpents' brood, who has assured you that you will escape the wrath to come? etc. Matt. 3, 7; Luke 3, 7.

In the same way Paul also preaches, Rom. 3, 10-12: There is none righteous, there is none that understandeth, there is none that seeketh after God, there is none that doeth good, no not one; they are all gone out of the way; they are together become unprofitable. And Acts 17, 30: God now commandeth all men everywhere to repent. "All men," he says; no one excepted who is a man. This repentance teaches us to discern sin, namely, that we are altogether lost, and that there is nothing good in us from head to foot [both within and without], and that we must absolutely become new and other men.

This repentance is not piecemeal [partial] and beggarly [fragmentary], like that which does penance for actual sins, nor is it uncertain like that. For it does not debate what is or is not sin, but hurls everything on a heap, and says: All in us is nothing but sin [affirms that, with respect to us, all is simply sin (and there is nothing in us that is not sin and guilt)]. What is the use of [For why do we wish] investigating, dividing, or distinguishing a long time? For this reason, too, this contrition is not [doubtful or] uncertain. For there is nothing left with which we can think of any good thing to pay for sin, but there is only a sure despairing concerning all that we are, think, speak, or do [all hope must be cast aside in respect of everything], etc.

In like manner confession, too, cannot be false, uncertain, or piecemeal [mutilated or fragmentary]. For he who confesses that all in him is nothing but sin comprehends all sins excludes none, forgets none. Neither can the satisfaction be uncertain, because it is not our uncertain, sinful work, but it is the suffering and blood of the [spotless and] innocent Lamb of God who taketh away the sin of the world.

Of this repentance John preaches, and afterwards Christ in the Gospel, and we also. By this [preaching of] repentance we dash to the ground the Pope and everything that is built upon our good works. For all is built upon a rotten and vain foundation, which is called a good work or law, even though no good work is there, but only wicked works, and no one does the Law (as Christ, John 7, 19, says), but all transgress it. Therefore the building [that is raised upon it] is nothing but falsehood and hypocrisy, even [in the part] where it is most holy and beautiful.

And in Christians this repentance continues until death, because, through the entire life it contends with sin remaining in the flesh, as Paul, Rom. 7, 14-25, [shows] testifies that he wars with the law in his members, etc.; and that, not by his own powers, but by the gift of the Holy Ghost that follows the remission of sins. This gift daily cleanses and sweeps out the remaining sins, and works so as to render man truly pure and holy.

The Pope, the theologians, the jurists, and every other man know nothing of this [from their own reason], but it is a doctrine from heaven, revealed through the Gospel, and must suffer to be called heresy by the godless saints [or hypocrites].

On the other hand, if certain sectarists would arise, some of whom are perhaps already extant, and in the time of the insurrection [of the peasants] came to my own view, holding that all those who had once received the Spirit or the forgiveness of sins, or had become believers, even though they should afterwards sin, would still remain in the faith, and such sin would not harm them, and [hence] crying thus: "Do whatever you please; if you believe, it all amounts to nothing; faith blots out all sins," etc.—they say, besides, that if any one sins after he has received faith and the Spirit, he never truly had the Spirit and faith: I have had before me [seen and heard] many such insane men, and I fear that in some such a devil is still remaining [hiding and dwelling].

It is, accordingly, necessary to know and to teach that when holy men, still having and feeling original sin, also daily repenting of and striving with it, happen to fall into manifest sins, as David into adultery, murder, and blasphemy, that then faith and the Holy Ghost has departed from them [they cast out faith and the Holy Ghost]. For the Holy Ghost does not permit sin to have dominion, to gain the upper hand so as to be accomplished, but represses and restrains it so that it must not do what it wishes. But if it does what it wishes, the Holy Ghost and faith are [certainly] not present. For St. John says, 1 Ep. 3, 9: Whosoever is born of God doth not commit sin, . . . and he cannot sin. And yet it is also the truth when the same St. John says, 1 Ep. 1, 8: If we say that we have no sin, we deceive ourselves and the truth is not in us.

IV. Of the Gospel.

We will now return to the Gospel, which not merely in one way gives us counsel and aid against sin; for God is superabundantly rich [and liberal] in His grace [and goodness]. First, through the spoken Word by which the forgiveness of sins is preached [He commands to be preached] in the whole world; which is the peculiar office of the Gospel. Secondly, through Baptism. Thirdly, through the holy Sacrament of the Altar. Fourthly, through the power of the keys, and also through the mutual conversation and consolation of brethren, Matt. 18, 20: Where two or three are gathered together, etc.

V. Of Baptism.

Baptism is nothing else than the Word of God in the water, commanded by His institution, or, as Paul says, a washing in the Word; as also Augustine says: Let the Word come to the element, and it becomes a Sacrament. And for this reason we do not hold with Thomas and the monastic preachers [or Dominicans] who forget the Word (God's institution) and say that

God has imparted to the water a spiritual power, which through the water washes away sin. Nor [do we agree] with Scotus and the Barefooted monks [Minorites or Franciscan monks], who teach that, by the assistance of the divine will, Baptism washes away sins, and that this ablution occurs only through the will of God, and by no means through the Word or water. Of the baptism of children we hold that children ought to be baptized. For they belong to the promised redemption made through Christ, and the Church should administer it [Baptism and the announcement of that promise] to them.

VI. Of the Sacrament of the Altar.

Of the Sacrament of the Altar we hold that bread and wine in the Supper are the true body and blood of Christ, and are given and received not only by the godly, but also by wicked Christians.

And that not only one form is to be given. [For] we do not need that high art [specious wisdom] which is to teach us that under the one form there is as much as under both, as the sophists and the Council of Constance teach. For even if it were true that there is as much under one as under both, yet the one form only is not the entire ordinance and institution [made] ordained and commanded by Christ. And we especially condemn and in God's name execrate those who not only omit both forms but also quite autocratically [tyrannically] prohibit, condemn, and blaspheme them as heresy, and so exalt themselves against and above Christ, our Lord and God [opposing and placing themselves ahead of Christ], etc.

As regards transubstantiation, we care nothing about the sophistical subtlety by which they teach that bread and wine leave or lose their own natural substance, and that there remain only the appearance and color of bread, and not true bread. For it is in perfect agreement with Holy Scriptures that there is, and remains, bread, as Paul himself calls it, 1 Cor.

10, 16: The bread which we break. And 1 Cor. 11, 28: Let him so eat of that bread.

VII. Of the Keys.

The keys are an office and power given by Christ to the Church for binding and loosing sin, not only the gross and well-known sins, but also the subtle, hidden, which are known only to God, as it is written in Ps. 19, 13: Who can understand his errors? And in Rom. 7, 25 St. Paul himself complains that with the flesh he serves the law of sin. For it is not in our power, but belongs to God alone, to judge which, how great, and how many the sins are, as it is written in Ps. 143, 2: Enter not into judgment with Thy servant; for in Thy sight shall no man living be justified. And Paul, 1 Cor. 4, 4, says: For I know nothing by myself; yet am I not hereby justified.

VIII. Of Confession.

Since Absolution or the Power of the Keys is also an aid and consolation against sin and a bad conscience, ordained by Christ [Himself] in the Gospel, Confession or Absolution ought by no means to be abolished in the Church, especially on account of [tender and] timid consciences and on account of the untrained [and capricious] young people, in order that they may be examined, and instructed in the Christian doctrine.

But the enumeration of sins ought to be free to every one, as to what he wishes to enumerate or not to enumerate. For as long as we are in the flesh, we shall not lie when we say: "I am a poor man [I acknowledge that I am a miserable sinner], full of sin." Rom. 7, 23: I see another law in my members, etc. For since private absolution originates in the Office of the Keys, it should not be despised [neglected], but greatly and highly esteemed [of the greatest worth], as [also] all other offices of the Christian Church.

And in those things which concern the spoken, outward Word, we must firmly hold that God grants His Spirit or grace to no one, except through or with the preceding outward Word, in order that we may [thus] be protected against the enthusiasts, i.e., spirits who boast that they have the Spirit without and before the Word, and accordingly judge Scripture or the spoken Word, and explain and stretch it at their pleasure, as Muenzer did, and many still do at the present day, who wish to be acute judges between the Spirit and the letter, and yet know not what they say or declare. For [indeed] the Papacy also is nothing but sheer enthusiasm, by which the Pope boasts that all rights exist in the shrine of his heart, and whatever he decides and commands with [in] his church is spirit and right, even though it is above and contrary to Scripture and the spoken Word.

All this is the old devil and old serpent, who also converted Adam and Eve into enthusiasts, and led them from the outward Word of God to spiritualizing and self-conceit, and nevertheless he accomplished this through other outward words. Just as also our enthusiasts [at the present day] condemn the outward Word, and nevertheless they themselves are not silent, but they fill the world with their pratings and writings, as though, indeed, the Spirit could not come through the writings and spoken word of the apostles, but [first] through their writings and words he must come. Why [then] do not they also omit their own sermons and writings, until the Spirit Himself come to men, without their writings and before them, as they boast that He has come into them without the preaching of the Scriptures? But of these matters there is not time now to dispute at greater length; we have elsewhere sufficiently urged this subject.

For even those who believe before Baptism, or become believing in Baptism, believe through the preceding outward Word, as the adults, who have come to reason, must first have heard: He that believeth and is baptized shall be saved, even though they are at first unbelieving, and receive the Spirit and Baptism ten years afterwards. Cornelius, Acts 10, 1 ff., had heard long before among the Jews of the coming Messiah, through whom he was righteous before God, and in such faith his prayers and alms were acceptable to God (as Luke calls him devout and God-fearing), and without such preceding Word and hearing could not have believed or been righteous. But St. Peter had to reveal to him that the Messiah (in whom, as one that was to come, he had hitherto believed) now had come, lest his faith concerning the coming Messiah hold him captive among the hardened and unbelieving Jews, but know that he was now to be saved by the present Messiah, and must not, with the [rabble of the] Jews deny nor persecute Him.

In a word, enthusiasm inheres in Adam and his children from the beginning [from the first fall] to the end of the world, [its poison] having been implanted and infused into them by the old dragon, and is the origin, power [life], and strength of all heresy, especially of that of the Papacy and Mahomet. Therefore we ought and must constantly maintain this point, that God does not wish to deal with us otherwise than through the spoken Word and the Sacraments. It is the devil himself whatsoever is extolled as Spirit without the Word and Sacraments. For God wished to appear even to Moses through the burning bush and spoken Word; and no prophet neither Elijah nor Elisha, received the Spirit without the Ten Commandments [or spoken Word]. Neither was John the Baptist conceived without the preceding word of Gabriel, nor did he leap in his mother's womb without the voice of Mary. And Peter says, 2. Ep. 1, 21: The prophecy came not by the will of man; but holy men of God spake as they were moved by the Holy Ghost. Without the outward Word, however, they were not holy, much less would the Holy Ghost have moved them to speak when they still were unholy [or profane]; for they were holy, says he, since the Holy Ghost spake through them.

IX. Of Excommunication.

The greater excommunication, as the Pope calls it, we regard only as a civil penalty, and it does not concern us ministers of the Church. But the lesser, that is, the true Christian excommunication, consists in this, that manifest and obstinate sinners are not admitted to the Sacrament and other communion of the Church until they amend their lives and avoid sin. And ministers ought not to mingle secular punishments with this ecclesiastical punishment, or excommunication.

X. Of Ordination and the Call.

If the bishops would be true bishops [would rightly discharge their office], and would devote themselves to the Church and the Gospel, it might be granted to them for the sake of love and unity, but not from necessity, to ordain and confirm us and our preachers; omitting, however, all comedies and spectacular display [deceptions, absurdities, and appearances] of unchristian [heathenish] parade and pomp. But because they neither are, nor wish to be, true bishops, but worldly lords and princes, who will neither preach, nor teach, nor baptize, nor administer the Lord's Supper, nor perform any work or office of the Church, and, moreover, persecute and condemn those who discharge these functions, having been called to do so, the Church ought not on their account to remain without ministers [to be forsaken by or deprived of ministers].

Therefore, as the ancient examples of the Church and the Fathers teach us, we ourselves will and ought to ordain suitable persons to this office; and, even according to their own laws, they have not the right to forbid or prevent us. For their laws say that those ordained even by heretics should be declared [truly] ordained and stay ordained [and that such ordination must not be changed], as St. Jerome writes of the Church at Alexandria, that at first it was governed in common by priests and preachers, without bishops.

XI. Of the Marriage of Priests.

To prohibit marriage, and to burden the divine order of priests with perpetual celibacy, they have had neither authority nor right [they have done out of malice, without any honest reason], but have acted like antichristian, tyrannical, desperate scoundrels [have performed the work of antichrist, of tyrants and the worst knaves], and have thereby caused all kinds of horrible, abominable, innumerable sins of unchastity [depraved lusts], in which they still wallow. Now, as little as we or they have been given the power to make a woman out of a man or a man out of a woman, or to nullify either sex, so little have they had the power to [sunder and] separate such creatures of God, or to forbid them from living [and cohabiting] honestly in marriage with one another. Therefore we are unwilling to assent to their abominable celibacy, nor will we [even] tolerate it, but we wish to have marriage free as God has instituted [and ordained] it, and we wish neither to rescind nor hinder His work; for Paul says, 1 Tim. 4, 1 ff., that this [prohibition of marriage] is a doctrine of devils.

XII. Of the Church.

We do not concede to them that they are the Church, and [in truth] they are not [the Church]; nor will we listen to those things which, under the name of Church, they enjoin or forbid. For, thank God, [to-day] a child seven years old knows what the Church is, namely, the holy believers and lambs who hear the voice of their Shepherd. For the children pray thus: I believe in one holy [catholic or] Christian Church. This holiness does not consist in albs, tonsures, long gowns, and other of their ceremonies devised by them beyond Holy Scripture, but in the Word of God and true faith.

XIII. How One is Justified before God, and of Good Works.

What I have hitherto and constantly taught concerning this I know not how to change in the least, namely, that by faith, as St. Peter says, we acquire a new and clean heart, and God will and does account us entirely righteous and holy for the sake of Christ, our Mediator. And although sin in the flesh has not yet been altogether removed or become dead, yet He will not punish or remember it.

And such faith, renewal, and forgiveness of sins is followed by good works. And what there is still sinful or imperfect also in them shall not be accounted as sin or defect, even [and that, too] for Christ's sake; but the entire man, both as to his person and his works, is to be called and to be righteous and holy from pure grace and mercy, shed upon us [unfolded] and spread over us in Christ. Therefore we cannot boast of many merits and works, if they are viewed apart from grace and mercy, but as it is written, 1 Cor. 1, 31: He that glorieth, let him glory in the Lord, namely, that he has a gracious God. For thus all is well. We say, besides, that if good works do not follow, faith is false and not true.

XIV. Of Monastic Vows.

As monastic vows directly conflict with the first chief article, they must be absolutely abolished. For it is of them that Christ says, Matt. 24, 5. 23 ff.: I am Christ, etc. For he who makes a vow to live as a monk believes that he will enter upon a mode of life holier than ordinary Christians lead, and wishes to earn heaven by his own works not only for himself, but also for others; this is to deny Christ. And they boast from their St. Thomas that a monastic vow is equal to Baptism. This is blasphemy [against God].

XV. Of Human Traditions.

The declaration of the Papists that human traditions serve for the remission of sins, or merit salvation, is [altogether] unchristian and condemned, as Christ says Matt. 15, 9: In vain they do worship Me, teaching for doctrines the commandments of men. Again, Titus 1, 14: That turn from the truth. Again, when they declare that it is a mortal sin if one breaks these ordinances [does not keep these statutes], this, too, is not right.

These are the articles on which I must stand, and, God willing, shall stand even to my death; and I do not know how to change or to yield anything in them. If any one wishes to yield anything, let him do it at the peril of his conscience.

Lastly, there still remains the Pope's bag of impostures concerning foolish and childish articles, as, the dedication of churches, the baptism of bells, the baptism of the altarstone, and the inviting of sponsors to these rites, who would make donations towards them. Such baptizing is a reproach and mockery of Holy Baptism, hence should not be tolerated. Furthermore, concerning the consecration of wax-tapers, palm-branches, cakes, oats, [herbs,] spices, etc., which indeed, cannot be called consecrations, but are sheer mockery and fraud. And such deceptions there are without number, which we commend for adoration to their god and to themselves, until they weary of it. We will [ought to] have nothing to do with them.

Dr. Martin Luther subscribed.

Dr. Justus Jonas, Rector, subscribed with his own hand.

Dr. John Bugenhagen, Pomeranus, subscribed.

Dr. Caspar Creutziger subscribed.

Nicholas Amsdorf of Magdeburg subscribed.

George Spalatin of Altenburg subscribed.

I, Philip Melanchthon, also regard [approve] the above articles as right and Christian. But regarding the Pope I hold that, if he would allow the Gospel, his superiority over the bishops which he has otherwise, is conceded to him by human right also by us, for the sake of the peace and general unity of those Christians who are also under him, and may be under him hereafter.

John Agricola of Eisleben subscribed.

Gabriel Didymus subscribed.

I, Dr. Urban Rhegius, Superintendent of the churches in the Duchy of Lueneburg, subscribe in my own name and in the name of my brethren, and of the Church of Hanover.

I, Stephen Agricola, Minister at Hof, subscribe.

Also I, John Draconites, Professor and Minister at Marburg, subscribe.

I, Conrad Figenbotz, for the glory of God subscribe that I have thus believed, and am still preaching and firmly believing as above.

I, Andrew Osiander of Nuernberg, subscribe.

I, Magister Veit Dieterich, Minister at Nuernberg, subscribe.

I, Erhard Schnepf, Preacher at Stuttgart, subscribe.

Conrad Oettinger, Preacher of Duke Ulrich at Pforzheim. Simon Schneeweiss, Pastor of the Church at Crailsheim.

I, John Schlagenhaufen, Pastor of the Church at Koethen, subscribe.

The Reverend Magister George Helt of Forchheim.

The Reverend Magister Adam of Fulda, Preacher in Hesse.

The Reverend Magister Anthony Corvinus, Preacher in Hesse.

I, Doctor John Bugenhagen, Pomeranus, again subscribe in the name of Magister John Brentz, as on departing from Smalcald he directed me orally and by a letter, which I have shown to these brethren who have subscribed.

I, Dionysius Melander, subscribe to the Confession, the Apology, and the Concordia on the subject of the Eucharist. Paul Rhodius, Superintendent of Stettin. Gerard Oemcken, Superintendent of the Church at Minden.

I, Brixius Northanus, Minister of the Church of Christ which is at Soest, subscribe to the Articles of the Reverend Father Martin Luther, and confess that hitherto I have thus believed and taught, and by the Spirit of Christ I shall continue thus to believe and teach.

Michael Caelius, Preacher at Mansfeld, subscribed.

The Reverend Magister Peter Geltner Preacher at Frankfort, subscribed.

Wendal Faber, Pastor of Seeburg in Mansfeld.

I, John Aepinus, subscribe.

Likewise, I, John Amsterdam of Bremen.

I, Frederick Myconius, Pastor of the Church at Gotha in Thuringia, subscribe in my own name and in that of Justus Menius of Eisenach.

I, Doctor John Lang, Preacher of the Church at Erfurt, subscribe with my own hand in my own name, and in that of my other coworkers in the Gospel, namely:

The Reverend Licentiate Ludwig Platz of Melsungen.

The Reverend Magister Sigismund Kirchner,

The Reverend Wolfgang Kiswetter,

The Reverend Melchior Weitmann

The Reverend John Thall.

The Reverend John Kilian.

The Reverend Nicholas Faber.

The Reverend Andrew Menser.

And I, Egidius Mechler, bave subscribed with my own hand.

MARTIN LUTHER'S 95 THESES

DISPUTATION OF DOCTOR MARTIN LUTHER ON THE POWER AND EFFICACY OF INDULGENCES

OCTOBER 31, 1517

Out of love for the truth and the desire to bring it to light, the following propositions will be discussed at Wittenberg, under the presidency of the Reverend Father Martin Luther, Master of Arts and of Sacred Theology, and Lecturer in Ordinary on the same at that place. Wherefore he requests that those who are unable to be present and debate orally with us, may do so by letter.

In the Name our Lord Jesus Christ. Amen.

1. Our Lord and Master Jesus Christ, when He said Poenitentiam agite, willed that the whole life of believers should be repentance.
2. This word cannot be understood to mean sacramental penance, i.e., confession and satisfaction, which is administered by the priests.
3. Yet it means not inward repentance only; nay, there is no inward repentance which does not outwardly work divers mortifications of the flesh.
4. The penalty [of sin], therefore, continues so long as hatred of self continues; for this is the true inward repentance, and continues until our entrance into the kingdom of heaven.

5. The pope does not intend to remit, and cannot remit any penalties other than those which he has imposed either by his own authority or by that of the Canons.

6. The pope cannot remit any guilt, except by declaring that it has been remitted by God and by assenting to God's remission; though, to be sure, he may grant remission in cases reserved to his judgment. If his right to grant remission in such cases were despised, the guilt would remain entirely unforgiven.

7. God remits guilt to no one whom He does not, at the same time, humble in all things and bring into subjection to His vicar, the priest.

8. The penitential canons are imposed only on the living, and, according to them, nothing should be imposed on the dying.

9. Therefore the Holy Spirit in the pope is kind to us, because in his decrees he always makes exception of the article of death and of necessity.

10. Ignorant and wicked are the doings of those priests who, in the case of the dying, reserve canonical penances for purgatory.

11. This changing of the canonical penalty to the penalty of purgatory is quite evidently one of the tares that were sown while the bishops slept.

12. In former times the canonical penalties were imposed not after, but before absolution, as tests of true contrition.

13. The dying are freed by death from all penalties; they are already dead to canonical rules, and have a right to be released from them.

14. The imperfect health [of soul], that is to say, the imperfect love, of the dying brings with it, of necessity, great fear; and the smaller the love, the greater is the fear.

15. This fear and horror is sufficient of itself alone (to say nothing of other things) to constitute the penalty of purgatory, since it is very near to the horror of despair.

16. Hell, purgatory, and heaven seem to differ as do despair, almost-despair, and the assurance of safety.
17. With souls in purgatory it seems necessary that horror should grow less and love increase.
18. It seems unproved, either by reason or Scripture, that they are outside the state of merit, that is to say, of increasing love.
19. Again, it seems unproved that they, or at least that all of them, are certain or assured of their own blessedness, though we may be quite certain of it.
20. Therefore by "full remission of all penalties" the pope means not actually "of all," but only of those imposed by himself.
21. Therefore those preachers of indulgences are in error, who say that by the pope's indulgences a man is freed from every penalty, and saved;
22. Whereas he remits to souls in purgatory no penalty which, according to the canons, they would have had to pay in this life.
23. If it is at all possible to grant to any one the remission of all penalties whatsoever, it is certain that this remission can be granted only to the most perfect, that is, to the very fewest.
24. It must needs be, therefore, that the greater part of the people are deceived by that indiscriminate and highsounding promise of release from penalty.
25. The power which the pope has, in a general way, over purgatory, is just like the power which any bishop or curate has, in a special way, within his own diocese or parish.
26. The pope does well when he grants remission to souls [in purgatory], not by the power of the keys (which he does not possess), but by way of intercession.
27. They preach man who say that so soon as the penny jingles into the money-box, the soul flies out [of purgatory].

28. It is certain that when the penny jingles into the money-box, gain and avarice can be increased, but the result of the intercession of the Church is in the power of God alone.
29. Who knows whether all the souls in purgatory wish to be bought out of it, as in the legend of Sts. Severinus and Paschal.
30. No one is sure that his own contrition is sincere; much less that he has attained full remission.
31. Rare as is the man that is truly penitent, so rare is also the man who truly buys indulgences, i.e., such men are most rare.
32. They will be condemned eternally, together with their teachers, who believe themselves sure of their salvation because they have letters of pardon.
33. Men must be on their guard against those who say that the pope's pardons are that inestimable gift of God by which man is reconciled to Him;
34. For these "graces of pardon" concern only the penalties of sacramental satisfaction, and these are appointed by man.
35. They preach no Christian doctrine who teach that contrition is not necessary in those who intend to buy souls out of purgatory or to buy confessionalia.
36. Every truly repentant Christian has a right to full remission of penalty and guilt, even without letters of pardon.
37. Every true Christian, whether living or dead, has part in all the blessings of Christ and the Church; and this is granted him by God, even without letters of pardon.
38. Nevertheless, the remission and participation [in the blessings of the Church] which are granted by the pope are in no way to be despised, for they are, as I have said, the declaration of divine remission.
39. It is most difficult, even for the very keenest theologians, at one and the same time to commend to the people the abundance of pardons and [the need of] true contrition.

40. True contrition seeks and loves penalties, but liberal pardons only relax penalties and cause them to be hated, or at least, furnish an occasion [for hating them].

41. Apostolic pardons are to be preached with caution, lest the people may falsely think them preferable to other good works of love.

42. Christians are to be taught that the pope does not intend the buying of pardons to be compared in any way to works of mercy.

43. Christians are to be taught that he who gives to the poor or lends to the needy does a better work than buying pardons;

44. Because love grows by works of love, and man becomes better; but by pardons man does not grow better, only more free from penalty.

45. Christians are to be taught that he who sees a man in need, and passes him by, and gives [his money] for pardons, purchases not the indulgences of the pope, but the indignation of God.

46. Christians are to be taught that unless they have more than they need, they are bound to keep back what is necessary for their own families, and by no means to squander it on pardons.

47. Christians are to be taught that the buying of pardons is a matter of free will, and not of commandment.

48. Christians are to be taught that the pope, in granting pardons, needs, and therefore desires, their devout prayer for him more than the money they bring.

49. Christians are to be taught that the pope's pardons are useful, if they do not put their trust in them; but altogether harmful, if through them they lose their fear of God.

50. Christians are to be taught that if the pope knew the exactions of the pardon-preachers, he would rather that St. Peter's church should go to ashes, than that it should be built up with the skin, flesh and bones of his sheep.

51. Christians are to be taught that it would be the pope's wish, as it is his duty, to give of his own money to very many of those from whom

certain hawkers of pardons cajole money, even though the church of St. Peter might have to be sold.

52. The assurance of salvation by letters of pardon is vain, even though the commissary, nay, even though the pope himself, were to stake his soul upon it.

53. They are enemies of Christ and of the pope, who bid the Word of God be altogether silent in some Churches, in order that pardons may be preached in others.

54. Injury is done the Word of God when, in the same sermon, an equal or a longer time is spent on pardons than on this Word.

55. It must be the intention of the pope that if pardons, which are a very small thing, are celebrated with one bell, with single processions and ceremonies, then the Gospel, which is the very greatest thing, should be preached with a hundred bells, a hundred processions, a hundred ceremonies.

56. The "treasures of the Church," out of which the pope. grants indulgences, are not sufficiently named or known among the people of Christ.

57. That they are not temporal treasures is certainly evident, for many of the vendors do not pour out such treasures so easily, but only gather them.

58. Nor are they the merits of Christ and the Saints, for even without the pope, these always work grace for the inner man, and the cross, death, and hell for the outward man.

59. St. Lawrence said that the treasures of the Church were the Church's poor, but he spoke according to the usage of the word in his own time.

60. Without rashness we say that the keys of the Church, given by Christ's merit, are that treasure;

61. For it is clear that for the remission of penalties and of reserved cases, the power of the pope is of itself sufficient.

62. The true treasure of the Church is the Most Holy Gospel of the glory and the grace of God.
63. But this treasure is naturally most odious, for it makes the first to be last.
64. On the other hand, the treasure of indulgences is naturally most acceptable, for it makes the last to be first.
65. Therefore the treasures of the Gospel are nets with which they formerly were wont to fish for men of riches.
66. The treasures of the indulgences are nets with which they now fish for the riches of men.
67. The indulgences which the preachers cry as the "greatest graces" are known to be truly such, in so far as they promote gain.
68. Yet they are in truth the very smallest graces compared with the grace of God and the piety of the Cross.
69. Bishops and curates are bound to admit the commissaries of apostolic pardons, with all reverence.
70. But still more are they bound to strain all their eyes and attend with all their ears, lest these men preach their own dreams instead of the commission of the pope.
71. He who speaks against the truth of apostolic pardons, let him be anathema and accursed!
72. But he who guards against the lust and license of the pardon-preachers, let him be blessed!
73. The pope justly thunders against those who, by any art, contrive the injury of the traffic in pardons.
74. But much more does he intend to thunder against those who use the pretext of pardons to contrive the injury of holy love and truth.
75. To think the papal pardons so great that they could absolve a man even if he had committed an impossible sin and violated the Mother of God—this is madness.
76. We say, on the contrary, that the papal pardons are not able to remove the very least of venial sins, so far as its guilt is concerned.

77. It is said that even St. Peter, if he were now Pope, could not bestow greater graces; this is blasphemy against St. Peter and against the pope.

78. We say, on the contrary, that even the present pope, and any pope at all, has greater graces at his disposal; to wit, the Gospel, powers, gifts of healing, etc., as it is written in I. Corinthians xii.

79. To say that the cross, emblazoned with the papal arms, which is set up [by the preachers of indulgences], is of equal worth with the Cross of Christ, is blasphemy.

80. The bishops, curates and theologians who allow such talk to be spread among the people, will have an account to render.

81. This unbridled preaching of pardons makes it no easy matter, even for learned men, to rescue the reverence due to the pope from slander, or even from the shrewd questionings of the laity.

82. To wit:—"Why does not the pope empty purgatory, for the sake of holy love and of the dire need of the souls that are there, if he redeems an infinite number of souls for the sake of miserable money with which to build a Church? The former reasons would be most just; the latter is most trivial."

83. Again:—"Why are mortuary and anniversary masses for the dead continued, and why does he not return or permit the withdrawal of the endowments founded on their behalf, since it is wrong to pray for the redeemed?"

84. Again:—"What is this new piety of God and the pope, that for money they allow a man who is impious and their enemy to buy out of purgatory the pious soul of a friend of God, and do not rather, because of that pious and beloved soul's own need, free it for pure love's sake?"

85. Again:—"Why are the penitential canons long since in actual fact and through disuse abrogated and dead, now satisfied by the granting of indulgences, as though they were still alive and in force?"

86. Again:—"Why does not the pope, whose wealth is to-day greater than the riches of the richest, build just this one church of St. Peter with his own money, rather than with the money of poor believers?"

87. Again:—"What is it that the pope remits, and what participation does he grant to those who, by perfect contrition, have a right to full remission and participation?"

88. Again:—"What greater blessing could come to the Church than if the pope were to do a hundred times a day what he now does once, and bestow on every believer these remissions and participations?"

89. "Since the pope, by his pardons, seeks the salvation of souls rather than money, why does he suspend the indulgences and pardons granted heretofore, since these have equal efficacy?"

90. To repress these arguments and scruples of the laity by force alone, and not to resolve them by giving reasons, is to expose the Church and the pope to the ridicule of their enemies, and to make Christians unhappy.

91. If, therefore, pardons were preached according to the spirit and mind of the pope, all these doubts would be readily resolved; nay, they would not exist.

92. Away, then, with all those prophets who say to the people of Christ, "Peace, peace," and there is no peace!

93. Blessed be all those prophets who say to the people of Christ, "Cross, cross," and there is no cross!

94. Christians are to be exhorted that they be diligent in following Christ, their Head, through penalties, deaths, and hell;

95. And thus be confident of entering into heaven rather through many tribulations, than through the assurance of peace.

Amore et studio elucidande veritatis hec subscripta disputabuntur Wittenberge, Presidente R. P. Martino Lutther, Artium et S. Theologie Magistro eiusdemque ibidem lectore Ordinario. Quare petit, ut qui non possunt verbis presentes nobiscum disceptare agant id literis absentes. In nomine domini nostri Hiesu Christi. Amen.

1. Dominus et magister noster Iesus Christus dicendo 'Penitentiam agite &c.' omnem vitam fidelium penitentiam esse voluit. 2. Quod verbum de penitentia sacramentali (id est confessionis et satisfactionis, que sacerdotum ministerio celebratur) non potest intelligi.
3. Non tamen solam intendit interiorem, immo interior nulla est, nisi foris operetur varias carnis mortificationes.
4. Manet itaque pena, donec manet odium sui (id est penitentia vera intus), scilicet usque ad introitum regni celorum.
5. Papa non vult nec potest ullas penas remittere preter eas, quas arbitrio vel suo vel canonum imposuit.
6. Papa non potest remittere ullam culpam nisi declarando, et approbando remissam a deo Aut certe remittendo casus reservatos sibi, quibus contemptis culpa prorsus remaneret.
7. Nulli prorus remittit deus culpam, quin simul eum subiiciat humiliatum in omnibus sacerdoti suo vicario.
8. Canones penitentiales solum viventibus sunt impositi nihilque morituris secundum eosdem debet imponi.
9. Inde bene nobis facit spiritussanctus in papa excipiendo in suis decretis semper articulum mortis et necessitatis.
10. Indocte et male faciunt sacerdotes ii, qui morituris penitentias canonicas in purgatorium reservant.
11. Zizania illa de mutanda pena Canonica in penam purgatorii videntur certe dormientibus episcopis seminata.
12. Olim pene canonice non post, sed ante absolutionem imponebantur tanquam tentamenta vere contritionis.
13. Morituri per mortem omnia solvunt et legibus canonum mortui iam sunt, habentes iure earum relaxationem.
14. Imperfecta sanitas seu charitas morituri necessario secum fert magnum timorem, tantoque maiorem, quanto minor fuerit ipsa.

15. Hic timor et horror satis est se solo (ut alia taceam) facere penam purgatorii, cum sit proximus desperationis horrori.
16. Videntur infernus, purgaturium, celum differre, sicut desperatio, prope desperatio, securitas differunt.
17. Necessarium videtur animabus in purgatorio sicut minni horrorem ita augeri charitatem.
18. Nec probatum videtur ullis aut rationibus aut scripturis, quod sint extra statum meriti seu augende charitatis.
19. Nec hoc probatum esse videtur, quod sint de sua beatitudine certe et secure, saltem omnes, licet nos certissimi simus. 20. Igitur papa per remissionem plenariam omnium penarum non simpliciter omnium intelligit, sed a seipso tantummodo impositarum.
21. Errant itaque indulgentiarum predicatores ii, qui dicunt per pape indulgentias hominem ab omni pena solvi et salvari.
22. Quin nullam remittit animabus in purgatorio, quam in hac vita debuissent secundum Canones solvere.
23. Si remissio ulla omnium omnino penarum potest alicui dari, certum est eam non nisi perfectissimis, i.e. paucissimis, dari.
24. Falli ob id necesse est maiorem partem populi per indifferentem illam et magnificam pene solute promissionem.
25. Qualem potestatem habet papa in purgatorium generaliter, talem habet quilibet Episcopus et Curatus in sua diocesi et parochia specialiter.
1. [26] Optime facit papa, quod non potestate clavis (quam nullam habet) sed per modum suffragii dat animabus remissionem.
2. [27] Hominem predicant, qui statim ut iactus nummus in cistam tinnierit evolare dicunt animam.
3. [28] Certum est, nummo in cistam tinniente augeri questum et avariciam posse: suffragium autem ecclesie est in arbitrio dei solius.
4. [29] Quis scit, si omnes anime in purgatorio velint redimi, sicut de s. Severino et Paschali factum narratur.

5. [30] Nullus securus est de veritate sue contritionis, multominus de consecutione plenarie remissionis.

6. [31] Quam rarus est vere penitens, tam rarus est vere indulgentias redimens, i. e. rarissimus.

7. [32] Damnabuntur ineternum cum suis magistris, qui per literas veniarum securos sese credunt de sua salute.

8. [33] Cavendi sunt nimis, qui dicunt venias illas Pape donum esse illud dei inestimabile, quo reconciliatur homo deo.

9. [34] Gratie enim ille veniales tantum respiciunt penas satisfactionis sacramentalis ab homine constitutas.

10. [35] Non christiana predicant, qui docent, quod redempturis animas vel confessionalia non sit necessaria contritio.

11. [36] Quilibet christianus vere compunctus habet remissionem plenariam a pena et culpa etiam sine literis veniarum sibi debitam.

12. [37] Quilibet versus christianus, sive vivus sive mortuus, habet participationem omnium bonorum Christi et Ecclesie etiam sine literis veniarum a deo sibi datam.

13. [38] Remissio tamen et participatio Pape nullo modo est contemnenda, quia (ut dixi) est declaratio remissionis divine.

14. [39] Difficillimum est etiam doctissimis Theologis simul extollere veniarum largitatem et contritionis veritatem coram populo.

15. [40] Contritionis veritas penas querit et amat, Veniarum autem largitas relaxat et odisse facit, saltem occasione.

16. [41] Caute sunt venie apostolice predicande, ne populus false intelligat eas preferri ceteris bonis operibus charitatis.

17. [42] Docendi sunt christiani, quod Pape mens non est, redemptionem veniarum ulla ex parte comparandam esse operibus misericordie.

18. [43] Docendi sunt christiani, quod dans pauperi aut mutuans egenti melius facit quam si venias redimereet.

19. [44] Quia per opus charitatis crescit charitas et fit homo melior, sed per venias non fit melior sed tantummodo a pena liberior.

20. [45] Docendi sunt christiani, quod, qui videt egenum et neglecto eo dat pro veniis, non idulgentias Pape sed indignationem dei sibi vendicat.

21. [46] Docendi sunt christiani, quod nisi superfluis abundent necessaria tenentur domui sue retinere et nequaquam propter venias effundere.

22. [47] Docendi sunt christiani, quod redemptio veniarum est libera, non precepta.

23. [48] Docendi sunt christiani, quod Papa sicut magis eget ita magis optat in veniis dandis pro se devotam orationem quam promptam pecuniam.

24. [49] Docendi sunt christiani, quod venie Pape sunt utiles, si non in cas confidant, Sed nocentissime, si timorem dei per eas amittant.

25. [50] Docendi sunt christiani, quod si Papa nosset exactiones venialium predicatorum, mallet Basilicam s. Petri in cineres ire quam edificari cute, carne et ossibus ovium suarum.

1. [51] Docendi sunt christiani, quod Papa sicut debet ita vellet, etiam vendita (si opus sit) Basilicam s. Petri, de suis pecuniis dare illis, a quorum plurimis quidam concionatores veniarum pecuniam eliciunt.

2. [52] Vana est fiducia salutis per literas veniarum, etiam si Commissarius, immo Papa ipse suam animam pro illis impigneraret.

3. [53] Hostes Christi et Pape sunt ii, qui propter venias predicandas verbum dei in aliis ecclesiis penitus silere iubent.

4. [54] Iniuria fit verbo dei, dum in eodem sermone equale vel longius tempus impenditur veniis quam illi.

5. [55] Mens Pape necessario est, quod, si venie (quod minimum est) una campana, unis pompis et ceremoniis celebrantur, Euangelium (quod maximum est) centum campanis, centum pompis, centum ceremoniis predicetur.

6. [56] Thesauri ecclesie, unde Pape dat indulgentias, neque satis nominati sunt neque cogniti apud populum Christi.

7. [57] Temporales certe non esse patet, quod non tam facile eos profundunt, sed tantummodo colligunt multi concionatorum.

8. [58] Nec sunt merita Christi et sanctorum, quia hec semper sine Papa operantur gratiam hominis interioris et crucem, mortem infernumque exterioris.

9. [59] Thesauros ecclesie s. Laurentius dixit esse pauperes ecclesie, sed locutus est usu vocabuli suo tempore.

10. [60] Sine temeritate dicimus claves ecclesie (merito Christi donatas) esse thesaurum istum.

11. [61] Clarum est enim, quod ad remissionem penarum et casuum sola sufficit potestas Pape.

12. [62] Verus thesaurus ecclesie est sacrosanctum euangelium glorie et gratie dei.

13. [63] Hic autem est merito odiosissimus, quia ex primis facit novissimos.

14. [64] Thesaurus autem indulgentiarum merito est gratissimus, quia ex novissimis facit primos.

15. [65] Igitur thesauri Euangelici rhetia sunt, quibus olim piscabantur viros divitiarum.

16. [66] Thesauri indulgentiarum rhetia sunt, quibus nunc piscantur divitias virorum.

17. [67] Indulgentie, quas concionatores vociferantur maximas gratias, intelliguntur vere tales quoad questum promovendum.

18. [68] Sunt tamen re vera minime ad gratiam dei et crucis pietatem comparate.

19. [69] Tenentur Episcopi et Curati veniarum apostolicarum Commissarios cum omni reverentia admittere.

20. [70] Sed magis tenentur omnibus oculis intendere, omnibus auribus advertere, ne pro commissione Pape sua illi somnia predicent.

21. [71] Contra veniarum apostolicarum veritatem qui loquitur, sit ille anathema et maledictus.

22. [72] Qui vero, contra libidinem ac licentiam verborum Concionatoris veniarum curam agit, sit ille benedictus.

23. [73] Sicut Papa iuste fulminat eos, qui in fraudem negocii veniarum quacunque arte machinantur,

24. [74] Multomagnis fulminare intendit eos, qui per veniarum pretextum in fraudem sancte charitatis et veritatis machinantur,

25. [75] Opinari venias papales tantas esse, ut solvere possint hominem, etiam si quis per impossibile dei genitricem violasset, Est insanire.

1. [76] Dicimus contra, quod venie papales nec minimum venialium peccatorum tollere possint quo ad culpam.

2. [77] Quod dicitur, nec si s. Petrus modo Papa esset maiores gratias donare posset, est blasphemia in sanctum Petrum et Papam.

3. [78] Dicimus contra, quod etiam iste et quilibet papa maiores habet, scilicet Euangelium, virtutes, gratias, curationum &c. ut 1. Co. XII.

4. [79] Dicere, Crucem armis papalibus insigniter erectam cruci Christi equivalere, blasphemia est.

5. [80] Rationem reddent Episcopi, Curati et Theologi, Qui tales sermones in populum licere sinunt.

6. [81] Facit hec licentiosa veniarum predicatio, ut nec reverentiam Pape facile sit etiam doctis viris redimere a calumniis aut certe argutis questionibus laicorm.

7. [82] Scilicet. Cur Papa non evacuat purgatorium propter sanctissimam charitatem et summam animarum necessitatem ut causam omnium iustissimam, Si infinitas animas redimit propter pecuniam funestissimam ad structuram Basilice ut causam levissimam?

8. [83] Item. Cur permanent exequie et anniversaria defunctorum et non reddit aut recipi permittit beneficia pro illis instituta, cum iam sit iniuria pro redemptis orare?

9. [84] Item. Que illa nova pietas Dei et Pape, quod impio et inimico propter pecuniam concedunt animam piam et amicam dei redimere, Et tamen propter necessitatem ipsius met pie et dilecte anime non redimunt eam gratuita charitate?

10. [85] Item. Cur Canones penitentiales re ipsa et non usu iam diu in semet abrogati et mortui adhuc tamen pecuniis redimuntur per concessionem indulgentiarum tanquam vivacissimi?

11. [86] Item. Cur Papa, cuius opes hodie sunt opulentissimis Crassis crassiores, non de suis pecuniis magis quam pauperum fidelium struit unam tantummodo Basilicam sancti Petri?

12. [87] Item. Quid remittit aut participat Papa iis, qui per contritionem perfectam ius habent plenarie remissionis et participationis?

13. [88] Item. Quid adderetur ecclesie boni maioris, Si Papa, sicut semel facit, ita centies in die cuilibet fidelium has remissiones et participationes tribueret?

14. [89] Ex quo Papa salutem querit animarum per venias magis quam pecunias, Cur suspendit literas et venias iam olim concessas, cum sint eque efficaces?

15. [90] Hec scrupulosissima laicorum argumenta sola potestate compescere nec reddita ratione diluere, Est ecclesiam et Papam hostibus ridendos exponere et infelices christianos facere.

16. [91] Si ergo venie secundum spiritum et mentem Pape predicarentur, facile illa omnia solverentur, immo non essent.

17. [92] Valeant itaque omnes illi prophete, qui dicunt populo Christi `Pax pax,' et non est pax.

18. [93] Bene agant omnes illi prophete, qui dicunt populo Christi `Crux crux,' et non est crux.

19. [94] Exhortandi sunt Christiani, ut caput suum Christum per penas, mortes infernosque sequi studeant,

20. [95] Ac sic magis per multas tribulationes intrare celum quam per securitatem pacis confidant.

M.D.Xvii.

CPSIA information can be obtained
at www.ICGtesting.com
Printed in the USA
LVHW081254100520
655301LV00018B/840